HARRAP'S
NEW GERMAN GRAMMAR

HARRAP'S
NEW
GERMAN GRAMMAR

By

CHARLES B. JOHNSON, M.A.

Based on *Harrap's Modern German Grammar*
by W. H. van der Smissen and W. H. Fraser

HARRAP   LONDON

First published in Great Britain 1971
by HARRAP LIMITED
19-23 Ludgate Hill, London EC4M 7PD

Reprinted 1976; 1977;1979; 1981; 1982

ISBN 0 245-52989-6

Printed in Great Britain by offset lithography by
Billings & Sons Ltd, Guildford, London and Worcester

PREFACE

This volume supersedes *Harrap's Modern German Grammar* by W. H. van der Smissen and W. H. Fraser, which, despite its many admirable qualities, was sadly out of date for present-day students. Much of the original explanatory material has been retained, but greater emphasis has been placed on illustrating grammatical points by situating them in meaningful contexts. The exercises and reading extracts have been discarded, thus making the new work one of reference only; hence the Index has been made as comprehensive as possible. The gothic type has been replaced throughout by roman. Another new feature is the Glossary of grammatical terms, which explains in simple English all the various terms used in the Grammar.

While the work does not claim to deal exhaustively with all points of grammar, it should provide a detailed enough guide to serve the purposes of students preparing for either the 'O' or the 'A' level examinations.

I am deeply indebted to Frau Ingrid de Haan, whose advice on innumerable points of detail, especially regarding modern German usage, was invaluable. I should also like to record my gratitude to Mr Trevor Jones, Editor of *Harrap's Standard German and English Dictionary*, and to members of the German Dictionary staff of George G. Harrap & Co., Ltd, for their unstinting assistance and many valuable suggestions; and to Mr R. P. L. Ledésert, Director and Editor of Harrap's Modern Languages Department, for much helpful advice. For reading the work in manuscript my thanks are due to Mr F. G. S. Parker, Mr J. R. Foster, and Dr B. J. Kenworthy. For his help with reading the proofs I am grateful to Herr Horst Sirges. Mr J. A. Porter and Mr J. A. Nicholson provided much useful advice based on their long experience as teachers of German. Miss Gillian Seymour typed the Index with consummate skill.

The principal authorities consulted in the preparation of the work were:

H. F. Eggeling: *A Dictionary of Modern German Prose Usage* (Oxford, 1961);

F. J. Stopp: *A Manual of Modern German* (London, 1963); *Duden-Grammatik* (Bibliographisches Institut, Mannheim; Harrap; 2., vermehrte und verbesserte Auflage, 1966);

Duden-Stilwörterbuch der deutschen Sprache (Bibliographisches Institut, Mannheim; Harrap; 5. Auflage, 1963);

Duden-Rechtschreibung der deutschen Sprache (Bibliographisches Institut, Mannheim; Harrap; 16., erweiterte Auflage, 1967);

Duden: Hauptschwierigkeiten der deutschen Sprache (Bibliographisches Institut, Mannheim; Harrap; 1966);

G. O. Curme: *A Grammar of the German Language* (New York, 1960).

C. B. J.

CONTENTS

I. INTRODUCTION

1. The German Alphabet

Roman form	Gothic form	Pronunciation	Roman form	Gothic form	Pronunciation
A, a	𝔄, 𝔞	[aː]	N, n	𝔑, 𝔫	[ɛn]
B, b	𝔅, 𝔟	[beː]	O, o	𝔒, 𝔬	[oː]
C, c	ℭ, 𝔠	[tseː]	P, p	𝔓, 𝔭	[peː]
D, d	𝔇, 𝔡	[deː]	Q, q	𝔔, 𝔮	[kuː]
E, e	𝔈, 𝔢	[eː]	R, r	𝔑, 𝔯	[ɛr]
F, f	𝔉, 𝔣	[ɛf]	S, s	𝔖, ſ, 𝔰	[ɛs]
G, g	𝔊, 𝔤	[geː]	T, t	𝔗, 𝔱	[teː]
H, h	𝔥, 𝔥	[haː]	U, u	𝔘, 𝔲	[uː]
I, i	𝔍, 𝔦	[iː]	V, v	𝔙, 𝔳	[ˈfau]
J, j	𝔍, 𝔧	[jot]	W, w	𝔚, 𝔴	[veː]
K, k	𝔎, 𝔨	[kaː]	X, x	𝔛, 𝔵	[iks]
L, l	𝔏, 𝔩	[ɛl]	Y, y	𝔜, 𝔶	[ˈypsilon]
M, m	𝔐, 𝔪	[ɛm]	Z, z	𝔷, 𝔷	[tsɛt]

NOTE: The notation is in accordance with the principles of the International Phonetic Association.

2. Remarks on the Alphabet

1. Three of the vowels may be modified by the sign ¨ (called 'umlaut'): ä [ɛː], ö [øː], ü [yː].

2. Diphthongs are: **ai** [ai], **au** [au], **ei** [ai], **eu** [oy], **äu** [oy], and the rarer forms **ay** [ai], **ey** [ai], **ui** [ui]; also **ie** finally after a stressed syllable—*e.g.*, **Tragödie** [traˈgøːdiə].

3. In gothic script the following change their form slightly when printed as one character: ch = ch; ck = ck; ſſ, ſʒ = ß; tʒ = ʒ.

4. The character ß replaces ſſ when final: Fuß, Haß, Fluß; within a word, it stands after long vowels, after diphthongs, and before another consonant: Füße, heißen, häßlich, mußte; *but* Flüſſe, müſſen, etc.

9

NOTE: 1. All vowels are to be pronounced short before ſſ.

2. In roman script the symbol ß is regularly used for the gothic ß; the symbol ſſ is replaced in roman by ss.

3. Surnames are often spelt with final   instead of -ß—*e.g.,* **Heuss, Grass.**

5. In gothic script the form ß occurs only as final in words or stems; elsewhere ſ: Haus, das, häuslich; Häuſer, leſen, haſt.

6. Since the sounds of German depend to a considerable extent upon syllabification, stress, and quantity, these subjects will be treated in the following paragraphs, before rules are given for the pronunciation of the alphabet.

3. Syllabification

A. SIMPLEX WORDS AND DERIVED FORMS

Simplex words—i.e., words of simple (as opposed to compound) form—and derived forms containing more than one syllable are divided in writing as they are in speaking: **Hän-de, kön-nen, Er-de, Leu-te, Sor-gen, Aus-gang.** Note the following special guiding principles:

1. Consonants

(*a*) A single consonant in a simplex word or derived form is written on the following line: **be-ten, ge-hen, Pu-der.**

NOTE: **ch, sch, ß** represent single sounds and are therefore not divided—*e.g.,* **ma-chen, Mu-schel, grü-ßen.**

(*b*) When there are two or more consonants the last consonant is carried over to the next line: **dan-ken, sin-gen, Gar-ten, Mül-ler, ret-ten, bes-ser, Wes-pen, kämp-fen, Ach-sel, steck-ten, Kat-zen, Städ-ter, Tisch-ler, gest-rig.**

NOTE: 1. **ck** is resolved into **k-k: Zuk-ker, bak-ken** (for **Zucker, backen**).

2. **st** is never divided in simplex words or derived forms: **la-sten, We-sten, Bast-ler, sech-ste, ge-stern;** *but* **Diens-tag** (see B, 1 below).

(*c*) Suffixes which begin with a vowel take over the preceding consonant: **Schaffne-rin, Lehre-rin, Freun-din, Bäcke-rei, Besteue-rung, Lüf-tung.**

2. Vowels

(*a*) A single vowel is not divided: **Ader** (not *A-der*), **Eber, Uhu.**

(*b*) Two vowels which are pronounced as if one, diphthongs, and vowels + lengthening **h** cannot themselves be divided, but the syllables which they comprise or in which they are included can be divided from other syllables: **Waa-ge, Mau-er, Ei-fel, Eu-le, oh-ne.** Two vowels may be divided if one of the elements is a prefix or a suffix: **Befrei-ung, Trau-ung, be-erben, bö-ig.**

B. COMPOUND WORDS

1. Compound words are divided into their component parts —i.e., their linguistic elements, based on their etymology: **Diens-tag, Ob-acht, Empfangs-tag, war-um, dar-auf, dar-in.** This means that the last etymological element remains intact. The components themselves are divided like simplex words according to the rules stated in section A above: **Hei-rats-an-zei-gen, voll-en-den.** Avoid divisions which, even though conforming to the rules, look strange—*e.g.*, **Spargel-der (Spargelder), beste-hende (bestehende).**

2. Compound words which logically would have three successive identical consonants drop one if followed by a vowel (*e.g.*, **Schiffahrt** for **Schifffahrt**), though the third consonant is restored if there is division at the end of a line—thus, **Schiff-fahrt, Brenn-nessel.** However, if the letter following the third consonant is also a consonant no letter is dropped—thus, **Auspuffflamme, Balletttruppe.**

C. LOAN WORDS

1. Simplex (not combined) loan words.

Simplex loan words are divided in exactly the same way as simplex words of true German origin (cf. section A above): **Bal-kon, Fis-kus, Ho-tel, Pla-net, Kon-ti-nent, Aku-stik.** However, the following special points should be observed:

(*a*) **ch, ph, rh, sh, th,** are single sounds and are therefore not divided: **Pro-phet, ka-tholisch.**

(*b*) Where combinations of certain consonants form a linguistic unity in the language of origin (*e.g.*, **bl, pl, fl, gl, cl, kl, phl; br, pr, dr, tr, fr, gr, cr, kr, phr, str, thr; chth, gn**) division is avoided: **Pu-bli-kum, Di-plom, Re-gle-ment, Zy-klus, Fe-bru-ar, De-pres-sion, Hy-drant, neu-tral, Re-greß, Sa-kra-ment, Ma-gnet.**

(*c*) Similarly, combinations of vowels which form a linguistic unity in the language of origin are not divided: **Moi-ré, Beef-steak.**

(*d*) Even if they do not form a linguistic unity, two vowels are better left undivided if dividing them results in an odd-looking form: thus, **asia-tisch** (rather than **asi-atisch**).

(*e*) Two vowels may be divided if there is a 'natural break' between them: **Muse-um, Individu-um, Oze-an, kre-ieren.**

2. Compound loan words.

Compound loan words (and words with a prefix), like compound words of pure German origin (section B above), are divided into their component parts—i.e. their linguistic elements: **Atmo-sphäre, Mikro-skop, Inter-esse.** The components themselves are divided like simplex words according to the rules stated above (section A): **At-mo-sphäre. Mi-kro-skop, In-ter-esse.** However, because the correct etymology of such words is not widely known, they are frequently found divided according to the rules pertaining to compound words of pure German origin—i.e. according to the way the syllables are divided in speaking; thus, **Epi-sode** (etymologically **Epis-ode**), **Tran-sit** (instead of **Trans-it**), etc.

4. Stress

The relative force with which a syllable in a group is uttered is called 'stress' (less properly 'accent'): **¹Freundschaft,** '¹friendship'; **mein ¹Vater ist schon ¹alt.** Several degrees of force may be distinguished in longer words and in phrases, but for present purposes it is sufficient to consider only the syllable of strongest or chief stress. In words of two or more syllables the chief stress is as follows:

1. In most German words of pure Germanic origin, on the stem: **¹Freundschaft, ¹Freundlichkeit, ¹lesen, ge¹lesen, ¹reinlich.**

2. In compounds, on the part most distinctive for the meaning: **¹Baumeister, ¹merkwürdig, ¹unangenehm.**

3. In compounded particles, often on the second component: **da¹her, her¹bei, ob¹gleich.**

4. In loan words, usually on the syllable stressed in the language from which the word has been taken: **Stu¹dent** (from

Latin *stu*|*dens*, -|*entis*), |**Logik** (from Latin |*logica*), **Philo**|**soph** (from Greek *philo*|*sophos*), **ele**|**gant** (from French *élé*|*gant*), **Nati**|**on** (from Latin *nati*|*o*, -|*onis*), **Sol**|**dat** (from French *sol*|*dat*, Italian *sol*|*dato*).

5. Always on the suffixes **-ei, -ieren**, and (when of foreign origin) **-ur, -ti**|**on, -ti**|**ent: Arz**|**nei, stu**|**dieren, Gla**|**sur, Nati**|**on, Pati**|**ent.**

6. Never on the inseparable prefixes **be-, emp-, ent-, er-, ge-, ver-, zer-.**

5. Quantity

1. Vowels in German may be distinguished as 'long', 'half long', and 'short': **loben** (long), **Mi***li***tär** (half long), **k***a***lt** (short).

NOTE: In practice it is sufficient to distinguish long and short (the latter including half long and short).

2. Vowels are normally long:

(*a*) in open stressed syllables; and a long stem vowel usually retains its length in inflection: **d***a***, loben; lobte.**

(*b*) when doubled, or followed by silent **h** or **e** (the latter only after **i**): **St***aa***t, Leh***r***er, S***o***hn, K***u***h, i***h***r, di***e***ser, s***ie***.**

(*c*) as diphthongs: **gl***au***ben, h***ei***ßen, L***eu***te.**

(*d*) in final stressed syllables ending in a single consonant (including monosyllables capable of inflection, or ending in **r**): **Geb***o***t, gen***u***g, d***e***m, R***a***t, b***o***t, g***u***t, w***a***r, w***i***r;** so also vowel before **ß** persisting in inflection: **s***a***ß (s***a***ßen), F***u***ß (F***ü***ße).**

3. Vowels are normally short:

(*a*) in unstressed syllables: **hab***e***n, g***e***habt,** |**unart***i***g.**

(*b*) in closed syllables (including monosyllables ending in more than one consonant): **S***o***mmer, W***i***nter, ***a***lt, f***e***st;** so also before **ß** *not* persisting in inflection: **Fl***u***ß (Fl***ü***sse).**

(*c*) In uninflected monosyllables ending in a single consonant (not **r**): **m***i***t, ***o***b, ***i***n, ***i***m, v***o***n, v***o***m;** *but* **f***ü***r, h***e***r** (long).

4. Before **ch**, some are long, some short: **Spr***a***che** (long), **l***a***chen** (short).

6. General Remarks on Pronunciation

The principal distinctions between German and English pronunciation are the following:

1. The action of the organs of speech, in general, is more energetic and precise in German than in English. The pronunciation of English strikes the German ear as slovenly. Great care should be taken not to obscure German vowels in unstressed syllables, which is the rule in English.

2. The tongue, both for vowels and consonants, is generally either further advanced or retracted than in the articulation of corresponding English sounds.

3. English long vowels (as **a** in 'fate', **oo** in 'poor') are usually diphthongal, particularly before liquids, whereas German long vowels are uniform in quality throughout.

4. The utterance of every German initial vowel, unless wholly unstressed, begins with the 'glottal stop', which consists in suddenly closing the glottis and forcing it open by an explosion of breath, as in slignt coughing: *a*us, *e*ssen, *o*hne, *ü*ber, *ü*berall, *a*ndersartig, *u*nterirdisch.

NOTE: 1. The glottis is the space between the vocal cords.

2. Corresponding English vowels begin with gradual closure of the glottis and strike the German ear as indistinct, since the German sound is fully resonant throughout. The learner may realize the nature of this sound by placing the hands to the sides and exerting a sudden, forcible pressure, the mouth being open as if to form a vowel. When this is done, the glottis closes automatically, and is at once forced open.

5. It must never be forgotten that the sounds of any two languages hardly ever correspond exactly, and hence that comparisons between German and English are only approximate. In describing the sounds below, brief cautions have been added in parenthesis, in order to help deal with this difficulty.

7. Pronunciation of the Alphabet

Vowels

1. Vowels are either 'front' or 'back', according to their place of articulation in the mouth, and are so grouped below.

2. They are pronounced long or short according to the rules given above (§5), the commonest exceptions only being noted.

3. All vowels must be distinctly uttered.

4. Do not drawl or diphthongize the long vowels.

5. Doubled vowels and those followed by e or **h**, as a sign of length, are omitted from the conspectus, but included in the examples.

1. Front Vowels

i 1. When long, like **i** in 'marine' (slightly closer; avoid diphthong, especially before **l** and **r**): M**i**ne, m**i**r, w**i**r; d**i**eser, L**i**ed, stud**i**eren, **i**hn, st**i**ehlst.

EXCEPTIONS: (short, see 2 below) A**l**pr**i**l, V**i**ertel, v**i**erzehn, v**i**erzig.

2. When short, like **i** in 'bit': K**i**nd, s**i**ngen, w**i**rd, b**i**st, geb**i**ssen, gel**i**tten; m**i**t, **i**m.

3. Like **y** in 'yes', when unstressed before **e** in loan words: Fa**l**mil**i**e, Pat**i**lent.

ü 1. When long, has no English counterpart; same tongue position as for **i**, 1, with tense lip rounding: Bl**ü**te, m**ü**de, gr**ü**n, s**ü**ß, F**ü**ße; M**ü**he, fr**ü**her.

2. When short, has no English counterpart; same tongue position as for **i**, 2, with slight lip rounding: h**ü**bsch, Gl**ü**ck, f**ü**nf, f**ü**rchten, K**ü**ste, M**ü**ller, m**ü**ssen.

y Like **ü** (see above): As**y**l (long), M**y**rte (short).

e 1. When long, like **a** in 'stated' (avoid diphthong, especially before **l** and **r**): l**e**sen, l**e**ben, r**e**den, schw**e**r, d**e**m, d**e**n; B**e**et, Schn**e**e, st**e**hen, f**e**hlen, l**e**hren.

EXCEPTIONS: (short, see 2 below) d**e**s, **e**s.

2. When short, like **e** in 'let' (avoid **e** as in 'her', before **r**): sch**e**nken, s**e**nden, g**e**stern, b**e**sser, B**e**tten, H**e**rr, g**e**rn.

EXCEPTIONS: (long, see 1 above) Dr**e**sden, **E**rde, **e**rst, Pf**e**rd, H**e**rd, Schw**e**rt.

3. In unstressed final syllables and in the prefixes **be-**, **ge-**, like **a** in 'soda' (tongue slightly advanced): hab**e**, Gab**e**, lob**e**n, arb**e**it**e**t, Brud**e**r, dies**e**r, dies**e**m, Vog**e**l; b**e**stell**e**n, g**e**lobt.

a 1. When long, like **a** in 'care' (avoid diphthong, especially before **l** and **r**): s**ä**en, w**ä**ren, Schl**ä**ge; **Ä**hre, m**ä**hen.

2. When short, identical with **e** short (**e**, 2, above): **Hände, Bäcker, Äpfel, hätte, längst.**
EXCEPTIONS: (long) **nächst, Städte.**

ö 1. When long, has no English counterpart; same tongue position as for **e**, 1, with tense lip rounding and protrusion: **hören, böse, schön, größer; Söhne.**

2. When short, has no English counterpart; same tongue position as for **e**, 2, with slight lip rounding: **Köpfe, Glöcklein, können, Götter.**
EXCEPTION: (long) **Österreich.**

2. Back Vowels

a   Like **a** in 'ah!', 'father' (tongue flat and mouth well open; lips neither rounded nor retracted).

1. Long: **sagen, da, bat, war, saß; Staat, nah, Bahn; Sprache, stach.**
EXCEPTIONS: (short) **das, was, hat.**

2. Short: **warten, hacken, lachen, niemand, Ball, hatte; als, ab, am.**
EXCEPTIONS: (long) **Jagd, Papst.**

o 1. When long, like **o** in 'omen' (tense lip rounding and protrusion; avoid diphthong, especially before **l** and **r**): **loben, Rose, groß, rot, hoch; Boot, Kohl, Ohr.**

2. When short, like **o** in 'not' (always definitely rounded; never lengthened, even before **r**): **klopfen, Gott, wollen, Sonne, morgen, Wort; ob, von.**
EXCEPTIONS: (long) **Lotse, Obst, Ostern.**
NOTE: The English short **o** has often very feeble rounding, especially in American English, approaching the sound of **a** in 'hat'.

u 1. When long, like **oo** in 'too' (tense lip rounding and protrusion; avoid diphthong, especially before **l** and **r**): **du, rufen, Blume, Fuß, guten, nur, zur; Kuh, Stuhl.**

2. When short, like **u** in 'put' (definitely rounded; never lengthened, even before **r**): **und, wurde, Mutter, Fluß; um, zum.**

Diphthongs

ai }   Like **i** in 'mile' (first element more deliberately uttered;
ay }   = German **a**, 2 + **i**, 2): **Kaiser, Bayern.**

au   Like **ou** in 'house' (first element more deliberately uttered; = German **a**, 2 + **u**, 2): H**au**s, Fr**au**, B**au**m, B**au**er.

äu   Like **oi** in 'boil' (first element more deliberately uttered; = German **o**, 2 + **i**, 2): R**äu**ber, M**äu**se, B**äu**me.

NOTE: The second element is sometimes slightly rounded.

ei⎫   The same sound as **ai**, above: m**ei**n, M**ei**le, s**ei**ner, kl**ei**ner,
ey⎭   **ei**nst; M**ey**er.

eu   The same sound as **äu**, above: n**eu**, h**eu**te, F**eu**er, **eu**er, s**eu**fzen.

ui   = German **u**, 2 + **i**, 2: h**ui**! pf**ui**!

CONSONANTS

1. It is very important to remember that all final consonants are short in German, although not always so in English; compare ma**n** and 'man', sa**ng** and 'sang'.

2. Double consonants have only a single sound, as also in English: gefa**ll**en, 'fallen'; but when two consonants come together through compounding the sound is doubled: mi**tt**eilen; Scha**ff**ell; in the case of contiguous final and initial consonant there is a distinct pause: Spor**t** **t**reiben.

3. When alternative pronunciations are given below the preferable one is put first.

Alphabetical List of Consonants

b 1. When initial in a word or syllable, or doubled, like **b** in 'ball': **b**ald, lie**b**en, ver**b**lei**b**en, E**bb**e.

2. When final in a word or syllable, or when followed by another consonant or other consonants, like **p** in 'ta**p**': a**b**, Wei**b**, lie**b**, a**b**geben, Schrei**b**tisch, lie**b**te, lie**b**lich, lie**b**ster, gi**b**st, le**b**t.

c 1. Before a front vowel, like **ts** in 'sets': **C**icero, **C**äsar.

2. Before a back vowel, like **c** in 'call': **C**anto, **C**anasta.

NOTE: **c** alone is now found only in loan words and proper nouns—otherwise replaced by **k**.

ch 1. After a back vowel, has no English counterpart; compare Scottish **ch** in 'loch' (formed by slight contact of

the back of the tongue with the soft palate; voiceless):
Ba*ch*, ma*ch*en, no*ch*, su*ch*en, rau*ch*en.

NOTE: 'Voiceless' means without vibration of the vocal cords;
compare 'fine' (voiceless) with 'vine' (voiced).

2. After a front vowel, after a consonant, and in -*ch*en, like
h in 'hue' very forcibly pronounced (avoid k as in
'kill' and sh as in 'ship'; it is best obtained by un-
voicing the y in 'yes'): i*ch*, schle*ch*t, wei*ch*, Bü*ch*er,
sol*ch*es, Mäd*ch*en; so also in *Ch*e¹mie, before a front
vowel.

3. Before s in a stem syllable, like k (page 19): La*ch*s,
O*ch*sen, wa*ch*sen; also some loan words, *Ch*rist, *Ch*or,
etc.

ck   Like k (page 19): di*ck*, schi*ck*en.

d 1. When initial in a word or syllable, or doubled, like d in
'day' (tongue advanced to the gums): *d*u, *d*rei, Fe*d*er,
Hän*d*e, wür*d*e, a*dd*ieren.

2. When final in a word or syllable, or when followed by
another consonant or other consonants, like t in 'take'
(tongue advanced to the gums): Lie*d*, Han*d*, un*d*,
Hän*d*chen, en*d*lich, Gesun*d*heit, lä*d*st, Kin*d*skopf.

dt   Like d, 2: Gesan*dt*e, Verwan*dt*schaft.

f   Like f in 'fall': kau*f*en, *F*rau, fün*f*, hof*f*en.

g 1. When initial in a word or syllable, or doubled, like g in
'began': *g*ab, Auf*g*abe, *g*ehen, *g*e*g*eben, *G*itter, *g*rün,
schmu*gg*eln.

NOTE: The place of contact between tongue and palate varies
along with the vowel or consonant of the syllable, as in English;
similarly also for the sounds of k, ng, nk.

2. When final in a word or syllable, or when followed by
another consonant or other consonants, like k (except
for the combination ng—see page 19): Ber*g*, sorg*los*,
mög*lich*.

3. In the suffix -ig, like ch, 2: Kön*ig*, Ess*ig*.

4. After a front vowel or a consonant within a word (and
followed by a vowel), like g, 1: le*g*en, Ber*g*e, Bür*g*er,
Schlä*g*e, Wie*g*e, Köni*g*e.

5. In many French loan words, like z in 'azure' (tongue advanced, lips protruded): E'tage (three syllables: [e: ˈta: ʒə]), Cou'rage (three syllables: [ku: ˈra: ʒə]).

h 1. Like h in 'have' (strongly and briefly uttered): *h*aben, ge*h*abt, *h*eißen, ge*h*olfen, ˈA*h*orn.

2. It is silent before the vowel of an ending and as a sign of length: ge*h*en, gese*h*en; Ku*h*, Re*h*, we*h*; see also ch, th, sch.

j 1. Regularly, like y in 'yes' (tongue closer to the palate; strongly buzzed): *j*a, *j*eder, *J*uni, *J*och, *j*auchzen.

2. In French loan words, like g, 5 above: *J*ournal, *J*alouˈsie.

k   Like c in 'can' or k in 'keen' (compare note to g, 1): *k*am, *k*ennen, *K*ind, *k*lein, san*k*.

l   Like l in 'lip' (tongue advanced to gums): *l*oben, *l*ieben, a*l*s, g*l*ück*l*ich, wo*ll*en, vo*ll*.

m   Like m in 'make': *m*it, Bau*m*, ko*mm*en, La*mm*.

n   Like n in 'name' (tongue advanced to gums): *n*en*n*en, u*n*d, Hä*n*de, a*n*, Ma*n*n, Mä*nn*er.

ng Like ng in 'sing' (abruptly uttered; compare note to g, 1; never as in English 'finger'): sa*ng*en, la*ng*, lä*ng*st, si*ng*, Fi*ng*er, E*ng*el.

nk Like nk in 'think' (abruptly uttered; compare note to g, 1): Da*nk*, da*nk*en, le*nk*en, si*nk*en.

p   Like p in 'pit' (pronounce fully before f): *P*u*pp*e, Siru*p*, *p*flanzen, *P*ferd.

ph Like f (page 18): *Ph*iloˈsoph, *Ph*ilosoˈ*ph*ie.

qu Like k + w: *Qu*elle, *qu*er.

r   Has no English counterpart; it is formed in careful speech by trilling the point of the tongue against the upper gums ('lingual' r) but more frequently by drawing the root of the tongue backward so as to cause the uvula to vibrate ('uvular' r): *R*at, *r*ot, *r*und, *r*ein, wa*r*, wi*r*, Her*z*, we*r*den.

NOTE: Either sound is correct in conversation. The lingual **r**, however, is more readily acquired by English-speaking students.

s 1. When initial in a word or syllable before a vowel, like **z** in
'zeal' (tongue advanced towards gums): *s*ehen, *s*o,
*s*ich, *s*üß, Ro*s*e, Zin*s*en, gele*s*en, ra*s*end.
2. When final in a word or syllable, and before most consonants, like **s** in 'seal' (tongue advanced, as above);
so also **ß**, always: Gra*s*, we*s*halb, fa*s*t, Ma*s*ke, We*s*pe,
e*ss*en, Fu*ß*, Fü*ß*e, Flü*ss*e, ge*s*tern.
3. When initial before **p** or **t**, like **sh** in 'ship' (tongue advanced, lips protruded): *s*tehen, ge*s*tanden, *s*pielen, ge-
*s*palten, *S*pott.

sch Like **sh** in 'ship' (see **s**, 3 above): *Sch*iff, *sch*reiben, Ti*sch*.

t 1. Like **t** in 'tame': *T*ag, *t*eilen, *T*isch, Mu*tt*er, ri*tt*, *t*ragen.
2. In loan words before **i** = **ts**: Na*t*i|on, Pa*t*i|ent.

th Same as **t**, 1: *Th*eater.

tz Same as **z**: Sa*tz*, si*tz*en.

v 1. Same as **f**: *V*ater, *v*iel, *v*on, bra*v*.
2. In most Latin or Romance loan words = **w**: *V*ase,
Pro*v*i|ant, Re|*v*ol*v*er, *V*e|randa, No|*v*ember.
3. When final (even in loan words), like **f**: Lär*v*chen [|lɛrf-
çən] but Larve [|larvə]; oli*v*(grün) [oː|liːf-] but Olive
[oː|liːvə].

w 1. Normally like **v** in 'vine' (less strongly buzzed): *w*ar, *w*o,
*w*ir, *w*eshalb, Sch*w*ester, z*w*ei.
2. When final in a syllable, like **f**: Lö*w*chen, Mö*w*chen.

x Like **k** + **s**, 2: A*x*t, Ni*x*e.

z Like **t**, 1 + **s**, 2: *z*u, Her*z*, Ski*zz*e.

Use of Capitals

Capital letters are required in German, contrary to English
usage, in the following cases:

1. As initial of all nouns and all words used as nouns: **die
Garage**, 'the garage'; **das Nützliche**, 'the useful'; **etwas Neues**,

'something new'; **das Reisen,** 'travelling'; nouns used with other functions take a small initial: **der Abend,** 'evening', but **abends,** 'in the evening'; **das Leid,** 'sorrow', but **es tut mir leid,** 'I am sorry'.

2. As initial of the pronoun **Sie** = 'you' (in all forms except **sich**), and of the corresponding possessives: **Haben Sie Ihren Hut?,** 'Have you got your hat?'

3. Similarly, but in correspondence only, **du, ihr** = 'you', and their possessives: **Wir erwarten Dich und Deine Schwester,** 'We expect you and your sister'.

4. Proper adjectives are not written with a capital unless formed from names of persons or forming part of a proper name: **das deutsche Buch,** 'the German book'; but **die Wagnerschen Opern,** 'Wagner's operas'; **das Deutsche Reich,** 'the German Empire'.

II. GENDER, AGREEMENT, ARTICLES, CASES

8. General Remarks

1. GENDER is a grammatical classification of nouns and pronouns into kinds comprising the *masculine*, to which names of males normally belong, the *feminine*, to which names of females normally belong, and the *neuter*, to which belong names that are neither masculine nor feminine, including all inanimate objects. The gender of German nouns is not, however, always decided by sex: neuter (inanimate) nouns in English are frequently masculine or feminine in German— *e.g.* **der Stein,** 'stone', **die Gabel,** 'fork'—while diminutives (see §43, 1) are always neuter in German irrespective of their being males or females—*e.g.* **das Männchen,** 'little man', **das Mädchen,** 'girl'. In German, gender affects not only the forms of nouns and pronouns themselves, but also the definite and indefinite articles, adjectives, and other modifying words accompanying them.

2. AGREEMENT shows how, in a given context, words are related to other words by means of variations in their forms; they are said to agree when their forms correspond in gender, number, case, or person—for example, 'I am a student' but 'We are students', where the singular verb ('am') agrees with the singular subject ('I') and the plural verb ('are') with the plural subject ('we'). In German, there is agreement between article and noun, verb and subject, etc.—*e.g.* the definite article agrees with its noun in gender, number, and case: **der Mann** (masculine nominative singular), **den Männern** (masculine dative plural), etc.

3. ARTICLES. In grammar there are two articles—the *definite* article and the *indefinite* article. In English, the definite article is the word 'the', used to denote a particular person or thing. Though invariable in English, the definite article in German changes its form to agree with its noun in gender, number, and case—for example, the nominative singular has the forms **der** (masculine), **die** (feminine), and **das** (neuter). The

22

indefinite article is, in English, the word 'a', not referring to a particular person or thing. Though invariable in English (except that, before a noun beginning with a vowel or silent h, 'a' becomes 'an' as in 'an animal', 'an hour'), the indefinite article in German changes its form to agree with its noun in gender and case—for example, the nominative singular has the forms **ein** (masculine), **eine** (feminine), and **ein** (neuter).

4. CASE is the form of a noun or pronoun which indicates the grammatical relation in which it stands to other words in a sentence. In German there are four cases: the Nominative, the Accusative, the Genitive, and the Dative.

9. Gender and Agreement

Der Mann ist alt.	The man is old.
Die Frau ist jung.	The woman is young.
Das Buch ist neu.	The book is new.
Das Mädchen ist hübsch.	The girl is pretty.
Der Hund ist groß.	The dog is large.
Der Winter ist kalt.	The winter is cold.
Die Tinte ist schwarz.	The ink is black.

1. There are three genders in German: masculine, feminine, and neuter. The gender of a noun does not necessarily have any connection with its meaning.

2. The definite article agrees with its noun in gender, number, and case, and has the following forms in the nominative singular:

Masc. **der**   *Fem.* **die**   *Neut.* **das**

3. The subject of a sentence is always in the nominative case, which answers the question 'who?' **(wer?)** or 'what?' **(was?)** placed before the main verb. The nominative case of **Mann** with the definite article is **der Mann,** of **Frau** is **die Frau,** and of **Buch** is **das Buch.**

4. Names of males are almost always masculine, and names of females feminine, but all nouns ending in the suffixes **-chen** and **-lein** (diminutives) are neuter, regardless of sex (see §43, 1).

5. Names of animals and things may be of any gender—each common noun should be learned together with its gender. (For such general rules of gender as can be formulated see §§41–43.)

6. Predicative adjectives—i.e., adjectives which do not immediately precede their noun—are not declined in German.

10. Declension of the Definite Article

	SINGULAR			PLURAL	
	Masc.	*Fem.*	*Neut.*	*All Genders*	
Nominative:	der	die	das	die,	the
Accusative:	den	die	das	die,	the
Genitive:	des	der	des	der,	of the
Dative:	dem	der	dem	den,	(to, for) the

11. Declension of Definite Article with Nouns (Singular)

	Masc.	*Fem.*	*Neut.*
Nom.:	der Mann	die Frau	das Kind
Acc.:	den Mann	die Frau	das Kind
Gen.:	des Mannes	der Frau	des Kindes
Dat.:	dem Manne	der Frau	dem Kinde

12. Declension of Definite Article with Nouns (Plural)

	Masc.	*Fem.*	*Neut.*
Nom.:	die Männer	die Frauen	die Kinder
Acc.:	die Männer	die Frauen	die Kinder
Gen.:	der Männer	der Frauen	der Kinder
Dat.:	den Männern	den Frauen	den Kindern

13. Repetition of the Definite Article, etc.

Der Mann und die Frau.	The man and woman.
Diese Gabel und dieser Löffel.	This fork and spoon.
Mein Vater und meine Mutter.	My father and mother.

In German, the article, possessive adjective, etc., must be repeated before each noun in the singular.

14. Various Uses of the Definite Article

The article is required before seasons, months, days of the week, streets, meals, and places of public resort:

Im Sommer; im Au¹gust.	In summer; in August.
Am Montag.	On Monday.
In der Bahnhofstraße.	In the Bahnhofstrasse.
Bei dem (Beim) Mittagessen.	At lunch.
Zur Schule gehen.	To go to school.
In die Kirche gehen.	To go to church.

NOTE: 1. The article is also used before **Stadt** (*f.*), 'town', **Himmel** (*m.*), 'sky; heaven', **Erde** (*f.*), 'earth', and **Hölle** (*f.*), 'hell'.
2. For the contraction of prepositions with the definite article, see §323.

15. Article with Noun in General Sense

Der Mensch ist sterblich.	Man is mortal.
Viele Menschen fürchten den Tod.	Many people are afraid of death.
Der Hund ist der treue Freund des Menschen.	The dog is the faithful friend of man.

1. A noun used in a general sense ('in general', 'all', 'every', etc., being implied with it) regularly has the definite article in German, though not usually in English.
2. Certain abstract nouns always take the article—*e.g.*, **die Natur,** 'nature', **das Schicksal,** 'fate, destiny', **die Ehe,** 'marriage', **der Tod,** 'death', **das Christentum,** 'Christianity'.

16. The Definite Article with Proper Names

Der Vesuv.	Mount Vesuvius.
Der Bodensee.	Lake Constance.
Der Rhein.	The (river) Rhine.
Die Pfalz.	The Palatinate.
Die Schweiz; die Tür¹kei.	Switzerland; Turkey.
Die Normandie.	Normandy.
Das schöne Frankreich.	Beautiful France.

Frankreich ist ein großes Land.	France is a big country.
Die Schweiz ist kleiner als Frankreich.	Switzerland is smaller than France.
Der kleine Robert.	Little Robert.

1. Geographical names always take the article when masculine or feminine, but *not* when neuter (except if preceded by an adjective)—exception: **das Elsaß,** Alsace.
2. Place names are neuter, except countries or regions ending in **-e, -ei, -ie,** or **-z** (which are feminine—see §42, 7) and a few others.
3. All proper names require the article when preceded by an adjective.

17. The Definite Article for Possessive Adjective

Gib mir die Hand!	Give me your hand.
Dreißig Leute hoben die Hand.	Thirty people raised their hands.

1. The definite article usually replaces the possessive adjective when no ambiguity would result as to the possessor.
2. With plurality of possessor, the object possessed is usually singular, if it is singular as regards the individual possessor.

18. Omission of Definite and Indefinite Article

1. The definite article with nouns used in a general sense is omitted
   (*a*) if an abstract noun expresses
      (i) a quality:

Geduld ist eine Tugend.	Patience is a virtue.
Schönheit ist vergänglich.	Beauty is transient.

      (ii) a state or action:

Schnelles Handeln ist jetzt angebracht.
Quick action is what is called for now.

Widerstand ist zwecklos.
Resistance is pointless.

(iii) time:

Anfang Juli (Mitte September, Ende des Monats) gehe ich auf Urlaub.
At the beginning of July (in the middle of September, at the end of the month) I am going on holiday.

Montag abend gehen wir ins Theater.
On Monday evening we are going to the theatre.

NOTE: If the abstract noun is qualified it takes the article—*e.g.*, **Das ist der reine Unsinn,** 'That is sheer nonsense', *but* **Das ist Unsinn.**

(*b*) in the plural:

Eltern lieben ihre Kinder.
Parents love their children.

Vorgesetzte sind auch nur Menschen!
One's superiors are only human, after all!

(*c*) in enumerations:

Gold und Silber sind Metalle.
Gold and silver are metals.

Ich kaufe Brot, Butter, Eier, Käse.
I buy bread, butter, eggs, cheese.

(*d*) in proverbs:

Not kennt kein Gebot.	Necessity knows no law.
Lügen haben kurze Beine.	Lies are short-lived.

(*e*) when the sense is partitive—i.e., when 'some' or 'any' is implied:

Können Sie mir Geld borgen?	Can you lend me some money?
Haben Sie Streichhölzer?	Have you any matches?

(*f*) with names of things:

Brot ist ein wichtiges Nahrungsmittel.
Bread is an important foodstuff.

Ich esse gern Kuchen.
I like (eating) cake.

Gold ist wertvoller als Silber.
Gold is more precious than silver.

But the article is used if reference to quantity is made—*e.g.*:

Herr Ober, einen Kaffee, bitte.
Waiter, a coffee (i.e., a cup of coffee), please.

Die Milch ist sauer.
The milk (i.e., the milk in a particular bottle) is sour.

Wieviel kostet das Brot?
How much does the bread (i.e., loaf of bread) cost?

(*g*) in numerous idiomatic expressions, *e.g.*:

Ich gehe jetzt nach Hause.
I'm going home now.

Wir essen zu Abend.
We are having supper.

Er verlor Haus und Hof.
He lost house and home.

Du mußt ihm guten Tag sagen.
You must say hello to him.

Nach getaner Arbeit.
After the work has been done.

(*h*) in officialese and clipped military language:

Auf Befehl des Königs.
At the King's command.

Nach Abschluß der Verhandlungen.
After the conclusion of the negotiations.

Es ist Aufgabe dieser Abteilung . . .
It is the task of this department . . .

Es ist nicht Sache dieses Gerichtes . . .
It is not the concern of this Court . . .

Hauptsache ist . . .
The main thing is . . .

2. The indefinite article is usually omitted before the un-qualified predicate after **sein** and **werden** when it indicates calling or profession:

Er ist (wurde) Arzt.
He is (became) a doctor.

but
Er ist ein guter Arzt.

19. Nominative of **ein** and **kein**

Ein Stein ist hart.	A stone is hard.
Eine Rose ist rot.	A rose is red.
Ein Flugzeug ist schnell.	An aeroplane is fast.
Kein Bahnhof ist sauber.	No railway station is clean.
Keine Rose ist grün.	No rose is green.
Kein Haus ist billig.	No house is cheap.

The indefinite article **ein** and its negative **kein** agree with their nouns, and have the following forms in the nominative singular:

Masc.: **ein** (*e.g.,* **ein Stein**)   *Masc.:* **kein** (*e.g.,* **kein Stein**)
Fem.: **eine** (*e.g.,* **eine Rose**)   *Fem.:* **keine** (*e.g.,* **keine Rose**)
Neut.: **ein** (*e.g.,* **ein Flugzeug**) *Neut.:* **kein** (*e.g.,* **kein Flug-zeug**)

NOTE: **Kein** is used to translate 'not a': **Barbara ist kein Kind,** 'Barbara is not a child'; **Er ist kein Lehrer,** 'He is not a teacher'.

20. Nominative of **welcher**

Welcher Mann ist reich?	Which man is rich?
Welche Blume ist rot?	Which flower is red?
Welches Auto ist schneller?	Which car is faster?

The interrogative adjective **welcher?** ('which?') has the following forms in the nominative singular, and agrees:

Masc.: **welcher**   *Fem.:* **welche**   *Neut.:* **welches**

NOTE: The adjectives **dieser** ('this'), **jener** ('that'), and **jeder** ('each' or 'every') take the same endings.

21. The Nominative Case

1. The nominative is the case of the subject, and is also used as a vocative.

2. Verbs indicating a state or transition, such as **sein, werden, bleiben, heißen, scheinen** (also, in literary usage, **sich dünken**), take a predicate nominative:

Er ist Student.	He is a student.
Er wird Lehrer.	He becomes a teacher.
Er blieb Soldat.	He remained a soldier.
Er heißt Richard.	His name is Richard.
Er scheint ein guter Lehrer zu sein.	He seems to be a good teacher.
Er dünkt sich ein großer Mann (*literary*).	He thinks himself a great man.

NOTE: With **werden, zu** is often used to indicate transition: **Das Wasser wurde zu Eis,** 'The water turned to ice'.

3. Other verbs require **als** before the nominative:

Er erwies sich als ein guter Freund.
He proved himself a good friend.

Er fühlt sich als Held.
He feels himself to be a hero.

22. The Accusative Case

1. The accusative is the case of the direct object of a verb. The direct object is put in the accusative case, which answers the question 'whom?' (**wen?**) or 'what?' (**was?**). It has the same form as the nominative, except in the masculine singular. Examples of the accusative as direct object:

Masc. sing.:	**Ich habe einen Bleistift.**	I have a pencil.
Fem. sing.:	**Er hat eine Mütze.**	He has a cap.
Neut. sing.:	**Wir haben ein Auto.**	We have a car.

2. Observe the following forms of the masculine singular accusative, and of the nominative and accusative plural (identical forms) of *all* genders:

Sing.: **den   einen   keinen   meinen,** etc.   **welchen**
(see §115, III) (see §115, II)
Plur.: **die   —   keine   meine,** etc.   **welche**

3. **Lehren,** 'to teach', and **kosten,** 'to cost', take the double accusative:

Ich lehre sie Physik.
I am teaching them physics.

Das Auto kostet ihn viel Geld.
The car costs him a lot of money.

NOTE: When both person and thing are mentioned, **unterrichten in** + dative is more usual than **lehren: Ich unterrichte sie in (der) Physik.**

4. **Fragen,** 'to ask', takes an accusative of the person, but only a neuter pronoun or clause as accusative of the thing:

Ich möchte Sie etwas fragen.
I should like to ask you something.

Er fragte mich alles mögliche.
He asked me all sorts of questions.

Er fragte, ob ich käme.
He asked whether I was coming.

23. Predicate Accusative

1. Verbs of naming, calling, etc., have a second accusative with predicative force:

Ich nannte ihn einen Dummkopf.
I called him a fool.

Er hieß (*literary; more usual:* **nannte**) **mich einen Lügner.**
He called me a liar.

Sie schalt ihn einen Faulenzer.
She called him a lazybones.

Man schimpfte ihn einen Verbrecher.
People called him a criminal.

2. Some verbs of regarding, considering, etc., take an accusative with **als**:

Ich betrachte ihn als einen Feind.
I regard him as an enemy.

Früher sah ich ihn als meinen treusten Freund an.
I used to consider him my most faithful friend.

NOTE: **Halten** takes **für**+accusative: **Ich halte ihn für einen guten Mann,** 'I consider him to be a good man'.

24. Adverbial Accusative

The accusative is used adverbially to express time 'when' and 'how long', price, and measure (see also §§284, 285); also way or road after verbs of motion:

Diesen Sommer fährt er ins Ausland.
This summer he is going abroad.

Er war einen Monat (or einen Monat lang) hier.
He was here for a month.

Die Zeitschrift kostet eine Mark.
The magazine costs one Mark.

Das Lineal ist einen Meter lang.
The ruler is one metre long.

Welchen Weg gehen Sie?
Which way are you going?

Sie fahren den Fluß hinunter.
They go down the river.

Er steigt den Berg hinauf.
He climbs up the mountain.

25. The Dative Case

1. The dative is the case of the indirect object, and answers the question 'to whom?' (wem?).

2. Observe the following examples of the dative as indirect object:

Er gibt dem Lehrer (*indirect object*) **das Buch** (*direct object*). He gives the teacher the book (= He gives the book *to* the teacher).

Ich erzähle dem Kind ein Märchen. I tell the child a fairy tale (= I tell a fairy tale *to* the child).

3. The dative denotes the person for whose advantage or disadvantage a thing is or is done, corresponding not only to the English 'to' or 'for' but also to 'from':

Er gab dem Kind Bonbons.	He gave the child sweets.
Mein Vater kauft mir die Bücher.	My father is buying the books for me.
Er hat mir Geld gestohlen.	He stole money from me.

4. The dative singular often has the same form as the nominative, and always in the case of feminine nouns; but masculine and neuter monosyllables sometimes add **-e** in the dative singular (*e.g.*, **dem Manne, dem Kinde**). Though once usual, this **-e** is now tending more and more to disappear.

26. Dative with Adjectives

German equivalents of English adjectives followed by 'to' (with some others) take the dative:

Er blieb mir treu.	He remained faithful to me.
Sie sieht ihrem Bruder ähnlich.	She looks like her brother.

27. Dative with Verbs

The dative stands as the personal and only object after many verbs, the equivalents of which are transitive in English:

Er begegnete (folgte) mir.	He met (followed) me.
Er hat mir gedroht.	He threatened me.
Womit kann ich Ihnen dienen?	Can I help you? (*in a shop*)
Er wird mir beistehen.	He will assist me.
Verzeihen Sie mir!	Forgive me.

28. The Genitive Case

Masc.	*Fem.*	*Neut.*
des Mann(e)s, of the man	der Frau, of the woman	des Kind(e)s, of the child
dieses Mann(e)s, of this man	dieser Frau, of this woman	dieses Kind(e)s, of this child
eines Mann(e)s, of a man	einer Frau, of a woman	eines Kind(e)s, of a child

—and similarly with jener, mein, sein, etc. (see §§61 and 114).

1. The use of the genitive in German is much the same as that of the English possessive, and answers the question 'whose?' (wessen?):

Wessen Tasche ist das? Das ist die Tasche meiner Mutter.
Whose bag is that? That is the bag of my mother (my mother's bag).

Wessen Auto ist in der Garage? Das Auto meines Onkels ist in der Garage.
Whose car is in the garage? My uncle's car is in the garage.

2. Most masculine and neuter nouns have the genitive singular optionally in -s or -es, but those which end in -el, -en, or -er have -s only.

3. The genitive singular of feminine nouns is identical in form with the nominative singular.

4. There is no apostrophe before the s in German to indicate the possessive as in 'the teacher's book', which in German is expressed in the form: 'the book of the teacher'—**das Buch des Lehrers.**

5. The genitive usually follows the governing noun, unless the genitive is a person's name:

Die Mutter des Kindes. The mother of the child, the child's mother.
Das Haus meines Freundes. My friend's house.
but **Roberts Buch.** Robert's book.

Note that **Vater, Mutter, Großvater** ('grandfather') and **Großmutter** (also **Tante,** 'aunt', and **Onkel,** 'uncle', with names only) also precede the governing noun in the genitive if they are associated with particular persons:

Vaters Hut hängt im Flur. Father's hat hangs in the hall.
Großmutters Brille liegt auf dem Tisch. Grandmother's spectacles are lying on the table.
Wo ist Tante Ninas Tasche? Where is Aunt Nina's bag?

NOTE: Instead of **Vaters Hut, Mutters Handtasche** ('handbag'), **Onkel Peters Auto,** etc., one can equally say **der Hut von Vater, die Handtasche von Mutter, das Auto von Onkel Peter.**

For prepositions with Genitive, see §321.

29. Genitive of Time

Ich höre des Abends gern Musik.
I like listening to music in the evening.

Ich ging eines Tages im Park spazieren.
I went walking one day in the park.

Viele Touristen nehmen sich kleine Stücke von der Ruine mit, und eines schönen Tages wird nichts mehr von ihr übrig sein.
Many tourists take away fragments of the ruin, and one of these days there will be nothing left of it.

Ich konnte sie nur mittwochs treffen.
I could only meet her on Wednesdays (*or* on a Wednesday—
cf. 'of a Wednesday').

1. Point of time is often expressed by an adverbial genitive
singular, when denoting indefinite time, or time with reference
to a habitual action, but only with **Tag,** 'day', days of the week,
and divisions of the day (like **morgens,** 'in the morning',
abends, 'in the evening'), used with or without the article.
2. When the article is omitted, the genitive is written with a
small initial letter, the word then acting as an adverb.
NOTE: 1. With determinatives (see §116, 1, note) other than the
article, the accusative must be used, except in the expression **dieser
Tage** (genitive plural)=(i) 'in a day or so'; (ii) 'the other day'.
2. While **des Abends** ('in the evening(s)') is still in common use,
des Tages ('by day'), though still possible, is best avoided; more usual
are **am Tage** and **tagsüber.** Similarly, **abends** (=**des Abends**) is
standard, but **tags** is little used nowadays.
3. **Nacht,** though feminine, is similarly used, with or without the
masculine article: **Des Nachts** (*or* **nachts**) **schläft man,** 'We sleep by
night'.

30. Position of Genitive

The genitive more usually follows the governing noun, unless
the genitive is a person's name:

Das Haus meines Freundes.   My friend's house.
Schillers Werke.   The works of Schiller.

31. Genitive with Adjectives and Verbs

1. Some German adjectives govern a genitive, usually corresponding to an 'of' construction in English:

Das ist ihrer nicht würdig.
That is not worthy of them.

Er wurde des Mordes schuldig befunden.
He was found guilty of murder.

Sein Handeln war bar aller Vernunft (*or* aller Vernunft bar).
His action was devoid of all reason.

Sie waren seiner Hilfe bedürftig. (*literary*)
They were in need of his help.

Wenn ich seiner habhaft werden könnte, dann würde ich ihm meine Meinung sagen!
If I could lay hands on him I would tell him what I think of him!

NOTE: **Los,** 'rid of', and **satt,** 'tired of', take the accusative: **Ich möchte ihn loswerden,** 'I'd like to get rid of him'; **Er hat (*or* ist) ihre ewige Nörgelei satt,** 'He is tired of her continual nagging' (cf. also §58, 5). With **voll,** 'full of', there are three possible constructions: (i) **Die Straße war voll Menschen;** (ii) **Die Straße war voll von Menschen;** (iii) **Die Straße war voller Menschen.**

2. The German equivalents of some English transitive verbs take a genitive:

Er gedachte seiner gestorbenen Freunde.
He remembered his dead friends.

Ich bedarf Ihrer Hilfe.
I need your help.

3. Verbs of accusing, convicting, acquitting, depriving, and some others, take a genitive of the remoter object:

Man klagt ihn des Mordes an.
He is accused of murder.

Man entband ihn seines Eides.
He was released from his oath.

4. Impersonal verbs expressing mental affection take a genitive of the remoter object (the cause of the emotion), though such constructions are now for the most part archaic:

Es jammert mich seiner.

I pity him.

(*modern:* **Ich bedaure ihn.**)

NOTE: 1. Some of these verbs are also used personally with the cause of the emotion as subject: **Er jammert mich** (*literary use*), 'I pity him'.

2. For the genitive after reflexive verbs, see §222, 4.

32. Adverbial Genitive

1. The genitive may express adverbial relations of place and manner, mostly confined to fixed phrases:

Seines Weges gehen.	To go on one's way.
Linker Hand.	On the left hand.
Meines Erachtens.	In my opinion.
Zweiter Klasse reisen.	To travel second class.
Guter (schlechter) Dinge sein.	To be in a good (bad) mood.
Du bist wohl des Teufels!	You must be mad!
Du wirst noch Hungers sterben, wenn du nicht mehr ißt!	You'll die of hunger if you don't eat more!

NOTE: For genitive of time, see §29.

2. The adverbial genitive with **-weise** is a common way of forming adverbs of manner from adjectives (**die Weise** = 'way, manner'; cf. English 'likewise', 'crosswise', etc.):

Glücklicherweise.	Fortunately.
Klugerweise.	Wisely, sensibly.

For further examples, see §249, 4.

III. NOUNS

33. General Remarks

A noun is a word which is the name of a living being or thing, such as a person, animal, or plant, of an inanimate object, such as a chair, gate, or book, or of a place, quality, idea, action, etc., such as 'village', 'bravery', 'theory', 'travel'. Whereas almost all English nouns form their plural in '-(e)s', only a very few—a handful of foreign borrowings—do in German. To form the nominative plural from the nominative singular the ending **-e** or **-er** or **-en** may be added or it may be left unchanged; furthermore, the root vowel may modify (i.e., take an umlaut). *All* nouns in German begin with a capital letter. There are various kinds of nouns, the most important of which are:

Abstract nouns: These are nouns which represent some quality, action, state, or general idea quite apart from any particular thing. Thus a green leaf, a green dress, and a green liquid all have the quality of 'greenness', which is an abstract noun—as are 'expulsion', the action of expelling, and 'poverty', the state of being poor. Many German abstract nouns end in **-heit** or **-keit** (both always feminine)—*e.g.* **die Schönheit,** 'beauty', and **die Tapferkeit,** 'gallantry'.

Concrete nouns: These are nouns which denote a particular thing, such as 'leaf', 'dress', 'liquid'—i.e., material objects as opposed to qualities, actions, states, or conditions, which are represented by abstract nouns.

Common nouns and *proper nouns:* Common nouns are names denoting any member of a group, as distinct from proper nouns, which denote one particular member of a group; thus 'river' is a common noun, while 'Thames' is a proper noun. Whereas in English only proper nouns begin with a capital letter, in German both common and proper nouns have an initial capital—*e.g.* **der Fluß** ('river'), **die Themse** ('the Thames'). Every proper noun has a corresponding common noun—*e.g.*

39

Hamlet (proper noun) is a play (common noun), Selborne (proper noun) is a village (common noun), Churchill (proper noun) was a statesman (common noun).

Collective nouns: These are nouns denoting a group-term, singular in form but plural in sense—*e.g.* 'a *number* of people', 'a *gaggle* of geese'. In German many collective nouns begin with **Ge-** and almost all of these are neuter—*e.g.* **das Gebirge,** 'mountain range', **das Gepäck,** 'luggage' (see §43, 4 and note). The agreement of a verb with a collective noun is in general the same in German as in English, with similar uncertainty and fluctuation.

Compound nouns: These are nouns made up of two or more nouns—*e.g.* **Zitronenlimonade** ('lemon-squash'), which is a combination of **Zitrone(n),** 'lemon(s)', and **Limonade,** 'lemonade'. The German language is very rich in compound nouns. In German, only the last component is declined, and the gender is that of the last component.

34. Strong Declension of Nouns

	I. **der Hund,** dog		II. **der Sohn,** son	
	Singular	*Plural*	*Singular*	*Plural*
Nom.:	der Hund	die Hunde	der Sohn	die Söhne
Acc.:	den Hund	die Hunde	den Sohn	die Söhne
Gen.:	des Hund(e)s	der Hunde	des Sohn(e)s	der Söhne
Dat.:	dem Hund(e)	den Hunden	dem Sohn(e)	den Söhnen

	III. **die Hand,** hand	
	Singular	*Plural*
Nom.:	die Hand	die Hände
Acc.:	die Hand	die Hände
Gen.:	der Hand	der Hände
Dat.:	der Hand	den Händen

NOTE: For classes of nouns so declined, see §37.

1. These three models are merely variations of the same type of noun declension (called the primary form of the 'strong declension').

2. Feminines are invariable in the singular; masculines and neuters take -(e)s in the genitive and sometimes -e in the dative singular. In modern usage, the e in both the genitive and dative singular is becoming less and less usual.

NOTE: 1. The e of the genitive and dative singular is mostly found in monosyllables (its inclusion or omission is often a matter of euphony), rarely in polysyllables (least of all in familiar language), but the e of the genitive is always retained after final -s, -ß, -sch, -tz, and -z.
2. The e of the dative singular is omitted when a preposition immediately precedes: aus Holz, 'of wood'; but exceptionally, zu Hause ('at home'), nach Hause ('home').
3. Nouns ending in -nis double the last consonant before an ending: das Bedürfnis, 'need', genitive singular des Bedürfnisses, nominative plural Bedürfnisse; so also ß=ss after a short stem-vowel: Fluß, 'river', Flusses, Flüsse.

3. All add -e in the plural with additional -n in the dative.
4. All feminine monosyllables of this model take umlaut in the plural.

IV. das Dorf, village

	Singular	Plural
Nom.:	das Dorf	die Dörfer
Acc.:	das Dorf	die Dörfer
Gen.:	des Dorf(e)s	der Dörfer
Dat.:	dem Dorf(e)	den Dörfern

NOTE: For classes of nouns so declined, see §37.

1. The singular is after the Hund model (I).
2. The Dorf model differs from the Hund model by adding -er in the plural (a, o, u, stems always with umlaut), and is called the 'enlarged form'.

V. der Maler, painter

	Singular	Plural
Nom.:	der Maler	die Maler
Acc.:	den Maler	die Maler
Gen.:	des Malers	der Maler
Dat.:	dem Maler	den Malern

VI. der Vater, father

	Singular	Plural
Nom.:	der Vater	die Väter
Acc.:	den Vater	die Väter
Gen.:	des Vaters	der Väter
Dat.:	dem Vater	den Vätern

NOTE: 1. For classes of nouns so declined, see §37.

2. Nouns ending in -n do not add -n in the dative plural: **Garten, Gärten.**

These models differ from **Hund** and **Sohn** only in the omission of **e** in the various endings, and are further variations of the strong declension—called the 'contracted form'.

35. Weak Declension of Nouns

VII. der Junge, boy

	Singular	Plural
Nom.:	der Junge	die Jungen
Acc.:	den Jungen	die Jungen
Gen.:	des Jungen	der Jungen
Dat.:	dem Jungen	den Jungen

VIII. der Graf, count

	Singular	Plural
Nom.:	der Graf	die Grafen
Acc.:	den Grafen	die Grafen
Gen.:	des Grafen	der Grafen
Dat.:	dem Grafen	den Grafen

IX. die Blume, flower

	Singular	Plural
Nom.:	die Blume	die Blumen
Acc.:	die Blume	die Blumen
Gen.:	der Blume	der Blumen
Dat.:	der Blume	den Blumen

NOTE: 1. For classes of nouns so declined, see §37.

2. **Herr** drops **e** before -n in the singular: accusative, etc.: **Herrn;** otherwise it follows the **Graf** model.

3. **Der Buchstabe,** 'letter (of the alphabet)', follows the **Junge** model, though the genitive singular **Buchstabens (Name** model, X) is now normally used.

1. These models are all variations of the same type of declension, called the 'weak declension'.

2. In masculines all cases of the singular, except the nominative, end in **-n** or **-en.**

3. The plurals end in **-n** or **-en** throughout.

36. Mixed Declension of Nouns

X. der Name, name

Singular	Plural
Nom.: **der Name**	**die Namen**
Acc.: **den Namen**	**die Namen**
Gen.: **des Namens**	**der Namen**
Dat.: **dem Namen**	**den Namen**

XI. der Vetter, cousin

Singular	Plural
Nom.: **der Vetter**	**die Vettern**
Acc.: **den Vetter**	**die Vettern**
Gen.: **des Vetters**	**der Vettern**
Dat.: **dem Vetter**	**den Vettern**

XII. das Ohr, ear

Singular	Plural
Nom.: **das Ohr**	**die Ohren**
Acc.: **das Ohr**	**die Ohren**
Gen.: **des Ohr(e)s**	**der Ohren**
Dat.: **dem Ohr(e)**	**den Ohren**

NOTE: For classes of nouns so declined, see §37.

1. Model X is a variation of the **Junge** model (VII), adding **-s** in the genitive singular.

2. Model XI follows the **Maler** model (V) in the singular and the **Junge** model in the plural.

3. Model XII follows the **Hund** model (I) in the singular and the **Graf** model (VIII) in the plural.

37. Summary of Noun Declension

A. STRONG DECLENSION

I. **Hund**
II. **Sohn** ⟩Models
III. **Hand**

[Primary Form]

	Masc.	*Fem.*	*Neut.*			*All genders*	
Sing. Nom.:	—	—	—	*Plur. Nom.:*	**-e**		(many
Acc.:	—	—	—	*Acc.:*	**-e**		with
Gen.:	**-(e)s**	—	**-(e)s**	*Gen.:*	**-e**		umlaut)
Dat.:	**-(e)**	—	**-(e)**	*Dat.:*	**-en**		

After I are declined: Masc. monosyllables in §38, 1; neut. monosyllables in §38, 2; nouns ending in **-at, -ich, -ig, -ing, -nis, -sal**; foreign mascs. ending in **-an, -ar, -ier**; also sometimes in **-or** and **-al** stressed. After II are declined: Masc. monosyllables, except as in §38, 1 and §38, 4; the neuts. **Floß** ('raft') and **Chor** ('choir, chancel'); those ending in **-ast**; those ending in **-al, -an, -ar** sometimes. After III are declined: Fems. in §38, 3.

IV. **Dorf** Model

[Enlarged Form]

	Masc.	*Neut.*			*Masc.*	*Neut.*	
Sing. Nom.:	—	—	*Plur. Nom.:*	**-er**	**-er**		(um-
Acc.:	—	—	*Acc.:*	**-er**	**-er**		laut)
Gen.:	**-(e)s**	**-(e)s**	*Gen.:*	**-er**	**-er**		
Dat.:	**-(e)**	**-(e)**	*Dat.:*	**-ern**	**-ern**		

After IV are declined: Mascs. in §38,4; neut. monosyllables, except those in §38,2; nouns ending in **-tum; das Regiment**

(= 'regiment'; pl. **Regimente** = 'régimes'), **das Spital** ('hospital');
no feminines; stems having **a, o, u,** take umlaut in the plural.

V. **Maler**⎫
          ⎬Models
VI. **Vater**⎭

[Contracted Form]

	Masc.	*Fem.*	*Neut.*			*Masc.*	*Fem.*	*Neut.*
Sing. Nom.:	—	—	—	*Plur. Nom.:*	—	∺	—
Acc.:	—	—	—	*Acc.:*	—	∺	—
Gen.:	-s	—	-s	*Gen.:*	—	∺	—
Dat.:	—	—	—	*Dat.:*	-n	∺n	-n

(some with umlaut)

After V are declined: Mascs. and neuts. ending in **-el, -en, -er**
(except those in §38, 5); diminutives ending in **-chen** and **-lein;**
neuter collectives beginning with **Ge-** and ending in **-e; der
Käse** ('cheese'). After VI are declined: The nouns in §38, 5,
including the feminines **Mutter, Tochter.**

NOTE: The modified vowel (i.e., the one taking the umlaut) is always
the vowel on which the stress occurs—*e.g.*, **der Mo'rast** ('bog,
quagmire'), *plur.* **die Mo'räste.**

B. WEAK DECLENSION

VII. **Junge**⎫
VIII. **Graf** ⎬Models
IX. **Blume**⎭

	Masc.	*Fem.*			*Masc.*	*Fem.*
Sing. Nom.:	-(e)	—	*Plur. Nom.:*	-(e)n	-n
Acc.:	-(e)n	—	*Acc.:*	-(e)n	-n
Gen.:	-(e)n	—	*Gen.:*	-(e)n	-n
Dat.:	-(e)n	—	*Dat.:*	-(e)n	-n

Thus are declined: After VII, mascs. ending in **-e** except **Käse**
(Model V); after VIII, mascs. of §38, 6, many foreign mascs.,
all fems. (except as in §38, 3, and those ending in **-e**); after IX,
all fems. ending in **-e.**

C. MIXED DECLENSION
X. **Name** Model

	Masc.		*Masc.*
Sing. Nom.:	—	*Plur. Nom.:*	-n
Acc.:	-n	*Acc.:*	-n
Gen.:	-ns	*Gen.:*	-n
Dat.:	-n	*Dat.:*	-n

(no umlaut)

Thus are declined: Those in §38, 7.

XI. **Vetter** } Models
XII. **Ohr**

	Masc.	*Neut.*		*Masc.*	*Neut.*
Sing. Nom.:	—	—	*Plur. Nom.:*	-(e)n	-(e)n
Acc.:	—	—	*Acc.:*	-(e)n	-(e)n
Gen.:	-(e)s	-(e)s	*Gen.:*	-(e)n	-(e)n
Dat.:	-(e)	-(e)	*Dat.:*	-(e)n	-(e)n

(no umlaut)

Thus are declined: After XI, the nouns in §38, 8, rejecting **-e**
throughout; after XII, those in §38, 9, foreign mascs. ending in
unstressed **-or.**

38. Reference Lists of Nouns

N.B. In the following lists words of less common occurrence
have been omitted.

1. **Masculine monosyllables of** *Hund* **model** (§34, I)

Aal, eel
Aar (*poetical*), eagle
Akt, act
Arm, arm
Bau, dwelling of animal
Docht, wick
Dolch, dagger
Dom, cathedral
Farn, fern
Golf, gulf (of sea)
Grad, degree
Hall, peal, clang

Halm, stalk, blade
Halt, halt, stop
Hauch, breath
Holm, beam, spar;
    islet
Horst, eyrie
Hort, hoard; refuge
Huf, hoof
Hund, dog
Kurs, course; rate of
    exchange
Lachs, salmon

Lauch, leek
Laut, sound
Mohn, poppy
Molch, salamander
Mond, moon
Pfad, path
Pol, pole (North or
    South)
Port (*poetical*), port,
    harbour
Puls, pulse
Punkt, point

Putsch, putsch
Ruf, call
Rutsch, landslip
Schuh, shoe
Spalt, split
Spuk, ghost

Stoff, material
Strand, beach
Strauß, ostrich
Sund, sound, strait
Tag, day
Takt, time, measure (in music)

Thron, throne
Trakt, tract, stretch
Wal, whale
Zoll, inch
Zuck, jerk

NOTE: The above list contains only nouns with stem vowel **a, o, u, au.**

2. Neuter monosyllables of *Hund* model (§34, I)

Band, tie, bond, link
Beet, garden-bed
Beil, hatchet
Bein, leg
Bier, beer
Boot, boat
Bord, shelf
Brot, loaf
Bund, bundle (of wood, straw); bunch (of radishes)
Ding[1], thing
Erz, ore
Fell, hide
Fest, festival
Gift, poison
Gleis, track
Haar, hair
Heer, army
Heft, handle; note-book

Jahr, year
Joch, yoke
Kreuz, cross
Los, lot
Lot, plumb-line
Mal, (point of) time
Maß, measure
Meer, sea
Moor, swamp
Moos, moss
Netz, net
Öhr, eye (of needle)
Öl, oil
Paar, pair, couple
Pferd, horse
Pfund, pound
Pult, desk
Recht, right
Reh, roe
Reich, empire
Riff, reef

Rohr, reed; pipe
Roß (*poetical*), horse, steed
Salz, salt
Schaf, sheep
Schiff, ship
Schwein, pig
Seil, rope
Sieb, sieve
Spiel, game
Stück, piece
Tau, rope, cable
Teil, share
Tier, animal
Tor, gate
Wehr, weir
Werk, work
Zelt, tent
Ziel, goal

[1] **Dinge** is the usual plural; **Dinger** is used of young girls, children and animals together with an adjective expressing pity, contempt, affection, etc.—*e.g.*, **die armen kleinen Dinger!** 'the poor little things!'

3. Feminines of *Hand* model (§34, III)

Angst, fear, anxiety
Ausflucht, evasion
Auskunft, information
Axt, axe
Bank, bench
Braut, fiancée; bride
Brust, breast; chest
Faust, fist

Frucht, fruit
Gans, goose
Geschwulst, swelling
Gruft, tomb, vault
Hand, hand
Haut, skin
Kluft, cleft
Kraft, strength

Kuh, cow
Kunst, art
Laus, louse
Luft, air
Lust, pleasure; desire
Macht, might
Magd, farm-girl
Maus, mouse

Nacht, night
Naht, seam
Not, need, necessity
Nuß, nut
Sau, sow

Schnur, string
Stadt, town, city
Wand, wall
Wulst, roll, pad
Wurst, sausage

Zunft, guild
Zusammenkunft, meeting

4. Masculines of *Dorf* model (§34, IV)
And nouns in -tum

Geist, spirit
Gott, god
Leib, body
Mann, man

Mund, mouth
Rand, edge
Schi *or* Ski, ski
Strauch, bush, shrub

Vormund, guardian
Wald, forest
Wurm, worm

5. Nouns of V*ater* model (§34, VI)

der Acker, (ploughed) field
der Apfel, apple
der Boden, floor; soil
der Bogen[1], bow
der Bruder, brother
der Faden, thread
der Garten, garden
der Graben, ditch
der Hafen, harbour
der Hammer, hammer

der Kasten[1], box
das Kloster, monastery; nunnery
der Kragen[1], collar
der Laden[2], shop; shutter
der Magen[1], stomach
der Mangel, lack
der Mantel, coat
die Mutter, mother
der Nagel, nail

der Ofen, stove
der Sattel, saddle
der Schaden, damage
der Schnabel, beak
der Schwager, brother-in-law
die Tochter, daughter
der Vater, father
der Vogel, bird

[1] Also of **Maler** model (§34, V).
[2] In the second meaning, also of **Maler** model (§34, V).

6. Nouns of *Graf* model (§35, VIII)
(all masculine)

Bär, bear
Bursch[1], lad
Christ, Christian
Elf, elf
Fink, finch
Fürst, prince
Geck, (conceited) ass

Gesell[1], fellow
Gnom, gnome
Graf, count
Held, hero
Herr[2], gentleman; master
Hirt[1], shepherd

Mensch, human being
Mohr, Moor
Narr, fool
Ochs[1], ox
Prinz, prince
Spatz, sparrow
Tor, fool

[1] More common with -e ending (**Bursche**, etc.)—**Junge** model, §37, VII.
[2] Singular adds -n only.

7. Nouns of *Name* model (§36, X)
(all masculine)

Friede, peace	**Glaube,** faith	**Name,** name
Funke, spark	**Haufe,** heap; crowd (of	**Same,** seed
Gedanke, thought	people)	**Wille,** will

And **das Herz,** 'heart', *Acc.:* **Herz,** *Gen.:* **Herzens,** *Dat.:* **Herzen,** *plural (all genders):* **Herzen.**

NOTE: All these words (except **Herz**) sometimes have the nominative singular ending in **-en**: in the case of **Friede** and **Funke**, both forms are commonly found; **Gedanke, Glaube, Name,** and **Wille** are less common with the **-en** form; **Haufe** (except in the second meaning above) and **Same** are more common with the **-en** form.

8. Nouns of *Vetter* model (§36, XI)

das Auge, eye	**das Interesse,** interest	**der See,** lake
der Bauer[1], peasant, farmer	**der Konsul,** consul	**der Stachel,** sting
das Ende, end	**der Muskel,** muscle	**der Vetter,** cousin
der Gevatter (*archaic*), godfather	**der Nachbar**[1], neighbour	
	der Pantoffel[2], slipper	

[1] Also adds **-n** throughout singular.   [2] Also **Maler** model (§34, 5).

9. Nouns of *Ohr* model (§36, XII)

der Ahn[1] (*poetical*), ancestor	**der Lorbeer,** laurel	**der Staat,** state
das Bett, bed	**der Mast**[2], mast	**der Strahl,** ray, beam
der Doktor, doctor	**der Nerv,** nerve	**der Untertan**[1], subject (of a king, etc.)
das Hemd, shirt	**das Ohr,** ear	**der Zins,** interest
das Insekt, insect	**der Psalm,** psalm	
	der Schmerz, pain	

[1] Also of **Graf** model (§35, VIII).   [2] Also of **Hund** model (§34, I).

39. Essential Parts of Nouns

The 'essential parts' of a noun are the nominative singular, genitive singular, and nominative plural; from these the full declension of any noun may be inferred. These are the forms usually given in dictionaries—*e.g.* **Sohn,** *m.* (-(e)s, ⸚e), meaning that the masculine noun **Sohn** has the genitive singular form **Sohnes** or **Sohns** and the nominative plural form **Söhne.**

40. Compound Nouns

In compound nouns the last component only is declined; they follow the gender of the last component:

Nom. Sing.	Gen. Sing.	Nom. Plur.
der Handschuh, glove	des Handschuh(e)s	die Handschuhe
der Obstbaum, fruit-tree.	des Obstbaum(e)s	die Obstbäume

NOTE: 1. Compounds with -mann have as plural -männer (individuals), or -leute (collectively): Staatsmänner, 'statesmen'; Landleute, 'country-people'; cf. der Kaufmann ('businessman, shopkeeper'), plural Kaufleute; der Seemann ('seaman'), plural Seeleute.
2. There are a *very* few compound nouns both of whose components are declined—*e.g.*, der Hohepriester ('high priest'): acc. den Hohenpriester, gen. des Hohenpriesters, dat. dem Hohenpriester; pl. die Hohenpriester; das Hohelied ('the Song of Solomon'), im Hohenlied ('in the Song of Solomon'); (figurative use) Schillers Gedicht „Die Bürgschaft" ist ein Hoheslied der Freundschaft, 'Schiller's poem "Die Bürgschaft" is a song in praise of friendship'.

41. Rules of Gender—Masculine Nouns

Masculine are:

1. Most nouns ending in -en (but not infinitives—see §43, 2), -er (especially in relation to trades and professions), -ich (except das Reich, 'empire'), -ig, -ing, -ling, -s. Examples:

der Garten, garden
der Kellner, waiter
der Teppich, carpet
der Essig, vinegar

der Hering, herring
der Jüngling, young man
der Knicks, curtsy

2. The days of the week:

der Sonntag, Sunday
der Montag, Monday
der Dienstag, Tuesday
der Mittwoch, Wednesday

der **Donnerstag,** Thursday
der **Freitag,** Friday
der **Samstag** *or* **Sonnabend,** Saturday

NOTE: **Samstag** is used mainly in the South and in the Rhineland; **Sonnabend** is used mainly in Central and North Germany.

3. The months of the year:

der **Januar,** January
der **Februar,** February
der **März,** March
der **A¹pril,** April
der **Mai,** May
der **Juni,** June
der **Juli,** July
der **Au¹gust,** August
der **September,** September
der **Oktober,** October
der **November,** November
der **Dezember,** December

NOTE: The names of the months are rarely inflected.

4. The four seasons:

der **Frühling,** spring
der **Sommer,** summer
der **Herbst,** autumn
der **Winter,** winter

NOTE: The days of the week, the months of the year, and the seasons usually require the article—**am Sonntag,** 'on Sunday', **im Dezember,** 'in December', **im Winter,** 'in winter'.

5. The cardinal points and all points of the compass:

der **Norden,** north
der **Süden,** south
der **Osten,** east
der **Westen,** west

NOTE: The shorter forms **der Nord, der Süd, der Ost, der West,** are occasionally found when referring to the wind—*e.g.*, **der Nord heulte um den Leuchtturm,** 'the north wind howled around the lighthouse'; cf. also **der Wind kommt aus** (*or* **von**) **Nord,** 'the wind is blowing from the north'. The longer forms (**der Nordwind,** etc.) are in far more frequent use.

der Südwesten, the south-west
der Nordosten, the north-east

6. Most monosyllabic nouns which form verb stems—*e.g.*:

  der Fall, fall, drop (*fallen*)
  der Lauf, course (*laufen*)
  der Haß, hatred (*hassen*)

7. The names of most mountains—*e.g.*:

  der Brocken, the Brocken
  der Montblanc, Mont Blanc
  der Mount Everest
  der Vesuv, Vesuvius
  der Ätna, Etna
  der Olymp, Olympus

8. (*a*) The names of most non-German rivers (except those ending in -a or -e, which are feminine—see §42, 8(*b*)—*e.g.*:

der Nil, the Nile	der Don
der Mississippi	der Po
der Ganges	der Tiber

  (*b*) The names of a few important German rivers—*e.g.*:

der Rhein, the Rhine	der Main
der Neckar	der Inn

9. Foreign nouns ending in

(*a*) -an—*e.g.*, der Vulkan, volcano.
(*b*) -ant—*e.g.*, der Fabrikant, manufacturer.
(*c*) -ast—*e.g.*, der Palast, palace.
(*d*) -ent—*e.g.*, der Dirigent, conductor (of orchestra).

EXCEPTIONS: All words in -ment except der Moment (=Augenblick, 'moment'), and der Zement, 'cement'; also das Äquivalent, 'equivalent' (in chemistry), and das Patent. See §43, 11 (*d*).

(*e*) -iker—*e.g.*, der Fanatiker, fanatic.
(*f*) -ist—*e.g.*, der Komponist, composer.
(*g*) -or—*e.g.*, der Traktor, tractor.
(*h*) -us—*e.g.*, der Organismus, organism.

EXCEPTIONS: das Genus, das Opus, das Tempus ('tense' (of a verb)), das Virus.

For rules of gender for feminine and neuter nouns, see §§42 and 43 respectively.

42. Rules of Gender—Feminine Nouns

Feminine are:

1. All nouns with the suffixes **-ei, -heit, -keit, -schaft, -ung.** Examples:

die Partei, (political) party
die Freiheit, freedom
die Eitelkeit, vanity

die Freundschaft, friendship
die Hoffnung, hope

NOTE: **Das Petschaft,** 'seal', 'signet', is a Czech-derived word, the **-schaft** of which is not a true suffix.

2. All nouns formed from masculine nouns denoting a person by adding **-in** to give the feminine equivalent. Examples:

die Freundin (from *der Freund,* friend)
die Engländerin (from *der Engländer,* Englishman)

NOTE: 1. Such feminine nouns double **-n** in the plural and often take umlaut: **der Koch,** cook, **die Köchin,** *plur.* **Köchinnen.**
2. The **e** present in weak nouns of nationality in the masculine (*e.g.,* **der Däne**) is replaced in the feminine by **-in (die Dänin);** exception: **der Deutsche—die Deutsche.**

3. Most trees. Examples:

die Eiche, oak
die Tanne, fir
die Fichte, pine

die Pappel, poplar
die Buche, beech
die Birke, birch

EXCEPTIONS: **der Ahorn,** maple, **der Flieder,** lilac, **der Holunder,** elder.

4. A large number of garden flowers. Examples:

die Orchidee, orchid
die Schwertlilie, iris
die Rose, rose

die Dahlie, dahlia
die Nelke, carnation
die Chrysantheme, chrysanthemum

5. Cardinal numerals, when used in the sense of 'the figure 6', 'the figure 4', etc. Examples:

<table>
<tr><td>Eine römische Drei.</td><td>A Roman three.</td></tr>
<tr><td>Eine Eins werfen.</td><td>To throw a one (at dice).</td></tr>
</table>

6. Nouns derived from adjectives of dimension. Examples:

<table>
<tr><td>die Breite, width (breit)</td><td>die Dichte, density (dicht)</td></tr>
<tr><td>die Größe, size (groß)</td><td>die Dicke, thickness (dick)</td></tr>
<tr><td>die Länge, length (lang)</td><td>die Schwere, weight (schwer)</td></tr>
<tr><td>die Ferne, distance (fern)</td><td>die Höhe, height (hoch)</td></tr>
</table>

7. The names of countries or regions ending in **-e, -ei, -ie,** or **-z.** Examples:

<table>
<tr><td>die Ukraine</td><td>die Normandie</td></tr>
<tr><td>die Türkei</td><td>die Schweiz, Switzerland</td></tr>
</table>

8. (*a*) The names of most German rivers (but see §41, 8 (*b*)).

Examples:

<table>
<tr><td>die Donau, the Danube</td><td>die Spree</td></tr>
<tr><td>die Oder</td><td>die Elbe</td></tr>
<tr><td>die Weser</td><td>die Mosel</td></tr>
</table>

(*b*) The names of most rivers ending in **-a** or **-e.** Examples:
die Wolga, the Volga   die Themse, the Thames

9. Foreign nouns ending in

(*a*) -a—*e.g.*, **die Kamera,** camera.
EXCEPTION: **der Wodka,** vodka; see also §43, 11 (*c*).

(*b*) -ade—*e.g.*, **die Schokolade,** chocolate.

(*c*) -age—*e.g.*, **die Garage,** garage.

(*d*) -anz—*e.g.*, **die Bilanz,** balance(-sheet).

(*e*) -ät—*e.g.*, **die Universität,** university.
EXCEPTION: **das Porträt,** portrait.

(*f*) -enz—*e.g.*, **die Konkurrenz,** competition.

(*g*) -ie—*e.g.*, **die Lotterie,** lottery.
EXCEPTION: **das Genie,** genius.

(*h*) -ik—*e.g.*, **die Politik,** politics.
EXCEPTION: **das Arsenik,** (white) arsenic.

(*i*) **-ine**—*e.g.*, **die Kabine,** cabin.

(*j*) **-ion**—*e.g.*, **die Religion,** religion.

EXCEPTIONS: **der Skorpion,** scorpion, **der Spion,** spy, **das Stadion,** stadium.

(*k*) **-isse**—*e.g.*, **die Kulisse,** wings (of theatre).

(*l*) **-tion**—*e.g.*, **die Nation,** nation.

(*m*) **-ur**—*e.g.*, **die Literatur,** literature.

EXCEPTION: **der Merkur,** Mercury.

For rules of gender for masculine and neuter nouns, see §§41 and 43 respectively.

43. Rules of Gender—Neuter Nouns

Neuter are:

1. All nouns ending in **-chen** and **-lein** (diminutives), regardless of sex. Examples:

> **das Städtchen,** small town (from *die Stadt*)
> **das Bärchen,** young bear (from *der Bär*)
> **das Fensterchen,** little window (from *das Fenster*)
>
> **das Fräulein,** young lady (from *die Frau*)
> **das Männlein,** little man (from *der Mann*)
> **das Büchlein,** little book (from *das Buch*)

NOTE: Such diminutives have identical forms in the plural and almost invariably take umlaut where possible.

2. Infinitives used as nouns. Examples:

> **das Rauchen,** smoking
> **das Schweigen,** silence

3. Adjectives used as abstract nouns. Examples:

> **das Böse in der Welt,** the evil in the world
> **das Braun,** (the colour) brown

4. Most collectives, and nouns with verbal force beginning with **Ge-,** denoting repeated performances of the act expressed by the verb. Examples:

das Gebirge, mountain range
das Gepäck, luggage

das Geflüster, whispering (*flüstern*, to whisper)
das Geschwätz, chattering (*schwätzen*, to chatter)
das Geschrei, shouting (*schreien*, to shout)

NOTE: Most other nouns with this prefix are also neuter, but there are a number of exceptions, notably those ending in -er which suggest an agent (*e.g.*, Gesellschafter, 'business associate', 'partner'), which are masculine, as also are der Gebrauch, 'use', der Gefallen, 'favour', der Genuß, 'enjoyment', der Geruch, 'smell', der Gesang, 'singing', der Geschmack, 'taste', der Gestank, 'stench', and several very common feminines, such as die Geschichte, 'story', 'history', die Gefahr, 'danger', and die Geduld, 'patience'.

5. Letters of the alphabet used as nouns. Examples:

das C, (the letter) C
Ich bin das A und das O (*biblical*), I am Alpha and Omega.

6. Nouns ending in -tel representing fractions (see §291, 1). Examples:

das Achtel, eighth (part)
ein Siebentel, one seventh

7. Nouns ending in -tum. Examples:

das Eigentum, property
das Christentum, Christianity
das Heldentum, heroism

EXCEPTIONS: der Irrtum, 'mistake', der Reichtum, 'wealth'.

8. The names of the young of animals. Examples:

das Junge, young (of animals)—puppy, cub, etc.
das Lamm, lamb
das Kalb, calf
das Fohlen *or* Füllen, foal

9. The names of all towns (except Den Haag, sometimes der Haag, 'the Hague') and of most countries (but see §42, 7).

Examples:

> **Nürnberg,** Nuremberg
> **Wien,** Vienna
> **das schöne Deutschland,** beautiful Germany
> **das heutige Frankreich,** modern France

10. (*a*) Names of chemical elements. Examples:

das Radium, radium	**das Chlor,** chlorine
das Jod, iodine	**das Chrom,** chromium
das Gold, gold	**das Silber,** silver

EXCEPTIONS: **der Phosphor,** phosphorus, and **der Schwefel,** sulphur; also **der Sauerstoff,** oxygen, **der Kohlenstoff,** carbon, **der Stickstoff,** nitrogen, and **der Wasserstoff,** hydrogen, which are masculine because the last component (**-stoff**) is masculine (see §40).

(*b*) Names of chemical substances ending in **-in.** Examples:

das Benzin, petrol	**das Insulin,** insulin
das Nikotin, nicotine	**das Vitamin,** vitamin

11. Foreign nouns ending in

(*a*) **-at**—*e.g.,* **das Zitat,** quotation.

EXCEPTIONS: **der Magistrat,** town *or* borough council, **der Salat,** salad, **der Renegat,** renegade.

(*b*) **-ett**—*e.g.,* **das Büfett,** refreshment bar.
EXCEPTION: **der Kadett,** cadet.

(*c*) **-ma**—*e.g.,* **das Klima,** climate.
(*d*) **-ment**—*e.g.,* **das Experiment,** experiment, **das Moment,** momentum.

EXCEPTIONS: **der Moment** (=**Augenblick**), moment, **der Zement,** cement. Cf. §41, 9 (*d*).

(*e*) **-um**—*e.g.,* **das Aquarium,** aquarium.

EXCEPTION: **der Konsum,** consumption.

For rules of gender for masculine and feminine nouns, see §§41 and 42 respectively.

44. Declension of Place Names

Nom.: **der Rhein,** the Rhine	*Nom.:* **die Schweiz,** Switzerland
Acc.: **den Rhein**	*Acc.:* **die Schweiz**
Gen.: **des Rhein(e)s**	*Gen.:* **der Schweiz**
Dat.: **dem Rhein**	*Dat.:* **der Schweiz**
Nom.: **Deutschland,** Germany	*Nom.:* **Berlin,** Berlin
Gen.: **Deutschlands**	*Gen.:* **Berlins**

1. Proper names of places which are never used without an article (§16) are declined like common nouns.

2. If not generally used with an article, they take no ending except **-s** in the genitive singular.

NOTE: **Von** may replace this genitive and must do so if the noun ends in a sibilant: **Die Straßen von Paris,** 'The streets of Paris'.

45. Place Names in Apposition

When a place name is defined by a common noun preceding it, the two nouns are in apposition, but the common noun only is inflected:

Nom.: **die Stadt London,** the city of London	*Nom.:* **das Königreich Dänemark,** the kingdom of Denmark
Gen.: **der Stadt London**	*Gen.:* **des Königreichs Dänemark**

NOTE: The word **Fluß** is regularly omitted in names of rivers: **Der Rhein, die Elbe,** 'The (river) Rhine, Elbe'.

46. Adjectives and Nouns of Nationality

1. Adjectives of nationality end in **-isch,** except **deutsch,** and are used substantively only of the language, being then written with a capital:

Deutsch; Französisch	German; French (the language)
Ich lerne Deutsch.	I am learning German.

NOTE: They are also written with a capital when forming part of a proper name: **Das Heilige Römische Reich Deutscher Nation,** 'The Holy Roman Empire'.

2. After the preposition **auf,** language names are used without article, remain undeclined, and are written with a small initial letter; after other prepositions they take the article, are declined, and are written with an initial capital letter:

Auf deutsch.	In German.
Etwas ins Deutsche, aus dem Deutschen, übersetzen.	To translate something into German, from German.

3. Nouns of nationality end either in **-e** (**Junge** model, §35, VII), or in **-er** (**Maler** model, §34, V), except **Deutsch,** which follows the adjective declension (§116):

Der Franzose; ein Russe.	The Frenchman; a Russian.
Ein Engländer (Amerikaner).	An Englishman (American).
Der Deutsche; ein Deutscher.	The German; a German.

NOTE: The English plural adjectival noun, indicating all people of a particular nationality, is always, except in the case of **Deutsch,** rendered in German by the noun of nationality: **Die Franzosen sind lebhafter als die Engländer oder die Deutschen,** 'The French are more vivacious than the English or the Germans'.

47. Declension of Personal Names

Ich habe Georgs Buch.	I have Georg's book.
Hier ist Erikas Puppe.	Here is Erika's doll.
Das ist das Buch von Max, von Luise.	That is Max's (Luise's) book.
Ich habe es Max gegeben.	I have given it to Max.
Des großen Cäsars Taten.	Great Caesar's deeds.
Die Briefe des Cicero (*better:* **Ciceros Briefe**).	The letters of Cicero.
Das Buch des kleinen Karl.	Little Karl's book.

1. Names of persons are inflected only in the genitive singular, usually by adding **-s.**

2. The genitive of those ending in a sibilant is usually formed with **von.** In written language the genitive is often indicated by

an apostrophe: **Max' Buch, Fritz' Haus.** The addition of **-ens** and, in the case of feminines in **-e,** of **-ns (Maxens, Luisens, Buch)** is now considered old-fashioned.

3. The genitive usually precedes its governing noun, and is then inflected; if the genitive follows, it has the article and remains uninflected.

NOTE: 1. The name "Jesus Christ" is usually declined thus: *Nom.:* **Jesus Christus,** *Vocative:* **Jesu Christe,** *Acc.:* **Jesum Christum,** *Gen.:* **Jesu Christi,** *Dat.:* **Jesu Christo.**

2. Family names are used in the plural with added **-s,** but usually without article: **Schmidts sind nach Paris gereist,** 'The Schmidts have gone to Paris'.

48. Personal Names with Titles

Personal names in the genitive, preceded by a common noun as a title, take the genitive ending, the title remaining uninflected and without article, if the governing word follows. But words standing in apposition to the name and following it are also inflected:

König Heinrichs Söhne.	King Henry's sons.
Frau Brauns Regenschirm.	Frau Braun's umbrella.
Am Hofe Kaiser Karls des Großen.	At the court of the Emperor Charlemagne.

NOTE: The title **Herr** always takes **-n** in the singular except in the nominative; throughout the plural it takes the article and **-en: Herrn Schmidts Haus,** 'Herr Schmidt's house'; **die Herren Schmidt und Braun,** 'Messrs. Schmidt and Braun' (for individuals, but not as a formal business mode of address, which would be rendered **Firma Schmidt und Braun**).

49. Nouns in Apposition

1. A noun in apposition with another agrees with it in case:

Peter, mein jüngster Bruder, ist krank. (*Nominative*)
Peter, my youngest brother, is ill.

Ich traf Peter, meinen jüngsten Bruder. (*Accusative*)
I met Peter, my youngest brother.

Wir wohnen in dem Haus meines Onkels, des ältesten Bruders meines Vaters. (*Genitive*)
We live in the house of my uncle, my father's eldest brother.

Könnte ich bitte mit Herrn Schmidt, dem Leiter der Abteilung, sprechen? (*Dative*)
Could I please speak to Herr Schmidt, the head of the department?

2. The case of a noun in apposition after **als** or **wie** depends on the sense, the indefinite article being omitted after **als** before an unqualified noun:

Ich kannte ihn schon als Junge (= als ich ein Junge war).
I knew him as a boy (when I was a boy).

Ich kannte ihn schon als Jungen (= als er ein Junge war).
I knew him as a boy (when he was a boy).

Er hat keinen besseren Freund als mich.
He has no better friend than me.

Er ist nicht so groß wie ich.
He is not as tall as I am.

NOTE: 1. **Als** indicates identity and **wie** comparison: **Er schreibt als Dichter,** 'He writes as a poet' (and is one); **Er schreibt wie ein Dichter,** 'He writes like a poet' (though he may not be one).
2. For apposition in expressions of quantity, see §285, 3; in place names and titles, §§45 and 48.

IV. PRONOUNS

50. General Remarks

A pronoun is a word used instead of a noun referring to a person or a thing. A pronoun always has the same gender as the noun it replaces. The adjective corresponding to the word 'pronoun' is *pronominal*. There are several kinds of pronouns, each described below:

Demonstrative pronouns: A demonstrative pronoun is one which distinctly points out that to which it refers—*e.g.* '*Those* whom the gods love die young', 'Of the two patterns I prefer *that* with the flower motif'.

Emphatic pronouns: An emphatic pronoun stresses or intensifies, as in the sentence 'He said so *himself*', **Er hat es selbst (or selber) gesagt.**

Indefinite pronouns: These are pronouns which do not stand for any particular noun, such as 'somebody', 'nobody', 'everybody', 'something', 'nothing'.

Interrogative pronouns: These are pronouns which are used to introduce a question, as in '*Who* goes there?', '*What* do you advise?', '*Which* came first, the chicken or the egg?'

Personal pronouns: A personal pronoun is a word used to represent nouns denoting persons or things—namely, 'I', 'you', 'he', 'she', 'it', and their plurals 'we', 'you', 'they'. In German, personal pronouns are declined, and a distinction is made when rendering 'you' between the **du** form (with its plural **ihr**) and the **Sie** form.

Possessive pronouns: These are pronouns which express possession, such as 'mine', 'yours', 'theirs', 'ours'.

Reciprocal pronouns: These denote a mutual (reciprocal) action or relation on the part of the persons indicated by the subject. In German, **einander** is used to denote a reciprocal action in preference to **sich** when there is a possibility of ambiguity—*e.g.* **sie zerkratzten einander (or sich gegenseitig) das Gesicht**, 'they scratched one another's faces': see §223, 1, 2.

Reflexive pronouns: These are pronouns which refer to the

subject of the sentence or clause in which they stand—*e.g.* 'We enjoyed *ourselves* at the Zoo', 'Put *yourself* in my position', 'To allow *oneself* such luxuries is to spoil *oneself*'—the action passing back to the doer.

Relative pronouns: These are pronouns which introduce a relative clause—*e.g.* 'Here is the man *who* can help you' (*who* here introducing the relative clause 'who can help you'), 'The girl *whom* he married was only sixteen' (relative clause: 'whom he married'), 'The person *whose* portrait hangs in the hall is my father', 'The books *which* he borrowed have now been returned'. The relative pronouns 'whoever' and 'whatever' are rendered in German by **wer** and **was,** which include the antecedent. Though it is possible to omit a relative pronoun in English (*e.g.* 'The books he borrowed . . .' for 'The books which he borrowed . . .'), it is never omitted in German.

51. Declension of Personal Pronouns

FIRST PERSON	SECOND PERSON
Sing. Nom.: **ich,** I	**du,** you (thou) (*familiar*)
Acc.: **mich,** me	**dich,** you
Gen.: **meiner,** of me	**deiner,** of you
Dat.: **mir,** (to, for) me	**dir,** (to, for) you
Plur. Nom.: **wir,** we	**ihr,** you
Acc.: **uns,** us	**euch,** you
Gen.: **unser,** of us	**euer,** of you
Dat.: **uns,** (to, for) us	**euch,** (to, for) you

Sing. and Plur. **Sie,** you (*formal*)
Sie, you
Ihrer, of you
Ihnen, (to, for) you

THIRD PERSON

Singular

	Masc.	Fem.	Neut.
Nom.:	**er,** he	**sie,** she	**es,** it
Acc.:	**ihn,** him	**sie,** her	**es,** it
Gen.:	**seiner,** of him	**ihrer,** of her	[**seiner**], of it
Dat.:	**ihm,** (to, for) him	**ihr,** (to, for) her	[**ihm**], (to, for) it

Plural

Nom.: **sie,** they
Acc.: **sie,** them
Gen.: **ihrer,** of them
Dat.: **ihnen,** (to, for) them

NOTE: 1. The genitive and dative of the 3rd person singular neuter do not occur, except when referring to persons (*e.g.*, **Mädchen, Männlein,** etc.) or animals—*e.g.*, **Das Rotkehlchen wird erfrieren, wenn wir uns seiner nicht annehmen,** 'The robin will freeze to death if we don't take care of it'.

2. **Dessen** (genitive of the demonstrative pronoun **das,** §63) replaces the neuter genitive **seiner,** referring to things: **Ich erinnere mich dessen nicht,** 'I don't remember it'. This use of **dessen** is, however, literary; the sentence would be more naturally expressed: **Ich erinnere mich nicht daran.**

3. **Dessen** is sometimes used instead of the possessive adjective of the third person, to avoid ambiguity: **Er brachte Michael und dessen Bruder mit,** 'He brought with him Michael and his (Michael's) brother'. See also §66, 1.

4. For the use of **da** before prepositions instead of personal pronouns of the 3rd person, see §328.

52. Use of the Personal Pronouns **du, ihr,** and **Sie**

1. **Du** is used in familiar address (cf. English 'thou' and French 'tu'), for example to a close relative, a friend, a child, or an animal. It is also used in exalted or archaic language, as in addressing the Supreme Being, and in poetry; also in fables and fairy tales. Its plural is **ihr,** and the corresponding possessive adjectives are **dein** and **euer** respectively, declined like **mein** (see §114):

Bist du es, Peter?	Is that you, Peter?
Seid ihr müde, Kinder?	Are you tired, children?
Ist das deine Mütze, Peter?	Is that your cap, Peter?
Ist das eure Schule, Kinder?	Is that your school, children?

2. **Sie** is used in formal address (cf. French 'vous') to strangers, mere acquaintances, and as a mark of respect to

older people. It is always written with a capital, and requires the verb in the third person plural, whether one person is addressed or more than one. Its corresponding possessive adjective is **Ihr**, declined like **ihr** ('her', 'its', 'their') but always written with a capital (see §114):

Sind Sie krank, Herr Fischer?	Are you ill, Herr Fischer?
Sind Sie zufrieden, meine Herren?	Are you satisfied, gentlemen?
Ist das Ihr Buch, Herr Fischer?	Is that your book, Herr Fischer?
Ist das Ihre Antwort, meine Herren?	Is that your answer, gentlemen?

NOTE: All pronouns of address, as well as the corresponding possessive adjectives, are spelt with initial capital letters when writing a letter.

53. Nominative of Personal Pronouns

Ist der Mann reich? Ja, *er* **ist reich.**	Is the man rich? Yes, he is rich.
Ist der Winter warm? Nein, *er* **ist kalt.**	Is the winter warm? No, it is cold.
Die Frau ist nicht alt; *sie* **ist jung.**	The woman is not old; she is young.
Die Tinte ist nicht rot; *sie* **ist schwarz.**	The ink is not red; it is black.
Das Buch ist alt; *es* **ist nicht neu.**	The book is old; it is not new.
Das Mädchen ist nicht klein; *es* **ist groß.**	The girl is not small; she is tall.

The third person singular of the personal pronoun agrees in gender with the noun to which it refers, and has the following forms in the nominative:

Masc. **er**   *Fem.* **sie**   *Neut.* **es**

54. Accusative of Personal Pronouns

Personal pronouns have the following forms in the accusative:

	Singular	*Plural*
1*st Person:*	**mich,** me	**uns,** us
2*nd Person:*	**dich,** you (*familiar*)	**euch,** you (*familiar*)
3*rd Person:*	⎧ **ihn,** him, it ⎨ **sie,** her, it ⎩ **es,** it	**sie,** them

Formal: *Sing.* and *Plur.*: **Sie,** you

EXAMPLES

Er boxt gegen mich.	He boxes against me.
Ich habe einen Brief für dich.	I have a letter for you.
Hat sie den Bleistift? Sie hat ihn.	Has she (got) the pencil? She has (got) it.
Hat er die Mütze? Er hat sie.	Has he (got) the cap? He has (got) it.
Das Buch ist für uns.	The book is for us.

55. Dative of Personal Pronouns

Personal pronouns have the following forms in the dative:

Singular

1*st Person:*	**mir,** (to, for) me
2*nd Person:*	**dir,** (to, for) you (*familiar*)
3*rd Person:*	⎧ **ihm,** (to, for) him ⎩ **ihr,** (to, for) her

Plural

uns,	(to, for) us
euch,	(to, for) you (*familiar*)
ihnen,	(to, for) them

Formal: *Sing.* and *Plur.*: **Ihnen,** (to, for) you

NOTE: For the use of the neuter dative **ihm** see §51, note 1.

EXAMPLES

Geben Sie mir (uns) Geld.	Give me (us) money.
Ich gebe dir (euch) Brot.	I give you bread (I give bread to you).
Sie gibt ihr ein Buch.	She gives her a book.
Er baut ihnen ein Haus.	He is building them a house (is building a house for them).
Er schreibt Ihnen einen Brief, Herr Brandt.	He is writing you a letter (is writing a letter to you), Herr Brandt.

The German dative forms are usually rendered into English by a pronoun simply before the direct object, and by a pronoun with 'to' or 'for' after the direct object.

56. Word Order of Pronoun Objects, etc.

1. Pronoun objects without prepositions precede all other objects, adverbs, etc.:

Ich habe ihm gestern ein Buch geschickt.
I sent him a book yesterday.

2. Personal pronouns precede other pronouns:

Ich schicke Ihnen dieses.
I send you this.

3. Of several personal pronouns, the accusative precedes:

Er hat es mir geschickt.
He sent it to me.

4. Of noun objects without prepositions, the person precedes the thing:

Ich habe meinem Sohn ein Buch geschickt.
I sent my son a book.

5. Prepositional objects follow other objects and adverbs:

Ich habe gestern ein Buch an ihn (an meinen Sohn) geschickt.
I sent a book to him (to my son) yesterday.

6. Adverbs of time usually precede everything, except pronouns not governed by a preposition:

Ich habe ihm gestern ein gutes Buch geschickt.
I sent him a good book yesterday.

57. Agreement

The pronouns of the third person singular must agree in gender and number with the nouns to which they refer—*e.g.*:

Das Zimmermädchen soll sich denken, was *es* will.
Let the maid think what she likes.

Mein Brüderchen ist krank, *es* hat die Masern.
My little brother is ill, he has the measles.

NOTE: **Fräulein**, 'young lady, miss', has for the feminine pronoun either **es** (grammatical gender) or **sie** (natural gender). Cf. §114, 4, note.

58. Idiomatic Uses of es

1. **Es** is often placed before a verb (especially **sein**) to represent the real subject, which follows the verb, and with which the verb agrees; thus used, it frequently = 'there':

Wer ist es? Es ist Richard.	Who is it? It is Richard.
Es waren meine Vettern.	It was my cousins.
Es leuchten die Sterne.	The stars are shining.
Es ist ein Mann an der Tür.	There is a man at the door.
Es liegen Bücher hier.	There are books lying here.

2. Whenever indefinite existence is to be expressed, or when the assertion is general, 'there is', 'there were', etc., must be rendered by **es gibt, es gab**, etc., and the English subject becomes the direct object (accusative) in German:

Es gibt viele Leute, die nicht gern Auto fahren.
There are many people who do not like driving a car.

Letztes Jahr gab es nicht sehr viel Obst.
Last year there was not very much fruit.

Es gibt nur einen Mann, der dir da helfen könnte.
There is only one man who could help you there.

Es gibt nur ein Mittel, um ihn wieder zur Vernunft zu bringen.
There is only one way to bring him back to reason.

3. With **sein**, 'to be', when the real subject is a personal pronoun, the English order is inverted, and the verb agrees with the real subject:

Ich bin es; du bist es, etc.	It is I; it is you, *etc.*
Sind Sie es?	Is it you?

4. After a verb, **es** often represents a predicate or clause, and corresponds to the English 'one', or 'so':

Ist er Arzt? Ja, er ist es.	Is he a doctor? Yes, he is (one).
Wir fangen an zu arbeiten, und ihr solltet es auch.	We are starting to work and you should (do so) too.
Bist du frei? Ich bin es.	Are you free? I am.
Er ist krank, du bist es nicht.	He is ill, you're not.

5. **Es** is also used in certain set expressions—*e.g.*:

Ich habe es satt, dich immer wieder daran erinnern zu müssen.
I am fed up with having to remind you of it time and again.

Ich bin es müde, jeden Tag in die Stadt zu fahren.
I am tired of driving into town every day.

59. Possessive Pronouns

1. They are formed as follows from the stems of the corresponding possessive adjectives (§114):

(*a*) with endings of the **dieser** model (see §61), without article:

	Masc.	Fem.	Neut.	Plural
Nom.:	**meiner** (mine)	**meine**	**mein(e)s**	**meine**
Acc.:	**meinen**	**meine**	**mein(e)s**	**meine**
Gen.:	**meines**	**meiner**	**meines**	**meiner**
Dat.:	**meinem**	**meiner**	**meinem**	**meinen**

(b) with definite article and weak adjective endings:

SINGULAR

Masc.	Fem.	Neut.
Nom.: der meine or der meinige	die mein(ig)e	das mein(ig)e
Acc.: den mein(ig)en	die mein(ig)e	das mein(ig)e
Gen.: des mein(ig)en	der mein(ig)en	des mein(ig)en
Dat.: dem mein(ig)en	der mein(ig)en	dem mein(ig)en

PLURAL

All Genders

Nom.: die mein(ig)en
Acc.: die mein(ig)en
Gen.: der mein(ig)en
Dat.: den mein(ig)en

Similarly:

deiner, yours (*familiar*)   Ihrer, yours (*formal, sing. and plur.*)
seiner, his, its   eurer, yours (*plur. of* deiner)
ihrer, hers, its, theirs   uns(e)rer, ours

NOTE: In **unsrige** and **eurige** the **e** of the stem is always omitted.

2. The possessive pronouns correspond to their antecedent like the possessive adjectives (§114, 2, 3, 4), but their case depends on their relation in the sentence:

Dieser Hut ist meiner (der meine, der meinige).
This hat is mine.

Ich habe meinen Hut, aber sie hat ihren (den ihren, den ihrigen) nicht.
I have my hat, but she does not have hers.

Dieses Haus ist größer als eures (das eure, das eurige).
This house is bigger than yours.

Wem gehört dieses Wörterbuch?—Es ist mein(e)s.
To whom does this dictionary belong?—It is mine.

NOTE: The three forms given are interchangeable, without difference of meaning, the first (or shortest) form being the most usual. In the nominative and accusative neuter singular the forms **meins, deins, seins,** etc. are much more common than the alternative forms **meines, deines, seines,** etc.

3. Observe the following idiomatic uses of the possessive pronoun:

(*a*) **die Mein(ig)en, die Sein(ig)en,** 'my (his) friends, family, etc.'

(*b*) **Ich werde das Mein(ig)e tun,** 'I shall do my bit'.

(*c*) **Wir werden seinesgleichen nie wieder erblicken,** 'We shall never see his like again'. In this construction the forms **meinesgleichen, deinesgleichen,** etc., meaning 'a person, or persons, like me, you, etc.', are indeclinable.

60. Demonstrative Pronouns

1. **dieser,** this (one), that (one)
2. **jener,** that (one) (yonder)
3. **der,** the one
4. **derjenige,** the one
5. **derselbe,** the same (one)
6. **(als) solcher,** (as) such
7. **dergleichen, desgleichen,** such a thing

61. Demonstrative Pronouns—**dieser** Model

SINGULAR

	Masc.	Fem.	Neut.
Nom.:	**dieser**	**diese**	**dieses,** this (one)
Acc.:	**diesen**	**diese**	**dieses,** this (one)
Gen.:	**dieses**	**dieser**	**dieses,** of this (one)
Dat.:	**diesem**	**dieser**	**diesem,** (to, for) this (one)

PLURAL

All Genders

Nom.:	**diese,** these (ones)
Acc.:	**diese,** these (ones)
Gen.:	**dieser,** of these (ones)
Dat.:	**diesen,** (to, for) these (ones)

Jener, 'that (one)' declines in the same way.

NOTE: 1. **Dieser** as a demonstrative adjective (§118) is declined in the same way.

2. The unchanged **dies** (also **jenes**) is also used, like **das** (§65), before the verb **sein**, irrespective of the gender or number of the subject, referring to a person or thing—*e.g.* **Dies ist meine Schwester,** 'This is my sister'; **Dies sind meine Streichhölzer, jenes sind Ihre,** 'These are my matches, those are yours'. Cf. a similar use of the demonstrative adjective (§118, 3).

62. Dieser, jener

1. Both follow the **dieser** model (§61).
2. The English demonstrative 'that (one)' is not rendered by **jener,** except when remoteness or contrast is indicated.
3. **Dieser** = 'the latter', the nearer or last mentioned of two objects; **jener** = 'the former', the more remote:

Inge und Helga sind Schwestern; diese ist älter als jene.
Inge and Helga are sisters; the latter is older than the former.

Dieses Haus ist viel näher dem Park als jenes (dort drüben).
This house (here) is much nearer the park than that one (over there).

63. Declension of der

As a demonstrative pronoun **der** is declined as follows:

	SINGULAR			PLURAL
	Masc.	*Fem.*	*Neut.*	*All Genders*
Nom.:	der	die	das	die
Acc.:	den	die	das	die
Gen.:	dessen	deren (derer)	dessen	derer (deren)
Dat.:	dem	der	dem	denen

Note the enlarged forms in the genitive, and in the dative plural.

64. Use of der

1. As a demonstrative pronoun it has the force of an emphasized personal pronoun of the 3rd person, and often implies contempt or disparagement:

Kennen Sie ¹den?	Do you know that man?
¹Die willst du heiraten?	You want to marry *her*?
¹Dem würde ich kein Geld leihen; ¹der bezahlt nie.	I wouldn't lend *him* any money; *he* never pays.

2. **Der** or **derjenige** (§§67, 68) renders the English 'that' before a genitive, and before a relative clause:

| Mein Hut und der meiner Frau. | My hat and that of my wife. |
| Dieser Band und der, welcher hier liegt. | This volume and that (the one) which is lying here. |

65. The Demonstrative Pronoun **das**

Das ist mein Vater.	That is my father.
Das ist ihre Mutter.	That is her mother.
Das sind meine Bücher.	Those are my books.

Das remains unchanged here; the verb agrees with the real subject, which follows (cf. **dies**, §61, note 2).

66. Use of the Demonstrative Pronouns **dessen, deren,** and **derer**

1. As a demonstrative pronoun **dessen,** which is used both for the masculine and the neuter singular of the genitive case, always refers to a preceding noun:

Ich will der Freund dessen sein, der mir helfen kann.
I want to be the friend of the man who can help me.

Er ging mit seinem Freund in dessen Wohnung.
He went with his friend to his (friend's) flat.

See also §51, notes 2 and 3.

2. As a demonstrative pronoun **deren** also always refers to a preceding noun. It may be used for both persons and things. It is used

(a) in the genitive singular feminine:

Sie traf ihre Freundin und deren Mutter.
She met her friend and her (friend's) mother.

(b) in the genitive plural of all three genders:

Auf der Party waren auch seine Eltern und deren Freunde.
At the party there were also his parents and their friends.

Angesichts der Einwände meines Vaters und deren seiner Freunde wurde der Antrag zurückgezogen.
In view of the objections of my father and those of his friends the proposition was withdrawn.

Er ist verantwortlich für das Drucken der Bücher und deren Vertrieb.
He is responsible for the printing of the books and their distribution.

NOTE: For the use of **dessen** and **deren** as relative pronouns, see §75.

3. **Derer** always points to a following relative clause. It is used only of persons. It is used

(a) in the genitive plural of all three genders:

Die Freude derer, die das Examen bestanden hatten, war groß.
The joy of those who had passed the examination was great.

Die Zahl derer, die mit dem Gesetz in Konflikt geraten, ist ungewöhnlich groß.
The number of those who come into conflict with the law is unusually great.

(b) in the genitive singular feminine; this use of **derer** is, however, literary and should be avoided, as it is likely to be confused with the genitive plural:

Er erinnerte sich derer, die er vor Jahren gekannt hatte.
He remembered those (the one?) whom he had known years before.

Er trank auf das Wohl derer, die fern von ihm war.
(*better:* **Er trank auf das Wohl der Frau, die . . .**)
He drank to the health of her who was far from him.

67. Declension of derjenige

| | SINGULAR | | | PLURAL |
	Masc.	*Fem.*	*Neut.*	*All Genders*
Nom.:	derjenige	diejenige	dasjenige	diejenigen
Acc.:	denjenigen	diejenige	dasjenige	diejenigen
Gen.:	desjenigen	derjenigen	desjenigen	derjenigen
Dat.:	demjenigen	derjenigen	demjenigen	denjenigen

These forms are made up of the definite article and **jenig** with weak adjective endings (see §115).

68. Use of derjenige

As in the case of **derjenige** used as a demonstrative adjective (§120), **derjenige** used as a demonstrative pronoun is considered rather clumsy, especially in speech, and the shorter, stressed demonstrative pronoun **der,** which is identical in meaning, is therefore generally preferred unless there is uncertainty of meaning or excessive repetition of **der.**

Alle diejenigen, die ein Fahrrad haben, können mitkommen.
All those who have a bicycle can come along.

Ich möchte denjenigen sehen, der damit etwas anfangen kann!
I should like to see the man who can do anything with that!

69. Declension of derselbe

| | SINGULAR | | | PLURAL |
	Masc.	*Fem.*	*Neut.*	*All Genders*
Nom.:	derselbe	dieselbe	dasselbe	dieselben
Acc.:	denselben	dieselbe	dasselbe	dieselben
Gen.:	desselben	derselben	desselben	derselben
Dat.:	demselben	derselben	demselben	denselben

These forms are made up of the definite article and **selb** with weak adjective endings (see §115), thus following the pattern of **derjenige** (§67).

70. Use of **derselbe**

1. As a demonstrative pronoun **derselbe** is used in the same way as the English 'the same (one)', 'the same (thing)':

Seitdem er die neue Stellung hat, ist er nicht mehr derselbe.
He has not been the same since he has been in his new job.

Es ist doch nicht dasselbe, wenn Vater kocht.
But it's not the same when father does the cooking.

Es läuft auf dasselbe hinaus, ob Sie den Bus oder die U-Bahn nehmen.
It comes to the same thing whether you take the bus or the Tube.

2. **Derselbe** is also frequently used in commercialese to render the English 'same':

Bitte, schicken Sie dasselbe (denselben, dieselbe) umgehend zurück.
Please send same by return of post.

For the use of **derselbe** as a demonstrative adjective, see §121.

71. Solcher

1. As a demonstrative pronoun **solcher** follows the **dieser** model (§61).

2. Though very common as a demonstrative adjective (§122), it is infrequent as a demonstrative pronoun except in the stylistically loose sense of 'as such':

Der Fall als solcher ist nicht sehr interessant, aber die Leute, die darin verwickelt sind, machen ihn zu etwas Besonderem.
The case as such is not very interesting, but the people who are involved in it make it something special.

Er ist nicht gegen die Kirche als solche, sondern gegen die Kirche als Institution.
He is not against the Church as such but against the Church as an institution.

72. Use of **dergleichen** and **desgleichen** as Demonstrative Pronouns

1. **Dergleichen** is used as an indeclinable neuter demonstrative pronoun:

Dergleichen ist noch nie dagewesen.
Such a thing is unprecedented.

Dergleichen sehe ich zum ersten Mal.
It is something the like of which I've never seen before.

Beim Trödler findet man alte Möbel, gebrauchte Kleider und dergleichen mehr.
At the second-hand dealer's one comes across old furniture, cast-off clothes and other things of that sort.

Er wurde nach geschmuggelten Uhren und Photoapparaten durchsucht, aber man fand nichts dergleichen.
He was searched for smuggled watches and cameras, but nothing of that kind was found.

2. **Desgleichen** is also used as an indeclinable neuter demonstrative pronoun, but is less common than **dergleichen**:

Desgleichen habe ich noch nie gehört.
I have never heard of such a thing.

For the use of **dergleichen** as a demonstrative adjective, see §123.

For the use of **desgleichen** as a conjunction, see §335, 4.

For the use of **dergleichen** and **desgleichen** as relative pronouns, see §78.

73. Relative Pronouns

1. **der,** who, which, that
2. **welcher,** who, which, that
3. **wer,** he (the one) who, whoever
4. **was,** what, that which
5. **desgleichen** ⎱ the like of whom *or* which
6. **dergleichen** ⎰

74. Declension of the Relative Pronoun der

	SINGULAR			PLURAL
	Masc.	*Fem.*	*Neut.*	*All Genders*
Nom.:	der	die	das	die, who, which, that
Acc.:	den	die	das	die, whom, which, that
Gen.:	dessen	deren	dessen	deren, whose, of which
Dat.:	dem	der	dem	denen, (to, for) whom, which

These forms are the same as those of the definite article, except for the added -en of the genitive singular and plural and the dative plural, and the double s of the masculine and neuter genitive singular.

For examples of the use of **der** as a relative pronoun, see §§79–81.

75. Use of the Relative Pronouns dessen and deren

1. As a relative pronoun **dessen** is used in the masculine and neuter singular of the genitive case; it always precedes the word on which it depends:

Hier ist der Mann, dessen Freund ich bin.
Here is the man whose friend I am.

Wo ist das Buch, dessen Umschlag zerrissen ist?
Where is the book the cover of which is torn?

2. As a relative pronoun **deren** is used
(*a*) in the genitive singular feminine:

Die Frau, deren Sohn bei dem Unfall verletzt wurde, war gestern hier.
The woman whose son was injured in the accident was here yesterday.

Die größte Kälte, deren (*literary; better:* an die) ich mich entsinnen kann, war vor drei Jahren.
The coldest spell I can remember was three years ago.

(*b*) in the genitive plural of all three genders:

Die Kinder, deren Eltern arbeiten, sind meistens sich selbst überlassen.
Children whose parents go out to work are mostly left on their own.

For the use of the demonstrative pronouns **dessen** and **deren** see §66.

76. Declension of the Relative Pronoun **welcher**

	SINGULAR			PLURAL
	Masc.	*Fem.*	*Neut.*	*All Genders*
Nom.:	**welcher**	**welche**	**welches**	**welche,** who, which, that
Acc.:	**welchen**	**welche**	**welches**	**welche,** whom, etc.
Gen.:	—	—	—	—
Dat.:	**welchem**	**welcher**	**welchem**	**welchen,** (to, for) whom, etc.

Welcher follows the **dieser** model (§61), but lacks the genitive, which is replaced by the genitive forms of **der (dessen,** etc.—see §74).

For examples of the use of **welcher** as a relative pronoun, see §79.

77. Use of the Relative Pronouns **wer** and **was**

1. **Wer** and **was** as relative pronouns are indefinite and compound in meaning, and include the antecedent:

Wer so etwas glaubt, ist ein Narr.
Whoever (= He who) believes such a thing is a fool.

Wer wagt, gewinnt.
He who ventures, wins (i.e., Nothing venture, nothing gain).

Was ich sage, ist wahr.
What (= That which) I say is true.

NOTE: 'Those who', 'he who', 'whoever', are rendered by **wer** in general statements only; otherwise by **der(jenige)** + relative (§§67–68).

2. (*a*) **Was** must replace the relative pronoun **das** or **welches** when the antecedent is a clause or a neuter pronoun (*e.g.* **alles,** 'all, everything', **nichts,** 'nothing', **vieles,** 'much'):

Er will nicht studieren, was schade ist.
He won't study, which is a pity.

Alles, was er sagt, ist wahr.
All (that) he says is true.

Es war nicht Haß gegen den alten Mann, was er empfand.
It was not hatred towards the old man that he felt.

(*b*) **Was** must also replace **das** or **welches** when the antecedent is a neuter adjective which does not refer back to anything specific, in which case the neuter adjective is spelt with an initial capital letter. If, however, the antecedent denotes clearly from the context what is being specified, or refers directly back to it,

das is used and the neuter adjective is spelt with a small initial letter. Compare the following two sentences, both of which would be translated by 'That is the best that he has ever written'; but whereas, in the first example, the antecedent is vague or indeterminate, the second is clearly understood from the context:

Das ist das *Beste, was* er je geschrieben hat.
Das ist das *beste, das* er je geschrieben hat.

Note that **was** introducing a relative clause always refers to the whole preceding idea, not just a word in it.

3. '-ever' = **auch** or **immer** or **auch immer** after a relative pronoun for additional emphasis:

Wer es auch gesagt hat,
Wer immer es gesagt hat, } **es ist falsch.**
Wer es auch immer gesagt hat,

Whoever (No matter who) said that, it is wrong.

For further examples of this construction, see §257, 3.

For the declension and use of **wer** and **was** as interrogative pronouns, see §§86, 87.

78. Use of the Relative Pronouns dergleichen and desgleichen

Dergleichen and **desgleichen** may be used as relative pronouns, though such a use is nowadays uncommon and regarded as literary:

Ein Fahrzeug, desgleichen man heutzutage nicht mehr sieht.
A vehicle the like of which one doesn't see nowadays.

Artige Kinder, dergleichen man nur in Büchern findet.
Nicely-behaved children such as one finds only in books.

The first example would be rendered more naturally in one of two ways:

(*a*) **Ein Fahrzeug, das man heutzutage nicht mehr sieht.**

(*b*) **Ein Fahrzeug, wie man es heutzutage nicht mehr sieht.**

(See §82.)

For the use of **dergleichen** and **desgleichen** as demonstrative pronouns, see §72.

For the use of **dergleichen** as a demonstrative adjective, see §123.

For the use of **desgleichen** as a conjunction, see §335, 4.

79. Relative Clauses

Der Arzt, der (welcher) Sie behandelt hat, war sehr tüchtig.
The doctor who treated you was very competent.

Hier ist der Stock, den (welchen) man gefunden hat.
Here is the stick which was found.

Hier sind die Bücher, die (welche) empfohlen wurden.
Here are the books which were recommended.

Kennen Sie die Dame, der (welcher) wir begegnet sind?
Do you know the lady whom we met?

Das Haus, worin (= in dem) ich wohne.
The house in which I live.

1. The relative pronoun agrees with its antecedent in gender and number; the case depends on its use in its own clause.

2. Since all relative clauses are dependent, the finite verb comes last (§163).

3. **Der** and **welcher** refer to both persons and things; **der** is very much more common than **welcher**, which, nowadays found predominantly in writing, and especially in officialese, is nevertheless sometimes used to avoid repetitions of **der**—*e.g.*, **Ein Buch, das mir gehörte, welches ich aber nie gelesen hatte,** 'A book which belonged to me but which I had never read'.

4. In finite clauses, **der** and **welcher**, referring to inanimate objects, are sometimes replaced by **wo** (**wor** before a vowel) preceding a preposition.

5. The relative pronoun is never omitted in German.

80. Agreement in Person

If the antecedent is in the first or second person, the relative pronoun (in this case always **der** or **die**) is followed by the personal pronoun of that person:

Ich, der ich dein Freund bin.
I who am your friend.

O Gott, der Du im Himmel bist!
O God, who art in heaven!

Du, die du geschworen hast, nie mehr zu rauchen, rauchst?
You, who swore never again to smoke, are smoking?

Ich, der ich unbedingt sparen wollte, habe mein ganzes Geld ausgegeben!
I, who was determined to cut down expenses, have spent all my money!

Mir, der ich dein Freund bin, kannst du doch trauen.
But me, who am your friend, you can trust.

81. Word Order of Relative Pronouns

1. A relative pronoun must immediately follow its antecedent when the latter precedes the verb of a principal clause:

Der Mann, der gestern hier war, ist wieder gekommen.
The man who was here yesterday has come again.

Den Mann, der jetzt redet, kenne ich nicht.
I do not know the man who is speaking now.

2. So also when a separation would cause ambiguity:

Ich traf einen Freund, den ich lange nicht gesehen hatte, bei seinem Bruder.
I met a friend, whom I had not seen for a long time, at his brother's.

3. Similarly when the antecedent is the subject of a dependent clause:

Ich glaube, der Mann, der vorhin hier war, ist ihr Vater.
I believe that the man who was here just now is her father.

4. In other cases the relative pronoun need not immediately follow, and the relative clause should not needlessly interrupt the sentence:

Er möchte wieder in die Stadt zurück, in der er geboren wurde.
He would like to go back again to the town where he was born.

Ich suchte den Hut aus, der mir am besten gefiel.
I picked out the hat I liked best.

82. Wie as a Relative

Solch ein or so ein ('such a') is often followed in German by wie ('as') and a personal pronoun or demonstrative, etc., agreeing in gender and number with its antecedent; solch or so may also be omitted:

Ein Mensch, wie man ihn nur selten trifft.
A man such as one seldom meets.

Solch (or So) einen Menschen wie diesen, trifft man nur selten.
One seldom comes across such a man as this.

Ein Schloß, wie man es sich nur in seinen kühnsten Träumen vorstellt.
A castle the like of which one pictures only in one's wildest dreams.

Solch (or So) ein Schloß wie dieses stellt man sich nur in seinen kühnsten Träumen vor.
Such a castle as this one pictures only in one's wildest dreams.

Solch (or So) eine schöne Goethe-Ausgabe wie diese hier findet man nicht alle Tage.
Such a beautiful edition of Goethe as this one is not to be found every day.

Solch (or So) eine Armbanduhr, wie du sie hast, möchte ich auch haben.
I too should like to have a wrist-watch like the one you have.

Das sind (solche) Früchte, wie sie in Indien wachsen.
Those are fruits such as grow in India.

83. Interrogative Pronouns

1. **welcher?** which? which one?
2. **wer?** who?
3. **was?** what?

84. Declension of welcher?

As an interrogative pronoun it is declined in exactly the same way as **welcher** as a relative pronoun—see §76.

85. Use of **welcher?**

1. **Welcher?** asks 'which?' of a number of persons or things, and agrees in gender with the noun for which it stands:

Welcher von euch beiden ist Peter?
Which of you two is Peter?

Welcher von diesen Damen gehört die Tasche?
To which of these ladies does the handbag belong?

2. The neuter singular **welches?** is used directly before the verb **sein,** irrespective of the gender or number of the subject, referring to a person or thing:

Welches ist der höchste Berg der Welt?
Which is the highest mountain in the world?

Welches (or Welche) sind ihre Lieblingsblumen?
Which are her favourite flowers?

86. Declension of the Interrogative Pronouns **wer?** and **was?**

	Masc. and Fem.	*Neuter*
Nom.:	**wer?** who?	**was?** what?
Acc.:	**wen?** whom?	**was?** what?
Gen.:	**wessen?** whose?	—
Dat.:	**wem?** (to, for) whom?	—

87. Use of the Interrogative Pronouns **wer?** and **was?**

Wer ist dieses Kind?	Who is this child?
Wer sind diese Männer?	Who are these men?
Wen meinen Sie?	Whom do you mean?
Wessen Füller ist das?	Whose pen is that?
Wem möchtest du die Uhr schenken?	To whom would you like to give the watch?
Mit wem hat er gesprochen?	With whom did he speak?
Was ist ein Chronometer?	What is a chronometer?
Was hat er gesagt?	What did he say?

For the use of **wer** and **was** as relative pronouns, see §77.

88. Indefinite Pronouns

1. **all,** all
2. **ander,** other
3. **beide,** both
4. **einer,** one, someone
5. **einige(s),** some, a few
6. **ein paar,** a few
7. **etliche(s),** some, quite a few
8. **etwas,** something, anything
9. **jeder(mann),** everybody
10. **jemand,** someone, anyone
11. **keiner,** no one, none, not one, not any
12. **man,** one, they, people, etc.
13. **manche(r),** some, many
14. **mehrere(s),** several
15. **nichts,** nothing
16. **niemand,** no one
17. **viel(e),** much, many
18. **welche(r),** some
19. **wenig(e),** little, few

89. All

1. This word expresses number as well as quantity:

Geld ist nicht alles.
Money is not everything.

Die Jungen sind alle hier.
The boys are all here.

Alle(s) einsteigen! Alle(s) aussteigen!
All aboard! All change!

Er hat alles, was man sich wünschen kann.
He has everything that one could wish for.

Note from the above example that 'everything that' is **alles, was;** cf. **nichts,** §103, 1.

2. **All** stands in apposition with a noun or pronoun:

Ich kenne sie alle.
I know all of them.

Er hat uns alle eingeladen.
He has invited all of us.

Unser aller (*genitive plural*) **Leben war in Gefahr.**
The lives of all of us were in danger.

3. When an adjective stands after **alles** it is used like a noun and given an initial capital, except for **ander** (see §128, 4):

Alles Böse.　　　**Alles Schöne.**
Everything evil.　　Everything (that is) beautiful.

Ich wünsche Ihnen alles Gute.
I wish you all the best.

Er ist alles andere als ein Held.
He is anything but a hero.

The adjectival ending here is weak; contrast **etwas** (§96, 4), **nichts** (§103, 2), **viel** (§105, 3), and **wenig** (§107, 3), where the adjectival ending is strong.

For **all** as an adjective, see §127.

90. Ander

1. This word indicates that a thing or person is different in kind or quality from what it is being contrasted with:

Die einen begeistern sich für Jazz, die anderen lieben nur klassische Musik.
Some are keen on jazz, others like only classical music.

Wir haben es gesehen, und andere haben es auch gesehen.
We have seen it, and others have seen it too.

2. As a pronoun it is declined like an adjective, and is weak after the personal pronouns **wir** and **ihr**:

Er begeht eine Dummheit nach der anderen.
He commits one blunder after another.

Das hätte jeder andere auch tun können.
Anyone else could have done that too.

Ihr anderen (or andren or andern) bekommt Tee anstatt Kaffee.
The rest of you are going to have tea instead of coffee.

Note from the last example that the e of **ander,** or of inflected forms ending in **-n,** is sometimes omitted, especially in colloquial speech.

For **ander** as an adjective, see §128.

91. Beide

1. This word, meaning 'both', suggests (as in English) a closer relationship between two things or persons than **zwei,** 'two':

Zwei Mädchen sitzen im Café. Beide sind blond.
Two girls are sitting in the café. Both are fair-haired.

Die Ähnlichkeit zwischen den beiden ist bemerkenswert.
The likeness between the two is remarkable.

Einer von euch beiden muß es gewesen sein.
It must have been one of you two.

2. As a pronoun it is declined like an adjective, and is strong after personal pronouns:

Kommt ihr beide?
Are you both coming?

But see §129, 3.

See also §280, 3.

For **beide** as an adjective, see §129.

92. Einer

See **man,** §100.

93. Einige(s)

1. This pronoun is used both in the singular and in the plural.

2. In the singular the neuter form **einiges** is used, with the meaning 'some', 'something', 'a few things':

Einiges davon scheint mir irreführend.
Some of it seems to me misleading.

Ich will noch einiges, was ich vorhin übergangen habe, nachtragen.
I want to add something (*or* a few things) which I previously omitted.

Note from the above example the use of the relative pronoun **was** (not *das*) with **einiges**.

3. The plural form **einige** means 'some', 'a few':

Nur einige waren da.
Only a few were there.

Einige gingen in Smokings umher, und andere sahen wie Land-streicher aus.
Some were walking about in dinner-jackets, and others looked like tramps.

See also **etliche(s), §95.**

For **einige** as an adjective, see §130.

94. Ein paar

As a pronoun **ein paar** is indeclinable; **paar** is not written with a capital letter:

Hundert Leute begannen das Rennen, zum Schluß blieben nur noch ein paar übrig.
A hundred people started the race, at the end only a few were left in it.

Wir brauchen keine Briefmarken zu kaufen, wir haben noch ein paar.
We don't need to buy any stamps, we still have a few.

For **ein paar** as an adjective, see §131.

95. Etliche(s)

Like the adjective **etliche** (§132), the pronoun has been largely replaced by **einige** (§93), but is still occasionally found, both in the singular and in the plural.

Etliche von ihnen waren leicht betrunken.
Some (quite a few) of them were tipsy.

Er hat schon etliches erlebt.
He has already been through quite a lot.

Es gefiel ihm etliches bei der Ausstellung.
At the exhibition quite a lot pleased him (more than he had expected).

NOTE: Whereas **einige von euch** may imply perhaps 3 or 4 out of ten, **etliche von euch** would be more—say 5 or 6.

96. Etwas

1. As a pronoun, **etwas** (colloquially shortened to **was**) is indeclinable and can be used in all cases except the genitive:

Das ist immerhin etwas!
That's something, anyway!

Etwas mußt du doch essen! Du hast den ganzen Tag gar nichts gegessen!
But you must eat something! You've eaten absolutely nothing all day!

Nun zu etwas anderem!
Now we'll turn to something else.

2. It is sometimes used colloquially to mean 'some':

Hat er Geld? Ja, etwas.
Has he any money? Yes, some.

3. **So etwas** (often abbreviated to **so was**) = 'such a thing', 'something of the kind':

Haben Sie je so (et)was gehört?
Have you ever heard of such a thing?

Er ist ein Kunsthistoriker oder so (et)was.
He is an art historian or something of the kind.

4. When an adjective stands after **etwas** it is used like a noun and given an initial capital:

Etwas Gutes.　　　**Etwas Schweres.**
Something good.　　　Something (that is) difficult.

Ich habe dir etwas Gutes zu erzählen.
I have something good to tell you.

As with **nichts** (§103, 2), **viel** (§105, 3), and **wenig** (§107, 3), the adjectival ending is strong; contrast **alles** (§89, 3), where the adjectival ending is weak.

For **irgend etwas,** see §263, 2 (*b*).
For **etwas** as an adjective, see §133.

97. Jeder(mann)

1. **Jeder,** a much commoner form than **jedermann,** may mean either 'each (one)', 'every one', or 'everybody':

Jeder von euch muß helfen.
Each one of you must help.

Hier kennt jeder jeden.
Here everybody knows everybody else.

2. **Jeder** is sometimes preceded by **ein,** and then follows the mixed adjective declension (§115):

Ein jeder hat die Pflicht zu helfen.
It is everyone's duty to help.

Er dankte einem jeden in der Gruppe. (*literary*)
He thanked each and every one in the group.

NOTE: **Jedweder** and **ein jeglicher** are less common, rather literary substitutes for **ein jeder,** but are sometimes still used when greater emphasis is required—*e.g.* **Ein jeglicher** (*or* **Jedweder**) **von uns hat die gleichen Rechte,** 'Each and every one of us has the same rights.'

3. **Jedermann** inflects only in the genitive, which has the form **jedermanns**:

Das ist nicht jedermanns Geschmack.
That is not everybody's taste.

For **jeder** as an adjective, see §136.

98. Jemand

This pronoun, which is used in the singular only, is inflected as follows:

Nom.: **jemand**
Acc.: **jemand** *or* **jemanden**
Gen.: **jemands** *or* **jemandes**
Dat.: **jemand** *or* **jemandem**

The case endings of the accusative and dative are optional, though they are usually omitted in colloquial speech, but inflexion in the genitive is essential:

Jemand fehlt (*or* **Es fehlt jemand).**
Somebody is missing.

Wir werden schon irgend jemand(en) am Bahnhof um Auskunft fragen können.
We shall be able to ask someone (or other) at the station for information.

Ich glaubte, ich hörte jemandes Stimme.
I thought I heard someone's voice.

Kann ich mit jemand anderem (*or* **jemand anders,** *or* **jemandem anders) sprechen?**
Can I speak to someone else?

For **irgend jemand,** see §263, 2 (*b*).
For **einer** in place of **jemand** (nominative), see §100, 4.

99. Keiner

1. When used as a pronoun **keiner** follows the strong declension (§115):

Keiner von uns glaubt ihm.
None (*or* Not one) of us believes him.

Ich kenne sonst keinen, der es tun könnte.
I don't know anyone else who could do it.

Es waren dort viele Gemälde, aber keine, die mir gefallen haben.
There were many paintings there, but none that I liked.

2. **Keiner** may replace **niemand** (§104):

Keiner wollte nach Hause gehen.
Nobody wanted to go home.

Dieses Stück gefällt keinem.
Nobody likes this play.

3. The form **keines** (nowadays nearly always contracted to **keins**) is often used in the accusative neuter singular:

Hast du Geld?—Nein, ich habe keins.
Have you any money?—No, I have none.

4. **Keiner von beiden** = 'neither':

Keiner von uns beiden wollte ins Theater gehen.
Neither of us wanted to go to the theatre.

Sie mag keinen von beiden.
She doesn't like either of them.

For **kein** as an adjective, see §137.

100. Man, einer

1. **Man** has the force of 'one', 'they', 'we', 'you', 'people', etc. (compare French '*on*'), and has this form only in the nominative:

Man sagt, daß es bald Neuwahlen geben soll.
They (people) say that there are to be new elections soon.

Öl und Wasser kann man nicht mischen.
One (we, you) cannot mix oil and water.

2. **Man** must not be replaced by a personal pronoun:

Man wird müde, wenn man lange arbeitet.
A man (one) gets tired when he (one) works a long time.

3. **Einer** sometimes replaces **man** in the nominative, and always in the other cases:

Wenn einer müde ist, kann er nicht gut arbeiten.
When a man (one) is tired, he (one) cannot work well.

Es muß einem leid tun, wenn man ihn so hilflos sieht.
It must make one feel sorry when one sees him so helpless.

4. **Einer** may replace **jemand** (§98):

Es klopft einer.
Someone is knocking.

Ich will die Meinung von einem, der besser urteilen kann.
I want the opinion of someone better able to judge.

5. As a pronoun **einer** has the plural form **die einen**:

Die einen sagen dies, die anderen das.
Some say this, the others that.

6. The possessive adjective and the reflexive pronoun corresponding to **man** are **sein** (§114) and **sich** (§109) respectively:

Man sollte sich bemühen, die Jugendlichen besser zu verstehen.
One (we) should endeavour to understand young people better.

7. The **man** construction may replace the passive forms with **werden** (§243) but only when the agent is indefinite or unknown:

Wie schreibt man das Wort? (*for* **Wie wird das Wort geschrieben?**)
How do you spell the word?

Wie spielt man Kricket? (*for* **Wie wird Kricket gespielt?**)
How is cricket played?

101. Manche(r)

1. As a pronoun it is used mainly in the nominative case, both in the singular and in the plural; it cannot be used in the genitive. When used with **von** + a personal pronoun (*e.g.* **von ihnen, von uns**) the singular (**mancher**) takes on the same meaning as the plural, namely 'some':

Mancher von euch kann sich vielleicht noch daran erinnern.
Some of you can still remember it perhaps.

Manche von uns haben viel durchgemacht.
Some of us have been through a great deal.

2. The neuter singular form **manches** is used in the sense of 'a great deal', and may be emphasized by the addition of **so**:

Der alte Mann sah aus, als hätte er manches durchgemacht.
The old man looked as though he had been through a great deal.

Man denkt an so manches, wenn es dunkel ist.
One thinks about such a lot of things when it is dark.

For **manch(er)** as an adjective, see §138.

102. Mehrere(s)

1. As a pronoun it is nowadays mainly used in the plural:

Mehrere von ihnen wurden krank.
Several of them fell ill.

**Mehrere ihrer Freunde sagten ihr, daß eine solche Unternehmung
    sehr gefährlich wäre.**
Several of her friends told her that such an enterprise would be
    very dangerous.

2. It is occasionally used in the neuter singular form **mehreres**, with the meaning 'several things':

Mehreres ist seit deiner Abreise passiert.
Several things have happened since your departure.

Ich habe dir mehreres zu sagen.
I have several things to tell you.

For **mehrere** as an adjective, see §140.

103. Nichts

1. **Nichts** is an indeclinable pronoun:

Nichts wird verschont werden.
Nothing will be spared.

Es hat nichts damit zu tun.
It has nothing to do with it.

Er besaß nichts, als das, was er auf dem Leibe trug.
He owned nothing but what he stood up in.

Das ist nichts gegen das, was wir gesehen haben.
That's nothing to what we have seen.

Du hast nichts, was ich brauche.
You have nothing that I need.

Note from the above example that 'nothing that' is **nichts, was;** cf. **alles,** §89, 1.

2. When an adjective stands after **nichts** it is used like a noun and given an initial capital:

Nichts Besonderes.   **Nichts Schweres.**
Nothing special.   Nothing (that is) difficult.

Ich habe Ihnen nichts Besonderes zu erzählen.
I have nothing special to tell you.

Die Stille hatte nichts Drohendes, nichts Dunkles an sich.
The stillness had nothing menacing, nothing sinister about it.

As with **etwas** (§96, 4), **viel** (§105, 3), and **wenig** (§107, 3), the adjectival ending is strong; contrast **alles** (§89, 3), where the adjectival ending is weak.

See also **gar,** §261, 2.

104. Niemand

Niemand, which is used in the singular only, is inflected as follows:

> *Nom.:* **niemand**
> *Acc.:* **niemand** *or* **niemanden**
> *Gen.:* **niemands** *or* **niemandes**
> *Dat.:* **niemand** *or* **niemandem**

The case endings of the accusative and dative are optional, though they are usually omitted in colloquial speech, but inflexion in the genitive is essential:

Niemand fehlt (*or* **Es fehlt niemand**).
Nobody is missing.

Ich habe niemand(en) gesehen.
I have seen no one.

Er ist niemandes Freund und niemandes Feind.
He is nobody's friend and nobody's enemy.

Ich habe es niemand(em) erzählt.
I have told it to nobody.

105. Viel(e)

1. **Viel** is always declined in the plural when used pronominally:

Es waren viele da.
There were many there.

Viele, die Frauen vor allem, reden immer wieder von den schönen Wohnungen, die sie gehabt haben.
Many, above all the women, talk again and again about the beautiful flats which they used to have.

Viele sind berufen, aber wenige sind auserwählt.
Many are called, but few are chosen. (*Matthew*, xxii, 14)

2. The neuter singular form **vieles** is often used with the meaning 'much', 'many things':

Vieles war zerstört.
Much was destroyed.

Er dachte, er müsse noch über vieles nachdenken.
He thought he still had a lot to reflect on.

3. When an adjective stands after **viel** it is used like a noun and given an initial capital:

Viel Wahres.   **Viel Gutes.**
Much that is true.   Much that is good.

Es ist viel Wahres daran.
There's a lot of truth in it.

As with **etwas** (§96, 4), **nichts** (§103, 2), and **wenig** (§107, 3), the adjectival ending is strong; contrast **alles** (§89, 3), where the adjectival ending is weak.

For **viel(e)** as an adjective, see §142.

106. Welcher

As an indefinite pronoun **welcher** means 'some', with the force of **etwas** (§96,2) in the singular and **einige** (§93,3) in the plural, and in this sense is mostly used in colloquial speech:

Haben Sie Geld?—Ja, ich habe welches.
Do you have any money?—Yes, I have some.

Haben Sie Streichhölzer?—Ja, ich habe welche.
Do you have any matches?—Yes, I have some.

For **welcher** as an interrogative pronoun, see §§84, 85.
For **welcher** as a relative pronoun, see §§76, 79.
For **welcher** as an interrogative adjective, see §§124, 125.

107. Wenig(e)

1. **Wenig** is always declined in the plural when used pronominally:

Es waren nur wenige da.
There were only a few there.

2. In the singular **wenig** is not usually declined:

Hast du Geld?—Nur noch ein wenig (nur noch wenig).
Do you have any money?—Only a little (only very little).

Nach Ansicht der Ärzte ist es für die Gesundheit besser, morgens und mittags viel, zu Abend aber nur wenig zu essen.
In the opinion of doctors it is better for one's health to eat lots in the morning and at lunchtime, but only little in the evening.

3. When an adjective stands after **wenig** it is used like a noun and given an initial capital:

Wenig Zuverlässiges.   **Wenig Schönes.**
Little that is reliable.   Little that is beautiful.

Es ist wenig Interessantes daran.
There is little in it that is interesting.

As with **etwas** (§96, 4), **nichts** (§103, 2), and **viel** (§105, 3), the adjectival ending is strong; contrast **alles** (§89, 3), where the adjectival ending is weak.

For **wenig(e)** as an adjective, see §143.

108. Emphatic Pronouns

1. The indeclinable **selbst** or **selber** is used to emphasize pronouns and nouns. Generally speaking, **selbst** belongs to the written language and formal speech while **selber** is more commonly used in conversation:

Du sagst es selbst (*or* selber).
You say so yourself.

Er sagte es mehr zu sich selber (*or* selbst) als zu den andern.
He said it more to himself than to the others.

Der Präsident selbst hat es gesagt.
The President himself said so.

Der Präsident hat es selbst gesagt.
The President said so himself.

2. **Selbst** is also used adverbially (= **auch** or **sogar,** 'even'), and then precedes:

Selbst der Präsident sagt es.
Even the President says so.

109. Reflexive Pronouns

1. In the 1st and 2nd persons singular and plural, reflexive pronouns are identical in form with personal pronouns (§51). Only the formal **Sie,** 'you', and the 3rd person dative and accusative, both singular and plural, have a special form, **sich.**

2. The following tables show examples of the reflexive pronoun forms both for reflexive verbs taking an accusative and for those taking a dative object:

> **sich** (*acc*.) **ergeben**, 'to surrender (oneself)'
> ich ergebe *mich*
> du ergibst *dich*
> er ergibt *sich*
> wir ergeben *uns*
> ihr ergebt *euch*
> Sie ergeben *sich*
> sie ergeben *sich*
>
> **sich** (*dat*.) **einbilden**, 'to think', 'to imagine'
> ich bilde *mir* ein
> du bildest *dir* ein
> er bildet *sich* ein
> wir bilden *uns* ein
> ihr bildet *euch* ein
> Sie bilden *sich* ein
> sie bilden *sich* ein

See §§220–222.

110. Word Order of Reflexive Pronouns

1. In simple sentences the reflexive pronoun follows the finite verb:

Du kannst *dir* leicht denken, wie entsetzt ich war.
You can easily imagine how horrified I was.

2. When a principal clause is inverted, the reflexive pronoun follows the subject if a pronoun; if a noun it may precede or follow the subject, more commonly following it in writing but not in speech:
Mit dreißig Jahren *läßt er sich* (but *läßt sich Peter* or *läßt Peter sich*) von seiner Mutter am Gängelband führen.
At thirty he (Peter) is still tied to his mother's apron-strings.

3. In questions the reflexive pronoun precedes or follows the subject:

Glaubst du, daß *jemand sich* (or *sich jemand*) etwas dabei denken würde?
Do you believe that anyone would see any harm in it?

Glaubst du, daß *sich dein Vater* (or *dein Vater sich*) etwas dabei denken würde?
Do you believe that your father would see any harm in it?

4. In dependent clauses, the reflexive pronoun immediately follows the subject if the verb is placed at the end of the clause, but follows the verb if **daß** is omitted (cf. §236,5):

Er sagte, *daß er sich* beleidigt *fühlte*.
He said that he felt insulted.
but
Er sagte, *er fühlte sich* beleidigt.

5. Reflexive pronouns usually follow personal pronouns used as direct objects or impersonally:

Kannst du *es dir* vorstellen?
Can you imagine it?

Aus diesem Glas trinkt *es sich* gut.
This is a good glass to drink out of.

Other pronouns, however, usually follow:

Ich hatte *mir das* so schön gedacht.
I had imagined it all so beautiful.

111. Possessive Dative

Es fiel ihm auf den Kopf.	It fell on his head.
Ein Nagel zerriß mir den Rock.	A nail tore my coat.
Er schüttelte seinem alten Freund die Hand.	He shook hands with his old friend.
Sie schnitt sich die Haare selbst.	She cut her own hair (She cut her hair herself).

1. With parts of the person, clothing, etc., the possessive adjective is commonly replaced by the dative of the personal pronoun or of a noun + the definite article.

2. If the possessor is the subject, the reflexive pronoun is used when the action is reflexive.

NOTE: But when there is no reflexive action, the reflexive pronoun is omitted: **Sie schüttelten den Kopf,** 'They shook their heads'.

112. Ethic Dative

The dative is used freely in German to denote the person who has some interest in an action or thing, and when so employed is called the 'ethic dative' or 'dative of advantage'; it is used colloquially to give a livelier tone to a sentence:

Komm mir nicht zu spät nach Hause!
See you don't come home too late!

Du bist mir ja ein nettes Bürschchen!
A nice fellow you are!

Das lobe ich mir—Kinder, die für Erwachsene aufstehen.
That's what I like to see—children who stand up for (give up their seats to) grown-ups.

Das ist dir ein Kerl!
There's an amazing fellow for you!

V. ADJECTIVES

113. General Remarks

There are two kinds of adjectives—qualifying and limiting. A qualifying adjective gives descriptive information about a noun—*e.g.* 'a *red* rose', 'a *heavy* suitcase'. Both 'red' and 'heavy' in these examples are used *attributively*—i.e., they qualify their noun directly. If, however, one says 'the rose is red', 'the suitcase is heavy', the adjectives are then said to form the *predicate* of the sentence—i.e., they qualify their noun indirectly by not standing immediately before it. In German, adjectives used predicatively are invariable—**die Rose ist *rot*, der Koffer ist *schwer*.** Used attributively, they must be declined. See also the Glossary under ATTRIBUTIVE ADJECTIVE, PREDICATIVE ADJECTIVE.

Besides including the definite and indefinite articles (see §8, 3), limiting adjectives (also known as 'determinatives') may be possessive ('*my* hat'), demonstrative ('*that* woman'), interrogative ('*which* address?'), indefinite ('*any* individual'), numeral ('*three* children'), or distributive ('*each* Sunday'). All these terms are treated separately in the Glossary.

114. **Mein** Model and Possessive Adjectives

	SINGULAR			PLURAL
	Masc.	*Fem.*	*Neut.*	*All Genders*
Nom.:	mein	meine	mein	meine, my
Acc.:	meinen	meine	mein	meine, my
Gen.:	meines	meiner	meines	meiner, of my
Dat.:	meinem	meiner	meinem	meinen, (to, for) my

1. Thus are declined the possessive adjectives:

mein, my	**sein,** his, its	**unser,** our	**Ihr,** your
dein, your	**ihr,** her, its, their	**euer,** your	

Also: **ein,** a, one (sing. only); **kein,** no, not any.

NOTE: 1. **Euer** usually refers to several persons **(euer Freund, eure Freundin)**—see §52, 1—though in very formal or archaic address it may refer to one person only **(Euer Gnaden,** 'Your Grace').

2. **Unser** and **euer** usually omit the **e** of the stem or the **e** of the inflectional endings: **unsrem, unserm; unsren, unsern; eures, eurem.**

2. Observe the correspondence between the pronoun of address and the possessive:

Du hast deine Bücher.	You have your books.
Ihr habt eure Bücher.	You have your books.
Sie haben Ihre Bücher.	You have your books.

3. Observe also the correspondence for the third person, especially for **sein** and **ihr,** of inanimate objects:

Die Blume verliert ihre Farbe.	The flower loses its colour.
Das Gras verliert seine Farbe.	The grass loses its colour.
Sie hat ihren Hut.	She has her hat.

4. The ending of the possessive adjective depends on the gender, number, and case of the noun it qualifies (the thing possessed); the stem depends on the gender and number of the noun or pronoun to which it refers (the possessor), as in the examples above.

NOTE: The neuter diminutive **das Mädchen,** 'the girl', takes the personal pronoun and possessive adjective referring to it in the neuter: **Das Mädchen liebt seine Mutter; es liebt sie,** 'The girl loves her mother; she loves her'. Cf. §57, note.

115. Attributive Adjective + Noun—
Strong, Weak, and Mixed Forms

I. STRONG FORM
Singular

	Good wine	Good soup	Good glass
	Good wine	Good soup	Good glass
Nom.:	**guter Wein**	**gute Suppe**	**gutes Glas**
Acc.:	**guten Wein**	**gute Suppe**	**gutes Glas**
Gen.:	**guten Weines**	**guter Suppe**	**guten Glases**
Dat.:	**gutem Wein**	**guter Suppe**	**gutem Glas**

Plural

Good wines, etc.

Nom.: gute Weine, Suppen, Gläser
Acc.: gute Weine, Suppen, Gläser
Gen.: guter Weine, Suppen, Gläser
Dat.: guten Weinen, Suppen, Gläsern

Adjectives after personal pronouns are strong except in the nominative plural, where weak endings are commoner: **Ihr armen Sünder!** 'You miserable sinners!' **Ihr lieben Leute!** 'You dear people!'

II. WEAK FORM
Singular

	The good man	The good woman	The good child
Nom.:	der gute Mann	die gute Frau	das gute Kind
Acc.:	den guten Mann	die gute Frau	das gute Kind
Gen.:	des guten Mannes	der guten Frau	des guten Kindes
Dat.:	dem guten Mann	der guten Frau	dem guten Kind

Plural

The good men, etc.

Nom.: die guten Männer, Frauen, Kinder
Acc.: die guten Männer, Frauen, Kinder
Gen.: der guten Männer, Frauen, Kinder
Dat.: den guten Männern, Frauen, Kindern

The same adjective endings occur after **dieser, jener, welcher, mancher, jeder.**

III. MIXED FORM
Singular

	My good resolution	My good watch
Nom.:	mein guter Vorsatz	meine gute Uhr
Acc.:	meinen guten Vorsatz	meine gute Uhr
Gen.:	meines guten Vorsatzes	meiner guten Uhr
Dat.:	meinem guten Vorsatz	meiner guten Uhr

My good dress

Nom.:	**mein**	**gutes Kleid**
Acc.:	**mein**	**gutes Kleid**
Gen.:	**meines**	**guten Kleides**
Dat.:	**meinem guten Kleid**	

Plural

My good resolutions, etc.

Nom.:	**meine guten Vorsätze, Uhren, Kleider**
Acc.:	**meine guten Vorsätze, Uhren, Kleider**
Gen.:	**meiner guten Vorsätze, Uhren, Kleider**
Dat.:	**meinen guten Vorsätzen, Uhren, Kleidern**

The same adjective endings occur after **ein, kein, dein, sein, unser, euer, ihr, Ihr.**

Two or more adjectives qualifying the same noun follow the same form: **Guter, alter, roter Wein; des guten, alten, roten Weines, mit gutem, altem, rotem Wein.**

116. Declension of Attributive Adjectives

1. When not preceded by a determinative, they take the endings of the **dieser** model (§61) throughout (Strong Form)—*e.g.*:

Echter Burgunder; echte Seide; echtes Gold.
Real Burgundy; real silk; real gold.

Er liebt schnelle Autos.
He loves fast cars.

NOTE: The articles, and possessive, interrogative, demonstrative and indefinite adjectives are called 'determinatives' or 'limiting adjectives'—see §113.

2. When preceded by the definite article or a determinative of the **dieser** model they take the ending **-e** in the nominative singular of all genders, and in the accusative singular feminine and neuter; otherwise **-en** throughout (Weak Form)—*e.g.*:

Der kluge Mann baut vor.
The prudent man provides for the future.

Ich mag diesen Wein nicht.
I don't like this wine.

3. When preceded by a determinative of the **mein** model
(§115, III) they take the endings **-er, -e, -es** in the nominative
singular, and **-en, -e, -es** in the accusative singular; otherwise
-en throughout (Mixed Form)—*e.g.*:

Gestern war kein schönes Wetter.
Yesterday the weather was not fine.

Meine eigenen Photos sind nicht so gut wie Ihre!
My own photographs are not as good as yours!

SUMMARY OF DECLENSION OF STRONG, WEAK, AND
MIXED ADJECTIVAL FORMS

	I. STRONG FORM			II. WEAK FORM			III. MIXED FORM		
	M.	*F.*	*N.*	*M.*	*F.*	*N.*	*M.*	*F.*	*N.*
Sing.: Nom.:	-er	-e	-es	-e	-e	-e	-er	-e	-es
Acc.:	-en	-e	-es	-en	-e	-e	-en	-e	-es
Gen.:	-en	-er	-en	-en	-en	-en	-en	-en	-en
Dat.:	-em	-er	-em	-en	-en	-en	-en	-en	-en

	All genders	*All genders*	*All genders*
Plur.: Nom.:	-e	-en	-en
Acc.:	-e	-en	-en
Gen.:	-er	-en	-en
Dat.:	-en	-en	-en

NOTE: In the mixed form, the adjective follows the **dieser** model
only in the three places where the **mein** model lacks distinctive
endings, namely, nominative singular masculine and neuter, and
accusative singular neuter; otherwise it is like the weak form.

117. Demonstrative Adjectives

1. **dieser,** this, that
2. **jener,** that
3. **der,** that (*stressed*)
4. **derjenige,** that
5. **derselbe,** the same
6. **solch(er),** such
7. **dergleichen,** such

118. Dieser, jener

1. Both follow the **dieser** model (§61).

2. The English demonstrative adjective 'that' is not rendered by **jener,** except when remoteness or contrast is indicated:

Mit diesen Worten verließ er das Zimmer.
With these (*or* those) words he left the room.

Ich war Student in diesen Jahren.
I was a student in those days.

Diese Äpfel schmecken gut, aber jene Birnen sind noch nicht reif.
These apples taste good, but those pears are not yet ripe.

3. The nominative and accusative neuter singular form **dieses** is sometimes contracted to **dies:**

Wer ist dies Kind?
Who is this child?

Dies alberne Geflüster kann ich nicht leiden.
I can't bear this silly whispering.

Cf. a similar use of the demonstrative pronoun (§61, note 2).

119. Der

1. As a demonstrative adjective **der** is declined in exactly the same way as the definite article (§10), but is always stressed, being pronounced with a long closed **e:**

Der Mann, the man (*unstressed*)
but **ˈDer Mann,** ˈthat man (*stressed*)

Die Leute, the people (*unstressed*)
but **'Die Leute,** 'those people (*stressed*)

Ich gehe nicht oft ins Kino, aber 'den Film muß ich sehen.
I don't often go to the cinema, but 'that film I must see.

'Die Frau ist eine Schauspielerin.
'That woman is an actress.

2. **'Der** is often used disparagingly or contemptuously:

'Den Mann willst du heiraten?!
You want to marry 'that man?!

For the use of **der** as a demonstrative pronoun, see §64.

120. Derjenige

1. **Derjenige** as a demonstrative adjective is declined in exactly the same way as **derjenige** as a demonstrative pronoun (§67).

2. Although regarded as rather clumsy, especially in speech, the use of **derjenige** is sometimes necessary in cases of uncertainty of meaning.

Sie zeigten ihm die Photos, die sie in der Schweiz aufgenommen hatten.

In this sentence the first **die** may be either the definite article or a demonstrative adjective; in the latter case it has a selective quality ('only those which . . .'). In speech this selective quality could be expressed by stressing the first **die,** but in writing the stress would be indicated by substituting **diejenigen:**

Sie zeigten ihm diejenigen Photos, die sie in der Schweiz aufgenommen hatten.
They showed him those photographs which they had taken in Switzerland.

121. Derselbe

1. **Derselbe,** 'the same', used as a demonstrative adjective is declined in exactly the same way as **derselbe** used as a demonstrative pronoun (§69). It expresses identity:

Das ist derselbe Mann, dem ich schon in der Stadt begegnet bin.
That is the same man whom I have already met in the town.

Treffen wir uns morgen um dieselbe Zeit!
Let's meet tomorrow at the same time.

Sie hat heute dasselbe Kleid an wie gestern.
She has the same dress on today as she was wearing yesterday.

Er wohnt in derselben Straße wie wir.
He lives in the same street as we do.

2. **Derselbe** may be replaced by **der gleiche** (two words), declined like **derselbe**:

Er fährt noch immer dasselbe (*or* das gleiche) Auto wie vor zehn Jahren.
He is still driving the same car as he was ten years ago.

3. If there is contraction of a preposition and the article of **derselbe**, the preposition and **selb-** are written separately:

Noch am selben Tag kaufte er sich eine Fahrkarte nach Frankreich.
On the very same day he bought a ticket to France.

Die Kinder sind im selben Alter.
The children are of the same age.

122. Solch(er)

1. When used alone, **solch** follows the **dieser** model (§61):

Ich habe schon lange nicht mehr solchen Durst gehabt.
It is a long time since I was so thirsty.

Es regnete mit solcher Heftigkeit, daß die Straßen bald überschwemmt waren.
It rained so hard that the streets were soon flooded.

2. After **ein** it follows the mixed declension of adjectives (§115, III):

Noch ein solcher Auftrag, und er kann ein eigenes Architektenbüro aufmachen!
Another order like this, and he can open an architect's office of his own!

3. Before **ein** it is undeclined:

Solch einen (*or* **Einen solchen**) **Wein haben Sie noch nicht getrunken.**
You have never drunk a wine like this.

Ich habe noch nie solch ein schlechtes Stück gesehen.
I have never seen such a bad play.

NOTE: **Solch** with **ein** is often replaced in colloquial speech by **so**:
Solch ein Regen! = So ein Regen! = Ein so starker Regen!

4. After the plural **solche** the adjective may be weak or strong (preferably weak):

Solche fromme(n) Leute. Such pious people.

After the uninflected singular form **solch,** however, the adjective must be strong:

Solch herrliches Wetter! Such splendid weather!

For **solcher** as a demonstrative pronoun, see §71.

123. Dergleichen

Dergleichen is used as an indeclinable demonstrative adjective (plural), with the meaning 'such':

Dergleichen Filme sollten Kindern nicht gezeigt werden.
Such films should not be shown to children.

Dergleichen Leute trifft man sehr häufig.
You meet people like that very often.

For the use of **dergleichen** as a demonstrative pronoun, see §72.
For the use of **dergleichen** as a relative pronoun, see §78.

124. Interrogative Adjectives

1. **welcher?** which? what?
2. **was für ein?** what kind of? what?

Declension: **welcher?** follows the **dieser** model (§61). **Was für ein** is declined as follows:

	SINGULAR			PLURAL
	Masc.	*Fem.*	*Neut.*	*All Genders*
Nom.:	was für ein	was für eine	was für ein	was für
Acc.:	was für einen	was für eine	was für ein	was für
Gen.:	was für eines	was für einer	was für eines	was für
Dat.:	was für einem	was für einer	was für einem	was für

Ein only is declined, agreeing with its noun, and being omitted in the plural.

125. Use of Interrogative Adjectives

(a)

Welcher Schauspieler hatte die Hauptrolle?
Which actor had the leading part?

Welche Schuhgröße haben Sie?
What size shoes do you take?

Mit welchem Zug sind Sie gefahren?
By which train did you go?

Von welcher Dame spricht er?
Which lady is he speaking of?

Über welches Thema werden Sie sprechen?
On which subject will you be speaking?

Welch Vergnügen für die Kinder! ⎫
Welches Vergnügen für die Kinder! ⎰
What a treat for the children!

Welch ein Unglück!
What a misfortune!

(b)

Was für einen Wagen hat er?
What sort of car has he got?

Auf was für eine Schule geht sie?
What sort of school does she go to?

Was sind das für seltsame Blumen?
What strange flowers are those?

Was für herrliches Wetter! }
Was für ein herrliches Wetter! }
What splendid weather!

Was er für Geld ausgibt! (*colloquial*)
It is incredible the amount of money he spends!

Note that **was für (ein)** is sometimes divided, the **für (ein)** with its noun following the verb, and that **welcher** and **was für (ein)** are also used in exclamations, the neuter **welches** often dropping the ending **-es,** and always before **ein.**

126. Indefinite Adjectives

1. **all,** all (the)
2. **ander,** other
3. **beide,** both
4. **einige,** some, a few
5. **ein paar,** a few
6. **etliche,** quite a few, quite a number of
7. **etwas,** some, a little
8. **ganz,** (the) whole (of)
9. **genug,** enough
10. **jeder,** each every
11. **kein,** no, not a
12. **manch(er),** many (a)
13. **mehr,** more
14. **mehrere,** several
15. **sämtlich(e),** all the
16. **viel(e),** much, many
17. **wenig(e),** little, few

127. All

1. This word expresses number as well as quantity (compare **ganz,** §134); when declined it follows the **dieser** model (§61):

Alles Geld. }
All das Geld. } All the money.

Alle Kinder.
All the children.

All die Mühe (*or* Alle Mühe) war umsonst.
All the trouble taken was in vain.

Das geschieht alle zwanzig Minuten.
That happens every twenty minutes.

Ich wünsche Ihnen alles Gute.
I wish you all the best.

NOTE: 1. 'All the' is translated either by inflected **all** without the definite article, or by uninflected **all** with the definite article.
2. The definite article is always unstressed after **all**.

2. With a possessive adjective or demonstrative adjective it always precedes, and remains uninflected in the singular; in the nominative and accusative plural the inflected forms are more usual, while in the genitive and dative plural inflected and uninflected forms are both commonly used:

Er hat all sein (dieses) Geld beim Spiel verloren.
He has lost all his (this) money gambling.

All(e) ihre Freundinnen waren verreist.
All her friends had gone away.

In dem Brief gedachte er all(er) seiner Freunde.
In the letter he remembered all his friends.

3. It is used with intensive force in a number of set expressions, such as **in aller Frühe**, 'very early in the morning', **in aller Eile**, 'post-haste', **mit aller Kraft**, 'with might and main', **was (wer) in aller Welt . . .**, 'what (who) on earth . . .'

4. After the plural **alle** the adjective may be weak or strong (preferably weak):

Alle guten Menschen, *occasionally* **alle gute Menschen.**
All good men.

For **all** as a pronoun, see §89.

128. Ander

1. This word has various shades of meaning when used as an adjective, the commonest of which are:

(*a*) 'other' (of two):

Die andere Hälfte.
The other half.

Die andere Seite der Straße.
The other side of the street.

(*b*) 'other(s)' (not already specified):

Die anderen Kandidaten.
The other candidates.

Erbsen und anderes Gemüse.
Peas and other vegetables.

(*c*) 'next', 'following':

Am anderen Tag.
(On) the next day.

Ein Jahr über (*or* um) das andere.
Every other year.

(*d*) 'different' (in kind or quality from what is being contrasted):

Ich bin ganz anderer Meinung als Sie.
I am of an entirely different opinion from you.

Das waren noch andere Zeiten, als Kinder ihren Eltern noch gehorchten.
Those were the days, when children were still obedient to their parents.

2. The **e** of **ander,** or of inflected forms ending in **-n,** is sometimes omitted, especially in colloquial speech:

Die anderen (*or* andren *or* andern) Kandidaten.

3. After the plural **andere** the adjective is strong:

Andere gute Leute.
Other good people.

4. The strong forms **etwas anderes** ('something else') and **nichts anderes** ('nothing else'), together with the weak form **alles andere** ('everything else'), are unique in that in no other instance where an adjective follows these indefinite neuter pronouns does it take a small letter (cf. **etwas Schweres**, 'something difficult', **nichts Schweres**, 'nothing difficult', **alles Schwere**, 'everything (that is) difficult').

5. The neuter forms **etwas anderes** and **nichts anderes** (nominative and accusative) must not be confused with the old genitive form **anders**, which has become an adverb, as in: **Wer anders könnte es gewesen sein?**, 'Who else could it have been?'; **Das ist anders!** 'That's different!'

For **ander** as a pronoun, see §90.

129. Beide

1. When stressed, this word means 'both':

Faß den Topf mit beiden Händen an!
Take hold of the pot with both hands.

Beide Damen traten ein ohne anzuklopfen.
Both ladies walked straight in without knocking.

Man muß immer beide Seiten anhören.
One must always listen to both sides.

2. When unstressed, it means 'two', no greater number being involved:

Meine beiden Freunde warten draußen.
My two friends are waiting outside.

(*Compare:* **Zwei meiner Freunde ...,** 'Two of my friends ...')

Die beiden Herren sind eben aus Paris angekommen.
The two gentlemen have just arrived from Paris.

3. When a noun follows the personal pronoun + **beide,** the latter follows the weak declension:

Ihr beiden Diebe!
You couple of thieves!

Similarly, attributive adjectives are weak:

Beide dunklen Anzüge müssen gereinigt werden.
Both dark suits must be cleaned.

For **beide** as a pronoun, see §91.

130. Einige

1. Plural = 'some', 'a few':

An einigen Orten kam es zu Zusammenstößen zwischen Polizei und Studenten.
In some places clashes broke out between police and students.

Ich bin einige Male dort gewesen.
I have been there a few times.

Die Reparatur wird ihn einige hundert Mark kosten.
The repair will cost him several hundred Marks.

Er beugte sich über die Landkarte und las den Namen des Ortes und noch einige andere.
He leaned over the map and read the name of the place and some others besides.

2. Singular = 'some', 'quite a lot':

In einiger Entfernung standen zwei Männer.
Some distance away stood two men.

Ich habe einiges Geld.
I have some money (not much).

Das hat einiges Geld gekostet.
That cost quite a lot of money.

NOTE: 1. The singular (**einiger, einige, einiges**) can denote a limited amount (of time, distance, etc.) or quite a lot, the sense being construed from the context or intonation (compare the last two examples).

2. Unless the idea of limited quantity is emphasized, 'some' and 'any' are omitted when rendering into German—cf. §133, note.

3. After the plural **einige** the adjective is strong, but the singular follows the weak declension:

Einige große Nägel. Some large nails.
Einiges innere Widerstreben. Some inner reluctance.

For **einige(s)** as a pronoun, see §93.

131. Ein paar

1. This form is indeclinable; **paar** is not written with a capital (see 3, below):

Ein paar tausend Mark würden ihn von seinen Schulden befreien.
A few thousand Marks would free him of his debts.

Schreiben Sie mir von Zeit zu Zeit ein paar Zeilen!
Write me a few lines from time to time.

In ein paar Tagen wird er das Ergebnis wissen.
In a few days he will know the result.

Er ließ sich durch ein paar Kritiken nicht von seinem Plan abbringen.
He did not allow himself to be dissuaded from his plan because of a few criticisms.

2. In colloquial language, **paar** is sometimes preceded by the stressed definite article, which gives a somewhat pejorative flavour:

Für ¹*die* paar Mark würde ich nicht so viel arbeiten.
For such a paltry sum I would not work so much.

NOTE: When not stressed, the sense is simply 'the few' as in **Er sehnte sich danach, mit ihr länger zusammenzusein als nur die paar Stunden am Nachmittag und Abend,** 'He longed to be together with her for longer than just the few hours in the afternoon and evening'.

3. Distinguish between **ein paar** and the neuter noun **ein
Paar** (with a capital), which means 'a pair of'—*e.g.* **ein Paar
Socken,** 'a pair of socks', **mit einem Paar Socken,** 'with a pair
of socks'.

For **ein paar** as a pronoun, see §94.

132. Etliche

As an adjective **etliche** is nowadays used almost exclusively in
the plural, but even then is little used, being replaced generally
by **einige** (§130). It is still found, however, in certain expressions.
with the meaning 'quite a few', 'quite a number of':

Er hat etliche hundert Mark dafür verlangt.
He wanted several hundred Marks for it.

Er hat etliche Glas Bier getrunken.
He drank quite a few glasses of beer.

Es ist etliche Tage her, seit ich ihn zuletzt gesehen habe.
It is quite a number of days since I last saw him.

For **etliche(s)** as a pronoun, see §95.

133. Etwas

As an adjective **etwas** is indeclinable; it is used only before
singular nouns, and is usually translated 'some', though the
implication is often 'not much':

Er spricht etwas Englisch.
He speaks some English (i.e., not much).

Ich habe noch etwas Zeit.
I still have some (i.e., a little) time.

Er hat etwas Geld.
He has ¹some money.

NOTE: The sentence 'Have you some (*or* any) money?', in which
'some', 'any', are not stressed, would be rendered simply by **Haben
Sie Geld?**—see §130, 2, note 2.

For **etwas** as a pronoun, see §96.

134. Ganz

1. This adjective expresses quantity, not number (compare **all**, §127), and denotes an object as complete and undivided; when, therefore, the English 'all'='the whole', it must be rendered by **ganz**; as an attributive adjective it always follows the determinative (§116, 1, note):

Ich arbeite den ganzen Tag lang.
I work all (the whole) day.

Er hat den ganzen Shakespeare gelesen.
He has read all (the whole of) Shakespeare.

Gewisse Tiere schlafen den ganzen Winter hindurch.
Certain animals sleep through the whole winter.

Sie schenkten ihm ihre ganze Aufmerksamkeit.
They gave him their undivided attention.

Der neue Sportwagen war sein ganzer Stolz.
The new sports car was his pride and joy.

2. Before proper names of places, unaccompanied by an article or other determinative, it may remain uninflected:

Ganz Europa war in Gefahr.
All (the whole of) Europe was in danger.

Ganz (*or* das ganze) Deutschland.
The whole of Germany.

but

Die ganze Schweiz.
The whole of Switzerland.   (Cf. §16.)

135. Genug

1. An as adjective **genug** is invariable.

2. Used with a noun, it may precede or follow, as in English:

Er hat Geld genug (*or* genug Geld).
He has money enough (*or* enough money).

3. It is most commonly found as a predicative adjective:

Das ist (schon) genug.
That's sufficient.

Zwei Koffer sind genug.
Two suitcases will do.

136. Jeder

1. **Jeder (dieser** model, §61) is used to denote each individual belonging to a class:

Jeder Baum hat Äste.
Every tree has branches.

Jedes Land hat eine Regierung.
Every country has a government.

2. It is sometimes preceded by **ein,** and then follows the mixed adjective declension:

Ein jeder Mensch hat dieses Recht.
Every person has this right.

NOTE: **Jedweder** and **jeglicher** are less common, rather literary substitutes for **jeder,** but are sometimes still used when greater emphasis is required—*e.g.* **Er verbot sich jedwede Kritik,** 'He refused to tolerate adverse criticism of any kind'; **Genug, daß ein jeglicher Tag seine eigne Plage habe**='Sufficient unto the day is the evil thereof'.

For **jeder** as a pronoun, see §97.

137. Kein

1. **Kein (mein** model, §114) is used adjectivally in German to render not only 'no' but also 'not a' and 'not any':

Es ist keine leichte Aufgabe.
It is no easy task.

Du bist kein Kind mehr.
You're not a child any longer.

Ich habe kein Geld mehr.
I haven't any money left.

Mach dir keine Hoffnungen!
Don't expect too much.

2. After uninflected **kein** (i.e., in the nominative singular masculine and neuter and in the accusative singular neuter) the following adjective is declined strong:

Kein großes Geschenk.
No big present.

After inflected **kein** (i.e., in all other cases) the following adjective is nowadays always weak:

Mit keinem großen Geschenk.
With no big present.

Keine großen Geschenke.
No big presents.

For **keiner** as a pronoun, see §99.

138. Manch(er)

1. It follows the **dieser** model (§61).

2. In the singular it means 'many a':

Mancher Politiker begnügt sich damit, sich an die allgemeine Linie der Partei zu halten.
Many a politician is (*or* Many politicians are) content to toe the party line.

NOTE: 1. **Mancher** is not inflected before (*a*) the indefinite article: **Manch ein Bergsteiger mußte seine Leidenschaft mit dem Leben bezahlen**, 'Many a mountaineer had to pay for his passionate enthusiasm with his life'; (*b*) adjective + noun: **Manch großes Schiff lag im Hafen**, 'Many a large ship was moored in the harbour'. (See 4, below.)

2. **Mancher** is often preceded by **gar** (§261, 6), **wie, so,** etc., providing sentimental or emotive force: **Gar mancher tapfere Soldat fiel im Rückzugsgefecht,** 'Many a brave soldier (*or* A great many brave soldiers) fell in the rearguard action', **Hier verbrachte ich so manche frohe Stunde,** 'I spent many a happy hour here'.

3. In the plural it means 'some':

Manche Leute wissen beim Trinken einfach nicht, wann sie genug haben.
Some people when they drink simply don't know when they've had enough.

In manchen Fällen mache ich eine Ausnahme.
I make an exception in some cases.

NOTE: **Manche** is sometimes used in a literary way with the meaning 'many', 'quite a number of' (*e.g.* **die Arbeit mancher Jahre,** 'the work of a good many years', but its usual meaning in the plural is merely 'some', unlike the singular where it always denotes 'many'.

4. After the uninflected singular **manch**, which is stylistically rather more elevated than the inflected form, the adjective is always strong:

Manch großes Schiff.
Many a large ship.

After the inflected form the adjective is weak in the singular, but in the plural may be weak or strong (preferably strong):

Manches große Schiff.
Manche große(n) Schiffe.

For **manche(r)** as a pronoun, see §101.

139. Mehr

As an adjective **mehr** is invariable:

Ich habe mehr Geld als Sie.
I have more money than you.

Für meine Arbeit habe ich jetzt mehr Interesse.
I now take a greater interest in my work.

Es gibt dieses Jahr mehr Tiere im Zoo.
There are more animals at the Zoo this year.

140. Mehrere

Mehrere is nowadays used only in the plural:

Mehrere Leute wurden krank.
Several people fell ill.

Der Zug kam mit mehreren Stunden Verspätung an.
The train arrived several hours late.

Er klopfte mehrere Male, bevor er hereingelassen wurde.
He knocked several times before he was let in.

Er besitzt mehrere gute Anzüge.
He has several good suits.

Note, from the last example above, that after **mehrere** the adjective is strong.

For **mehrere(s)** as a pronoun, see §102.

141. Sämtlich(e)

1. As an adjective **sämtlich** contains the idea of 'the whole thing' in the singular (which is rarely used, the usual construction nowadays being **ganz** preceded by article, §134, 2), and 'all (things *or* persons)' in the plural:

Sie riß sämtliches (*better:* **das ganze) Unkraut heraus.**
She pulled up all the weeds.

E.T.A. Hoffmanns sämtliche Werke sind neu verlegt worden.
E. T. A. Hoffmann's complete works have just been republished.

Sämtliche Nachbarn waren empört.
All the neighbours were indignant.

Sämtliche Theaterkarten waren ausverkauft.
All the theatre tickets were sold out.

NOTE: The related adjective **gesamt** is used attributively with collective *singular* nouns—*e.g.* **die gesamte Verwandtschaft,** 'all the relatives'.

2. After the singular **sämtlich** the adjective is weak:

Sämtliches ausgerissene Unkraut.
All the pulled-up weeds.

After the plural **sämtliche** the adjective is declined sometimes strong, more often weak:

Sämtliche ordentliche(n) Mitglieder.
All the regular members.

In the genitive plural, however, the strong ending is more frequent:

Einschließlich sämtlicher ordentlicher Mitglieder.
Inclusive of all the regular members.

142. Viel(e)

1. It usually remains uninflected in the singular when used adjectivally:

Ich habe viel Geld.
I have a lot of money.

Du mußt viel Milch trinken.
You must drink plenty of milk.

In dieser Gegend gab es im Mittelalter viel Blutvergießen.
In this region there was much bloodshed in the Middle Ages.

2. It is usually inflected in the plural:

Waren viele Leute anwesend?
Were many people present?

Ich habe noch viel(e) Briefe zu schreiben.
I still have many letters to write.

3. In the singular the following adjective is usually declined strong:

Vieler schöner Schmuck.
Much beautiful jewellery.

In the nominative and accusative neuter singular and the dative masculine and neuter singular, however, the adjective is more often declined weak:

Vieles unnötige Verzögern.
Much unnecessary delay.

Mit vielem unnötigen Verzögern.
With much unnecessary delay.

In the plural the following adjective is usually declined strong:

Viele schöne Mädchen.
Many beautiful girls.

4. Note the adjectival forms **soviel** ('so much', 'as much') and **zuviel** ('too much'), both written as one word:

Ich habe nicht soviel Geld wie du.
I don't have as much money as you.

Es ist zuviel Milch im Kaffee.
There is too much milk in the coffee.

For **viel(e)** as a pronoun, see §105.

143. Wenig(e)

1. It usually remains uninflected in the singular when used adjectivally:

Ich habe wenig Geld.
I have little money.

Er hatte wenig Gewinn von seinem Berufswechsel.
He did not gain much by changing his job.

Die Welt bringt ihm wenig Verständnis entgegen.
The world shows him little understanding.

2. It is usually inflected in the plural:

Nur wenige Leute waren bei der Feier anwesend.
Only a few people were present at the ceremony.

Die wenigen Schaufenster des Städtchens verrieten das nahe Weihnachtsfest.
The few shop-windows of the little town told of approaching Christmas.

3. **Ein wenig** (uninflected) = 'a little':

Mit ein wenig Geduld kann man alles erreichen.
With a little patience one can achieve anything.

4. In the singular the following adjective is always declined strong except in the dative singular masculine and neuter:

Weniges unnötiges Verzögern.
Little unnecessary delay.

In the dative singular masculine and neuter the following adjective is always declined weak:

Mit wenigem unnötigen Verzögern.
With little unnecessary delay.

In the plural the following adjective is always declined strong:

Wenige treue Freunde.
Few faithful friends.

For **wenig(e)** as a pronoun, see §107.

144. The Suffix -lei with Indefinite Adjectives

1. Some of the indefinite adjectives listed in §126 have forms ending with the suffix **-lei,** signifying 'kinds', 'sorts of'. They are all invariable:

(*a*) **allerlei** = 'all kinds of', 'of all kinds':

Im Zoo sahen wir allerlei fremde Tiere.
At the Zoo we saw all kinds of strange animals (strange animals of all kinds).

(*b*) **anderlei** = 'of another (different) kind', 'other kinds of':

Sie hatten Äpfel da; anderlei Obst war nicht erhältlich.
They had apples there; other kinds of fruit were not available.

NOTE: **Anderlei** is not in common use; **ander** is used instead—thus, the above example would read more naturally if expressed ... **anderes Obst war nicht erhältlich.**

(c) **beiderlei** = 'of both kinds':

Die Zeitschrift ist für Leser beiderlei Geschlechts.
The magazine is for readers of both sexes.

(d) **jederlei** = 'of every kind':

Dort findet man jederlei Stoffe.
You can find every kind of material there.

(e) **mancherlei** = 'all kinds of', 'quite a few':

Es gibt mancherlei Dinge, die ich nicht verstehe.
There are quite a few things I don't understand.

(f) **vielerlei** = 'many kinds of':

In seinem Garten sind vielerlei Blumen.
In his garden there are many kinds of flowers.

2. Note also that by adding **-erlei** to any number the sense 'of (one, two, three, etc.) kinds, sorts, varieties' is conveyed— e.g., **zweierlei Kuchen,** 'two kinds of cake', **Dieses Problem kann auf dreierlei (viererlei, fünferlei, etc.) Art und Weise gelöst werden,** 'This problem can be solved in three (four, five, etc.) ways', **aus zweierlei Leder,** 'made of two different sorts of leather'. In practice, one does not go beyond **sechserlei;** thus, **zwanzigerlei Schmetterlinge** ('twenty kinds of butterflies'), though theoretically correct, would be more naturally expressed by **zwanzig Arten Schmetterlinge** and **achterlei Kuchen** ('eight kinds of cake') by **acht Sorten Kuchen.**

Einerlei, 'of one kind', 'of the same kind', is also used in certain idiomatic expressions (in which cases the stress is transferred from the first to the last syllable) such as **Mir ist alles einer'lei,** 'It's all the same to me', **Es ist mir ziemlich einer'lei, ob er kommt oder nicht,** 'It matters little to me whether he comes or not', and as a noun, **das Einerlei,** meaning 'monotony', 'humdrumness'.

Zweierlei, apart from its literal meaning 'of two kinds', is also used colloquially in such expressions as **Versprechen und Halten ist zweierlei,** 'Making a promise and keeping it are two different things'.

145. Adjective stems in -el, -en, -er

1. Adjectives ending in **-el** drop the **e** of the inflectional ending if they precede a noun or if they are used in the comparative:

dunkel: der dunkle Keller, the dark cellar.
eitel: mit einer eitlen Frau, with a vain woman.
edel: von edlerer Herkunft, of nobler descent.

2. Adjectives ending in **-en** and **-er** usually keep the **e** of the inflectional ending:

golden: das goldene Vlies, the golden fleece.
irden: eine irdene Pfeife, a clay pipe.

heiser: eine heisere Stimme, a hoarse voice.
finster: mit finsterem Gesicht, with a scowling face.

Note, however, that adjectives ending in **-er** preceded by a vowel usually drop the **e**:

teuer: in einem teuren Wagen, in an expensive car.

NOTE: Adjectives ending in **-er** may drop the **e** (i) in literary language: **mit finstren Zügen,** 'with dark features'; **Er hat ein heitres Wesen,** 'He has a happy disposition'; (ii) if they are of foreign origin: **ein makabres Schauspiel,** 'a macabre spectacle'.

See also §150, 7.

146. Special Cases

1. The adjective **hoch,** 'high', drops the **c** when inflected:

> **der hohe Baum,** the tall tree
> **die hohen Bäume,** the tall trees

2. Adjectives ending in **-er** from names of cities are indeclinable, and are written with a capital:

die Londoner Zeitungen	**Pariser Moden**
the London newspapers	Paris fashions

147. Adjective-Nouns

Ein altes Buch und ein neues.	An old book and a new one.
Der Alte; die Alte.	The old man; the old woman.
Die Alten.	The old people.
Das Gute und das Schöne.	The good and the beautiful.

1. The English 'one' after adjectives, as in the first example, is not to be translated into German.

2. Attributive adjectives may be used to form adjective-nouns, and are then written with a capital.

148. Adjectives as Nouns

Adjectives and participles used as nouns vary their declension according to the rules for adjective declension (§§115, 116)—*i.e.* they are declined exactly as if a noun followed: 'the foreign (man)', 'of a foreign (woman)', 'foreign (people)', etc.— but are written with initial capital letters:

	The stranger (*m.*).	The stranger (*f.*).	The strangers.
Nom.:	**der Fremde**	**die Fremde**	**die Fremden**
Acc.:	**den Fremden**	**die Fremde**	**die Fremden**
Gen.:	**des Fremden**	**der Fremden**	**der Fremden**
Dat.:	**dem Fremden**	**der Fremden**	**den Fremden**

	A stranger (*m.*).	A stranger (*f.*).	Strangers.
Nom.:	**ein Fremder**	**eine Fremde**	**Fremde**
Acc.:	**einen Fremden**	**eine Fremde**	**Fremde**
Gen.:	**eines Fremden**	**einer Fremden**	**Fremder**
Dat.:	**einem Fremden**	**einer Fremden**	**Fremden**

NOTE: Many adjectives and participles are thus used in German, the English equivalents of which are nouns only: **fremd**, 'strange', **der (die) Fremde**, 'the stranger'; **reisend**, 'travelling', **der (die) Reisende**, 'the traveller'; **verwandt**, 'related', **der (die) Verwandte**, 'the relative'.

149. Adjectival Suffixes

The following are among the commonest adjectival suffixes in German:

1. **-bar** (*often rendered in English by '-able' or '-ible' when added to verb stems, and by '-ful' when added to nouns*):

eßbar, edible	**dankbar,** thankful
erkennbar, recognizable	**furchtbar,** frightful
lesbar, readable	**wunderbar,** wonderful

2. **-en, -ern** (*denoting material,* = '(made) of'):

metallen, (made of) metal	**eisern,** (made of) iron
golden, golden	**bleiern,** (made of) lead
irden, earthen	**gläsern,** (made of) glass
seiden, silk(en)	**hölzern,** (made of) wood
eichen, oak(en)	**steinern,** (made of) stone

3. **-haft** (= 'full of', 'containing', *or, when suffixed to nouns,* 'resembling'):

ernsthaft, earnest	**engelhaft,** angelic
boshaft, malicious	**launenhaft,** moody
krankhaft, morbid	**traumhaft,** dreamlike

4. **-ig** ('having the nature or characteristics of'; *often* = '-y'):

gierig, greedy	**eisig,** icy
schwarzhaarig, blackhaired	**schmutzig,** dirty
hügelig, hilly	**zugig,** draughty

5. **-isch**

(*a*) *often* = '-ish':

kindisch, childish	**weibisch,** womanish
sklavisch, slavish	**teuflisch,** devilish

(*b*) = 'originating from' (a country):

englisch, English	**schweizerisch,** Swiss
französisch, French	**russisch,** Russian

(*c*) *in words of foreign origin* = '-ic(al)':

musikalisch, musical	**historisch,** historic *or*
statistisch, statistical	historical
akademisch, academic	**klassisch,** classic *or* classical

(d) *formed from personal names:*

Lutherisch, Lutheran   **Wagnerisch,** Wagnerian

6. **-lich** (*often* = '-like', '-ly'):

kindlich, childlike   **herrlich,** glorious
freundlich, friendly   **herbstlich,** autumnal
fürstlich, princely   **altertümlich,** ancient,
tödlich, deadly   antiquated

7. **-los** (*cf. English* '-less'):

sinnlos, senseless   **haarlos,** hairless
kinderlos, childless   **hoffnungslos,** hopeless
achtlos, heedless   **geldlos,** without money

8. **-reich** (= 'rich in'):

bilderreich, richly   **fischreich,** (river, etc.)
   illustrated (book);   abounding in fish
   ornate (style)   **glorreich,** glorious
ideenreich, full of ideas   **kinderreich,** large (family)
geistreich, ingenious;   **einflußreich,** influential
   witty   **hilfreich,** helpful

9. **-sam** ('having an inclination towards what is implied in the stem'):

gewaltsam, violent   **einsam,** lonely
sparsam, economical   **schweigsam,** taciturn
biegsam, pliant   **gemeinsam,** common, joint

10. **-voll** (*cf. English* '-ful'):

gedankenvoll, thoughtful   **erbarmungsvoll,** merciful
kraftvoll, powerful   **hoffnungsvoll,** hopeful
wundervoll, wonderful   **wertvoll,** valuable

For adverbial suffixes, see §249.

150. Comparison of Adjectives

Positive	*Comparative*	*Superlative* (cf. §153, 1)
reich, rich	**reicher,** richer	**reichst,** richest
arm, poor	**ärmer,** poorer	**ärmst,** poorest

Positive	Comparative	Superlative
neu, new	neuer, newer	neuest, newest
alt, old	älter, older	ältest, oldest
klein, small	kleiner, smaller	kleinst, smallest
süß, sweet	süßer, sweeter	süßest, sweetest
breit, broad	breiter, broader	breitest, broadest
edel, noble	edler, nobler	edelst, noblest
klug, intelligent	klüger, more intelligent	klügst, most intelligent
teuer, dear	teurer, dearer	teuerst, dearest
müde, tired	müder, tireder	müdest, tiredest
angenehm, agreeable	angenehmer, more agreeable	angenehmst, most agreeable
schnell, quick	schneller, quicker	schnellst, quickest

Du bist *kleiner* als ich.
You are smaller than I am.

Er ist *älter* als sein Freund.
He is older than his friend.

Wer ist *reicher* als mein Onkel?
Who is richer than my uncle?

Je (or Desto) *länger* die Nacht ist, desto (or je or um so) *kürzer* ist der Tag.
The longer the night is, the shorter the day is.

Er ist einer der *reichsten* Männer der Welt.
He is one of the richest men in the world.

Die Strauße sind nicht nur die *größten* Vögel, sie sind auch die *schnellsten* Läufer unter den Vögeln.
Ostriches are not only the largest birds, they are also the fastest runners among birds.

1. Except for a few irregular forms (see §157), adjectives form their comparative and superlative stems by adding **-(e)r** and **-(e)st** to the positive stem.

2. Many monosyllabic adjectives with stem vowel **a, o, u,** have umlaut (**ä, ö, ü,** respectively) in the comparative and superlative.

3. 'Than' = **als** in a comparison of inequality; '(not) as . . . as' or '(not) so . . . as' = **(nicht) so . . . wie** in a comparison of equality.

4. The noun after **als** has the same case as that which precedes.

5. 'The ... the' before comparatives = **je** or **desto ... je** or **desto** or **um so,** and in complete clauses the former clause has the word order of a dependent clause (verb last), the latter of a principal clause (verb second).

6. Stems ending in a vowel (except **e**) or a sibilant retain **e** in the superlative; so usually do those ending in **d** or **t.**

7. Stems ending in **-el** always drop **e** in the stem of the comparative; so sometimes (especially in poetry) do those ending in **-en** or **-er**—*e.g.,* **selt(e)ner,** 'rarer'; **finst(e)rer,** 'darker'. Cf. §145.

8. Stems ending in **e** add **-r** and **-st** only.

9. The endings are added regardless of length.

NOTE: 1. The form with **mehr,** 'more', is used when two qualities of the same object are compared: **Sie ist mehr hübsch als schön,** 'She is more pretty than beautiful '; **Er ist mehr unwissend als dumm,** 'He is more ignorant than stupid'.

2. The English 'more and more' before a noun = **immer mehr: Die Leute geben immer mehr Geld aus,** 'People are spending more and more money'.

3. The English 'more and more' before an adjective = **immer +** comparative: **Der Sturm wird immer heftiger,** 'The storm grows more and more violent'. (Similarly with adverbs: **Der Sturm heult immer heftiger,** 'The storm howls more and more violently'.)

4. As in English, adjectives in the comparative may be preceded by adverbs: **Sie ist noch schöner als ihre Schwester,** 'She is even more beautiful than her sister'; **Er ist viel (etwas, nur wenig) älter als ich,** 'He is much (somewhat, only a little) older than I am'.

151. Declension of Comparative and Superlative

The attributive adjective has the same endings in the comparative and superlative as in the positive (see §§115, 116).

Ein breiterer Fluß.	A broader river.
Der breitere Fluß.	The broader river.
Der breiteste Fluß.	The broadest river.

152. The Comparative Absolute of Adjectives

Ein *längerer* Spaziergang.
A fairly long ('longish') walk.

Ein *älterer* Herr.
An elderly gentleman.

Seit *längerer* Zeit.
For some time now.

(*Compare:* **Seit ziemlich langer Zeit,** 'for quite some time now').

1. Sometimes when in English an adjective + noun construction is preceded by 'rather' or 'fairly', expressed or implied, the comparative absolute is used in German instead of **etwas** or **ziemlich.**

2. The comparative absolute is used to denote a higher degree than is expressed by the simple adjective, although no direct comparison is made.

For the comparative absolute of adverbs, see §275.

153. The Superlative Relative of Adjectives

Ein Auto ist gewöhnlich schneller als ein Motorrad, jedoch (*or* aber) ein Flugzeug ist *am schnellsten*.
A car is usually faster than a motor-bike, but an aeroplane is the fastest.

Im Juni sind die Tage *am längsten*.
The days are longest in June.

Dieser Fluß ist *der breiteste* (Fluß) in England.
This river is the broadest (river) in England.

Der Mount Everest ist *der höchste* Berg der Welt.
Mount Everest is the highest mountain in the world.

1. The superlative relative of adjectives does not occur in uninflected form, even in the predicate.

2. When no previously expressed noun can be supplied, the superlative adjective is expressed in the predicate by the form with **am.**

3. If a noun can be supplied from the context, the superlative is expressed in the predicate by the definite article + the superlative with adjective inflection.

NOTE: 1. The superlative adjective is regularly preceded by the definite article or other determinative (§116, 1, note).

2. Most monosyllabic adjectives and those adjectives which have the stress on the last syllable (*e.g.*, **berühmt,** 'famous') ending in **-d, -s, -sch, -st, -t, -tz, -x, -z,** take **der (die, das) -este**—*e.g.*, **der (die, das) hübscheste,** 'the prettiest'.

3. Adjectives having an umlaut in the comparative have the same in the superlative.

For the superlative relative of adverbs, see §276.

154. Umlaut in Monosyllables

	Comparative	*Superlative*
alt, old	**älter**	**ältest**
jung, young	**jünger**	**jüngst**
dumm, stupid	**dümmer**	**dümmst**
klug, intelligent	**klüger**	**klügst**
kurz, short	**kürzer**	**kürzest**
lang, long	**länger**	**längst**
stark, strong	**stärker**	**stärkst**
schwach, weak	**schwächer**	**schwächst**
warm, warm	**wärmer**	**wärmst**
kalt, cold	**kälter**	**kältest**

1. Most monosyllables with **a, o, u** (not **au**) in the stem take umlaut.

2. The above are conveniently paired as opposites. Other examples are: **arm,** poor, **ärmer, ärmst; grob,** coarse, **gröber, gröbst; hart,** hard, **härter, härtest; krank,** ill, **kränker, kränkst; scharf,** sharp, **schärfer, schärfst; schwarz,** black, **schwärzer, schwärzest.**

155. No Umlaut in Monosyllables

	Comparative	*Superlative*
blank, shining	**blanker**	**blankst**
brav, well-behaved	**braver**	**bravst**

	Comparative	Superlative
bunt, brightly-coloured	bunter	bunt(e)st
falsch, wrong	falscher	falschest
flach, shallow	flacher	flachst
froh, happy	froher	froh(e)st
kahl, bare	kahler	kahlst
klar, clear	klarer	klarst
knapp, scanty	knapper	knappst
platt, flat	platter	platt(e)st
rasch, quick	rascher	raschest
roh, raw	roher	roh(e)st
rund, round	runder	rund(e)st
sanft, soft	sanfter	sanft(e)st
schlank, slim	schlanker	schlank(e)st
stolz, proud	stolzer	stolzest
toll, mad	toller	tollest
voll, full	voller	vollst
zahm, tame	zahmer	zahmest
zart, tender	zarter	zart(e)st

156. Optional Umlaut in Monosyllables

	Comparative	Superlative
bang, afraid	banger or bänger	bangst or bängst
blaß, pale	blasser or blässer	blassest or blässest
fromm, pious	frommer or frömmer	frommst or frömmst
gesund, healthy	gesünder or gesunder	gesündest or gesundest
glatt, smooth	glatter or glätter	glattest or glättest
karg, scanty	karger or kärger	kargst or kärgst
krumm, crooked	krummer or krümmer	krummst or krümmst
naß, wet	nasser or nässer	nassest or nässest
schmal, narrow	schmaler or schmäler	schmalst or schmälst

NOTE: The unmodified forms are preferable, except in the case of **gesund.**

157. Irregular Comparison

	Comparative	Superlative
groß, great	**größer**	**größt**
gut, good	**besser**	**best**
hoch, high	**höher**	**höchst**
nah(e), near	**näher**	**nächst**
viel, much	**mehr**	**meist**
wenig, little	**minder**	**mindest**

NOTE: 1. **Groß** is regular in the comparative but irregular in the superlative (**größt** for *größest*).
2. **Mehr** and **minder** are invariable.
3. **Wenig** has usually the regular forms **weniger** (invariable), **wenigst**.

158. Word Order

1. The predicative adjective comes at the end of a principal clause in simple tenses:

Das Wetter ist heute schön.
The weather is fine today.

Fahrpläne sind am Schalter erhältlich.
Timetables are obtainable at the counter.

2. In compound tenses, however, it is followed by the past participle and/or the infinitive:

Das Wetter ist heute schön gewesen.
The weather has been fine today.

Diese Leute müssen reich (gewesen) sein.
These people must be (must have been) rich.

159. Adjectives and Participles in Apposition

1. An uninflected adjective or participle may stand in apposition to a noun (usually the subject):

Die Stadt, im Kriege zerstört, wurde wieder aufgebaut.
The town, destroyed in the war, was rebuilt.

Er hielt an, erschreckt durch den Unfall.
He stopped, shocked by the accident.

Ihr werdet ein Kind finden, eingewickelt in Windeln und in einer Krippe liegend.

You will find a child wrapped in swaddling-clothes and lying in a manger.

2. Unless the apposition is with the subject, the English appositive construction should be rendered into German by a subordinate clause:

Ich habe die Uhr verloren, die mein Vater mir geschenkt hat.

I have lost the watch given me by my father.

NOTE: 1. The appositive adjectival construction, frequent in English, is sparingly used in German.

2. The appositive construction may be replaced by the attributive construction, for which see §216, 2.

VI. VERBS

160. General Remarks

A verb is a word or group of words denoting either an action (*e.g.* 'The hen *laid* an egg') or a state (*e.g.* 'I *am resting*'), referring to past, present or future time. A *finite* verb is a word which has person, number and tense and says something about something else, being distinctly limited to the subject (see Glossary).

Verbs are either *transitive* or *intransitive*. A transitive verb is a verb requiring an object—which may be a noun ('I like *chocolate*'), a pronoun ('I like *it*'), or a clause ('I know *what I like*')— to complete the sense, in contrast to an intransitive verb, which has no object. An intransitive verb may be defined as a verb which cannot take an object, or which denotes a state or action without reference to an object—*e.g.* 'The storm raged', 'The sun shone', 'The ice-cream melted'. Intransitive verbs have no passive forms. Many verbs can be used either transitively or intransitively—*e.g.* 'He rows a boat...' (transitive, 'boat' being the object) but 'He rows well' (intransitive—no object). Some transitive verbs have equivalent intransitive forms—*e.g.* 'to lay' **(legen)** (transitive, as in 'He lays his head on the pillow', where 'head' is the object) and 'to lie' **(liegen)** (intransitive, as in 'He lies on the bed'—no object). Sometimes verbs which are normally intransitive become transitive by taking an object which repeats and expands the idea expressed by the verb— 'He *lived a gay life* but *died a miserable death*'; such objects are known as cognate accusatives.

Verbs may be *weak* (or *regular*), *strong*, or *mixed*.

A *weak verb* is a verb which in English forms its past tense (imperfect) and past participle by the addition to the infinitive of the ending '-ed' (*e.g.* call—called—called) or (when the infinitive ends in '-e', as in 'to love') '-d', and in German by the addition to the stem of **-te** or **-ete** (*e.g.* **ich liebte,** 'I loved', **er arbeitete,** 'he worked') to form the imperfect, and the prefixing to the stem of **ge-** followed by the ending **-t** or **-et** (*e.g.* **geliebt, gearbeitet**) to

139

form the past participle. There also exist in German a number of irregular weak verbs, which change the stem vowel to **a** in the imperfect indicative and past participle—see §197. The *weak conjugation*, in German, is that class of verbs (also known as 'regular verbs') characterized by the features described above.

A *strong verb* is a verb the infinitive form of which undergoes an internal vowel change in its past tense (imperfect) and, usually, in its past participle also—*e.g.* 'to write, wrote, written', **schreiben, schrieb, geschrieben.** Note that in German the past participle of all strong verbs ends in **-en;** the past participle of many English strong verbs also ends in '-en' (*e.g.* 'taken', 'given'), though often this has either been replaced in the course of time by a weak ending (*e.g.* 'strived' for 'striven') or has become restricted to adjectival use (*e.g.* 'drunken', 'bounden'). The *strong conjugation*, in German, is that class of verbs (also known as 'irregular verbs') characterized by the vowel changes described above—see §246.

A *mixed verb* is a verb which shows characteristics of both the weak and the strong verb conjugations. All the modal auxiliary verbs (**dürfen, können, mögen, müssen, sollen, wollen**), also the verb **wissen,** 'to know', belong to the mixed conjugation. They all lack the typical weak **-e** and **-t** endings in the first and third persons singular of the present indicative, though the imperfect indicative and past participle have the weak endings **-te, -t.** Except for **sollen,** they also show variations in the stem vowel in the singular and plural forms respectively of the present tense (*e.g.* **ich kann** but **wir können).**

For other terms relating to verbs, see the Glossary.

161. Verb Tables

N.B. In the tables no special English forms are given for the subjunctive, as such forms are only occasionally correct, and often misleading.

1. AUXILIARIES OF TENSE
haben, to have

PRINCIPAL PARTS

haben, hatte, gehabt

PRESENT

I have, etc.

Indicative		*Subjunctive*	
ich	habe	ich	habe
du	hast	du	habest
er		er	
sie }	hat	sie }	habe
es		es	
wir	haben	wir	haben
ihr	habt	ihr	habet
sie	haben	sie	haben

IMPERFECT

I had, etc.

ich	hatte	ich	hätte
du	hattest	du	hättest
er		er	
sie }	hatte	sie }	hätte
es		es	
wir	hatten	wir	hätten
ihr	hattet	ihr	hättet
sie	hatten	sie	hätten

PERFECT

I have had, etc.

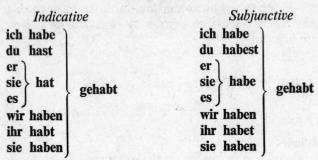

Indicative		*Subjunctive*	
ich habe		ich habe	
du hast		du habest	
er		er	
sie } hat	gehabt	sie } habe	gehabt
es		es	
wir haben		wir haben	
ihr habt		ihr habet	
sie haben		sie haben	

PLUPERFECT

I had had, etc.

ich hatte		ich hätte	
du hattest		du hättest	
er		er	
sie } hatte	gehabt	sie } hätte	gehabt
es		es	
wir hatten		wir hätten	
ihr hattet		ihr hättet	
sie hatten		sie hätten	

FUTURE

I shall have, etc.

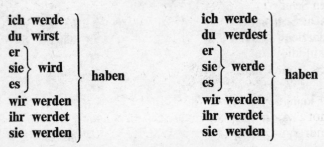

ich werde		ich werde	
du wirst		du werdest	
er		er	
sie } wird	haben	sie } werde	haben
es		es	
wir werden		wir werden	
ihr werdet		ihr werdet	
sie werden		sie werden	

FUTURE PERFECT

I shall have had, etc.

Indicative			*Subjunctive*		
ich	werde		ich	werde	
du	wirst		du	werdest	
er			er		
sie	wird	gehabt haben	sie	werde	gehabt haben
es			es		
wir	werden		wir	werden	
ihr	werdet		ihr	werdet	
sie	werden		sie	werden	

CONDITIONAL

Simple			*Compound*		
I should have, etc.			I should have had, etc.		
ich	würde		ich	würde	
du	würdest		du	würdest	
er			er		
sie	würde	haben	sie	würde	gehabt haben
es			es		
wir	würden		wir	würden	
ihr	würdet		ihr	würdet	
sie	würden		sie	würden	

Better: **ich hätte,** etc. See p. 159, note 1, and p. 141.

Better: **ich hätte gehabt,** etc. See p. 159, note 1, and p. 142.

IMPERATIVE

Have! etc.

hab(e)!
habt!
haben Sie!

INFINITIVES

Pres., **haben,** to have
Perf., **gehabt haben,** to have had

PARTICIPLES

Pres., **habend,** having
Past, **gehabt,** had

sein, to be   **werden,** to become

PRINCIPAL PARTS

sein, war, gewesen   **werden, wurde, geworden**

PRESENT

Indicative	Subjunctive		Indicative	Subjunctive
I am, etc.			I become, etc.	
ich bin	ich sei		ich werde	ich werde
du bist	du sei(e)st		du wirst	du werdest
er ⎫	er ⎫		er ⎫	er ⎫
sie ⎬ ist	sie ⎬ sei		sie ⎬ wird	sie ⎬ werde
es ⎭	es ⎭		es ⎭	es ⎭
wir sind	wir seien		wir werden	wir werden
ihr seid	ihr sei(e)t		ihr werdet	ihr werdet
sie sind	sie seien		sie werden	sie werden

IMPERFECT

Indicative	Subjunctive		Indicative	Subjunctive
I was, etc.			I became, etc.	
ich war	ich wäre		ich wurde	ich würde
du warst	du wär(e)st		du wurdest	du würdest
er ⎫	er ⎫		er ⎫	er ⎫
sie ⎬ war	sie ⎬ wäre		sie ⎬ wurde	sie ⎬ würde
es ⎭	es ⎭		es ⎭	es ⎭
wir waren	wir wären		wir wurden	wir würden
ihr wart	ihr wär(e)t		ihr wurdet	ihr würdet
sie waren	sie wären		sie wurden	sie würden

PERFECT

I have been, etc.   I have become, etc.

Indicative   *Indicative*

ich bin ⎫		ich bin ⎫	
du bist ⎪		du bist ⎪	
er ⎫ ⎪		er ⎫ ⎪	
sie ⎬ ist ⎬ gewesen		sie ⎬ ist ⎬ geworden	
es ⎭ ⎪		es ⎭ ⎪	
wir sind ⎪		wir sind ⎪	
ihr seid ⎪		ihr seid ⎪	
sie sind ⎭		sie sind ⎭	

Subjunctive

ich sei ⎞
du sei(e)st ⎟
er ⎤ ⎟
sie ⎬ sei ⎬ gewesen
es ⎦ ⎟
wir seien ⎟
ihr sei(e)t ⎟
sie seien ⎠

Subjunctive

ich sei ⎞
du sei(e)st ⎟
er ⎤ ⎟
sie ⎬ sei ⎬ geworden
es ⎦ ⎟
wir seien ⎟
ihr sei(e)t ⎟
sie seien ⎠

PLUPERFECT
I had been, etc.

PLUPERFECT
I had become, etc.

Indicative

ich war ⎞
du warst ⎟
er ⎤ ⎟
sie ⎬ war ⎬ gewesen
es ⎦ ⎟
wir waren ⎟
ihr wart ⎟
sie waren ⎠

Indicative

ich war ⎞
du warst ⎟
er ⎤ ⎟
sie ⎬ war ⎬ geworden
es ⎦ ⎟
wir waren ⎟
ihr wart ⎟
sie waren ⎠

Subjunctive

ich wäre ⎞
du wär(e)st ⎟
er ⎤ ⎟
sie ⎬ wäre ⎬ gewesen
es ⎦ ⎟
wir wären ⎟
ihr wär(e)t ⎟
sie wären ⎠

Subjunctive

ich wäre ⎞
du wär(e)st ⎟
er ⎤ ⎟
sie ⎬ wäre ⎬ geworden
es ⎦ ⎟
wir wären ⎟
ihr wär(e)t ⎟
sie wären ⎠

FUTURE
I shall be, etc.

FUTURE
I shall become, etc.

Indicative

ich werde ⎞
du wirst ⎟
er ⎤ ⎬ sein
sie ⎬ wird
es ⎦

Indicative

ich werde ⎞
du wirst ⎟
er ⎤ ⎬ werden
sie ⎬ wird
es ⎦

Future Indicative (contd.)

wir werden
ihr werdet } sein
sie werden

Future Indicative (contd.)

wir werden
ihr werdet } werden
sie werden

Subjunctive

ich werde
du werdest
er
sie } werde } sein
es
wir werden
ihr werdet
sie werden

Subjunctive

ich werde
du werdest
er
sie } werde } werden
es
wir werden
ihr werdet
sie werden

FUTURE PERFECT
I shall have been, etc.

Indicative

ich werde
du wirst
er
sie } wird } gewesen sein
es
wir werden
ihr werdet
sie werden

FUTURE PERFECT
I shall have become, etc.

Indicative

ich werde
du wirst
er
sie } wird } geworden sein
es
wir werden
ihr werdet
sie werden

Subjunctive

ich werde
du werdest
er
sie } werde } gewesen sein
es
wir werden
ihr werdet
sie werden

Subjunctive

ich werde
du werdest
er
sie } werde } geworden sein
es
wir werden
ihr werdet
sie werden

CONDITIONAL	CONDITIONAL
Simple	*Simple*
I should be, etc.	I should become, etc.

ich würde	ich würde
du würdest	du würdest
er	er
sie } würde	sie } würde
es	es } werden
} sein	
wir würden	wir würden
ihr würdet	ihr würdet
sie würden	sie würden

Better: ich wäre, etc. See p. 159, note 1, and p. 144.

Compound	*Compound*
I should have been, etc.	I should have become, etc.

ich würde	ich würde
du würdest	du würdest
er	er
sie } würde	sie } würde
es } gewesen	es } geworden
sein	sein
wir würden	wir würden
ihr würdet	ihr würdet
sie würden	sie würden

Better: ich wäre gewesen, etc.   *Better:* ich wäre geworden, etc.
See p. 159, note 1, and p. 145.   See p. 159, note 1, and p. 145.

IMPERATIVE
sei! seid! seien Sie! be!
werde! werdet! werden Sie! become!

INFINITIVES

Pres., **sein,** to be

werden, to become

Perf., **gewesen sein,** to have been

geworden sein, to have become

PARTICIPLES

Pres., **seiend,** being
werdend, becoming

Past, **gewesen,** been
geworden, become

2. AUXILIARIES OF MOOD

PRINCIPAL PARTS

dürfen	durfte	gedurft	(dürfen	after infinitive)
können	konnte	gekonnt	(können	after infinitive)
mögen	mochte	gemocht	(mögen	after infinitive)
müssen	mußte	gemußt	(müssen	after infinitive)
sollen	sollte	gesollt	(sollen	after infinitive)
wollen	wollte	gewollt	(wollen	after infinitive)

PRESENT INDICATIVE

ich	darf	kann	mag	muß	soll	will
du	darfst	kannst	magst	mußt	sollst	willst
er sie es	darf	kann	mag	muß	soll	will
wir	dürfen	können	mögen	müssen	sollen	wollen
ihr	dürft	könnt	mögt	müßt	sollt	wollt
sie	dürfen	können	mögen	müssen	sollen	wollen

PRESENT SUBJUNCTIVE

ich	dürfe	könne	möge	müsse	solle	wolle
du	dürfest	könnest	mögest	müssest	sollest	wollest
er sie es	dürfe	könne	möge	müsse	solle	wolle
wir	dürfen	können	mögen	müssen	sollen	wollen
ihr	dürfet	könnet	möget	müsset	sollet	wollet
sie	dürfen	können	mögen	müssen	sollen	wollen

IMPERFECT INDICATIVE

ich	durfte	konnte	mochte	mußte	sollte	wollte
du	durftest	konntest	mochtest	mußtest	solltest	wolltest
er sie es	durfte	konnte	mochte	mußte	sollte	wollte
wir	durften	konnten	mochten	mußten	sollten	wollten
ihr	durftet	konntet	mochtet	mußtet	solltet	wolltet
sie	durften	konnten	mochten	mußten	sollten	wollten

IMPERFECT SUBJUNCTIVE

ich	dürfte	könnte	möchte	müßte	sollte	wollte
du	dürftest	könntest	möchtest	müßtest	solltest	wolltest

er ⎱					
sie ⎬	dürfte	könnte	möchte	müßte	sollte	wollte
es ⎰					

wir	dürften	könnten	möchten	müßten	sollten	wollten
ihr	dürftet	könntet	möchtet	müßtet	solltet	wolltet
sie	dürften	könnten	möchten	müßten	sollten	wollten

COMPOUND TENSES

Perfect: ich habe gedurft (gekonnt, gemocht, gemußt, gesollt, gewollt)

ich habe bleiben dürfen (können, mögen, müssen, sollen, wollen)

Pluperfect: ich hatte gedurft (gekonnt, gemocht, gemußt, gesollt, gewollt)

ich hatte bleiben dürfen (können, mögen, müssen, sollen, wollen)

Future: ich werde dürfen (können, mögen, müssen, sollen, wollen)

Future Perfect: ich werde gedurft (gekonnt, gemocht, gemußt, gesollt, gewollt) haben

3. WEAK CONJUGATION

PRINCIPAL PARTS
loben, lobte, gelobt

INFINITIVES

Pres., **loben,** to praise   *Perf.*, **gelobt haben,** to have praised

PRESENT		IMPERFECT	
Indicative	*Subjunctive*	*Indicative*	*Subjunctive*
I praise, etc.		I praised, etc.	
ich lobe	ich lobe	ich lobte	ich lobte
du lobst	du lobest	du lobtest	du lobtest
er ⎱ sie ⎬ lobt es ⎰	er ⎱ sie ⎬ lobe es ⎰	er ⎱ sie ⎬ lobte es ⎰	er ⎱ sie ⎬ lobte es ⎰
wir loben	wir loben	wir lobten	wir lobten
ihr lobt	ihr lobet	ihr lobtet	ihr lobtet
sie loben	sie loben	sie lobten	sie lobten

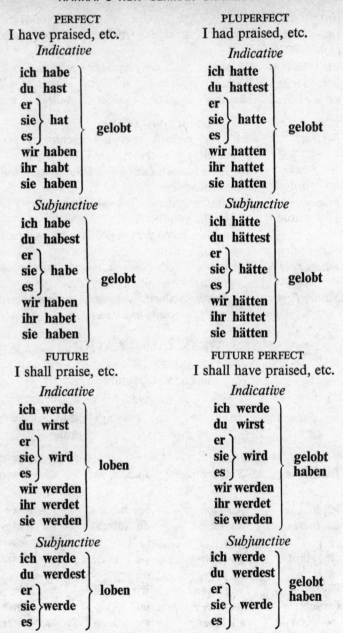

PERFECT
I have praised, etc.

Indicative

ich habe ⎫
du hast ⎪
er ⎫ ⎪
sie ⎬ hat ⎬ gelobt
es ⎭ ⎪
wir haben ⎪
ihr habt ⎪
sie haben ⎭

Subjunctive

ich habe ⎫
du habest ⎪
er ⎫ ⎪
sie ⎬ habe ⎬ gelobt
es ⎭ ⎪
wir haben ⎪
ihr habet ⎪
sie haben ⎭

PLUPERFECT
I had praised, etc.

Indicative

ich hatte ⎫
du hattest ⎪
er ⎫ ⎪
sie ⎬ hatte ⎬ gelobt
es ⎭ ⎪
wir hatten ⎪
ihr hattet ⎪
sie hatten ⎭

Subjunctive

ich hätte ⎫
du hättest ⎪
er ⎫ ⎪
sie ⎬ hätte ⎬ gelobt
es ⎭ ⎪
wir hätten ⎪
ihr hättet ⎪
sie hätten ⎭

FUTURE
I shall praise, etc.

Indicative

ich werde ⎫
du wirst ⎪
er ⎫ ⎪
sie ⎬ wird ⎬ loben
es ⎭ ⎪
wir werden ⎪
ihr werdet ⎪
sie werden ⎭

Subjunctive

ich werde ⎫
du werdest ⎪
er ⎫ ⎬ loben
sie ⎬werde ⎪
es ⎭

FUTURE PERFECT
I shall have praised, etc.

Indicative

ich werde ⎫
du wirst ⎪
er ⎫ ⎪ gelobt
sie ⎬ wird ⎬ haben
es ⎭ ⎪
wir werden ⎪
ihr werdet ⎪
sie werden ⎭

Subjunctive

ich werde ⎫
du werdest ⎪ gelobt
er ⎫ ⎬ haben
sie ⎬ werde ⎪
es ⎭

Future Subjunctive (*contd.*)	*Future Perfect Subjunctive* (*contd.*)
wir werden ⎫	wir werden ⎫
ihr werdet ⎬ loben	ihr werdet ⎬ gelobt
sie werden ⎭	sie werden ⎭ haben

CONDITIONAL

Simple	*Compound*
I should praise, etc.	I should have praised, etc.

ich würde		ich würde	
du würdest		du würdest	
er ⎫		er ⎫	
sie ⎬ würde	loben	sie ⎬ würde	gelobt
es ⎭		es ⎭	haben
wir würden		wir würden	
ihr würdet		ihr würdet	
sie würden		sie würden	

Better: **ich hätte gelobt,** etc. See p. 159, note 1, and p. 150.

IMPERATIVE

lob(e)! praise!
lobt! praise!
loben Sie! praise

PARTICIPLES

Pres., **lobend,** praising
Past, **gelobt,** praised

4. STRONG CONJUGATION

PRINCIPAL PARTS

singen, sang, gesungen

INFINITIVES

Pres., **singen,** to sing   *Perf.*, **gesungen haben,** to have sung

PRESENT	IMPERFECT
Indicative	*Indicative*
I sing, etc.	I sang, etc.

ich singe	ich sang
du singst	du sangst
er ⎫	er ⎫
sie ⎬ singt	sie ⎬ sang
es ⎭	es ⎭
wir singen	wir sangen
ihr singt	ihr sangt
sie singen	sie sangen

Subjunctive	*Subjunctive*
ich singe	ich sänge
du singest	du sängest
er ⎫	er ⎫
sie ⎬ singe	sie ⎬ sänge
es ⎭	es ⎭
wir singen	wir sängen
ihr singet	ihr sänget
sie singen	sie sängen

PERFECT	PLUPERFECT
I have sung, etc.	I had sung, etc.
Indicative	*Indicative*

ich habe ⎫		ich hatte ⎫	
du hast ⎪		du hattest ⎪	
er ⎫ ⎪		er ⎫ ⎪	
sie ⎬ hat ⎬ gesungen	sie ⎬ hatte ⎬ gesungen
es ⎭ ⎪		es ⎭ ⎪	
wir haben ⎪		wir hatten ⎪	
ihr habt ⎪		ihr hattet ⎪	
sie haben ⎭		sie hatten ⎭	

Subjunctive	*Subjunctive*

ich habe ⎫		ich hätte ⎫	
du habest ⎪		du hättest ⎪	
er ⎫ ⎬ gesungen	er ⎫ ⎬ gesungen
šie ⎬ habe ⎪		sie ⎬ hätte ⎪	
es ⎭ ⎭		es ⎭ ⎭	

Subjunctive

wir haben ⎫
ihr habet ⎬ gesungen
sie haben ⎭

Subjunctive

wir hätten ⎫
ihr hättet ⎬ gesungen
sie hätten ⎭

FUTURE
I shall sing, etc.

Indicative

ich werde ⎫
du wirst ⎪
er ⎫ ⎪
sie ⎬ wird ⎬ singen
es ⎭ ⎪
wir werden ⎪
ihr werdet ⎪
sie werden ⎭

FUTURE PERFECT
I shall have sung, etc.

Indicative

ich werde ⎫
du wirst ⎪
er ⎫ ⎪
sie ⎬ wird ⎬ gesungen
es ⎭ ⎪ haben
wir werden ⎪
ihr werdet ⎪
sie werden ⎭

Subjunctive

ich werde ⎫
du werdest ⎪
er ⎫ ⎪
sie ⎬ werde ⎬ singen
es ⎭ ⎪
wir werden ⎪
ihr werdet ⎪
sie werden ⎭

Subjunctive

ich werde ⎫
du werdest ⎪
er ⎫ ⎪
sie ⎬ werde ⎬ gesungen
es ⎭ ⎪ haben
wir werden ⎪
ihr werdet ⎪
sie werden ⎭

CONDITIONAL

Simple
I should sing, etc.

ich würde ⎫
du würdest ⎪
er ⎫ ⎪
sie ⎬ würde ⎬ singen
es ⎭ ⎪
wir würden ⎪
ihr würdet ⎪
sie würden ⎭

Compound
I should have sung, etc.

ich würde ⎫
du würdest ⎪
er ⎫ ⎪
sie ⎬ würde ⎬ gesungen
es ⎭ ⎪ haben
wir würden ⎪
ihr würdet ⎪
sie würden ⎭

Better: ich hätte gesungen, etc.
See p. 159, note 1, and pp. 152–3.

IMPERATIVE

sing(e)! sing!
singt! sing!
singen Sie! sing!

PARTICIPLES

Pres., **singend**, singing
Past, **gesungen**, sung

5. CONJUGATION WITH *SEIN*

PRINCIPAL PARTS
fallen, fiel, gefallen

INFINITIVES

Pres., **fallen**, to fall   *Perf.*, **gefallen sein**, to have fallen

PRESENT	IMPERFECT
Indicative	*Indicative*
I fall, etc.	I fell, etc.
ich falle	**ich fiel**
du fällst	**du fielst**
er	**er**
sie } **fällt**	**sie** } **fiel**
es	**es**
wir fallen	**wir fielen**
ihr fallt	**ihr fielt**
sie fallen	**sie fielen**
Subjunctive	*Subjunctive*
ich falle	**ich fiele**
du fallest	**du fielest**
er	**er**
sie } **falle**	**sie** } **fiele**
es	**es**
wir fallen	**wir fielen**
ihr fallet	**ihr fielet**
sie fallen	**sie fielen**

PERFECT
I have fallen, etc.

Indicative

ich bin	
du bist	
er	
sie } ist	gefallen
es	
wir sind	
ihr seid	
sie sind	

PLUPERFECT
I had fallen, etc.

Indicative

ich war	
du warst	
er	
sie } war	gefallen
es	
wir waren	
ihr wart	
sie waren	

Subjunctive

ich sei	
du sei(e)st	
er	
sie } sei	gefallen
es	
wir seien	
ihr sei(e)t	
sie seien	

Subjunctive

ich wäre	
du wär(e)st	
er	
sie } wäre	gefallen
es	
wir wären	
ihr wär(e)t	
sie wären	

FUTURE
I shall fall, etc.

Indicative

ich werde	
du wirst	
er	
sie } wird	fallen
es	
wir werden	
ihr werdet	
sie werden	

FUTURE PERFECT
I shall have fallen, etc.

Indicative

ich werde	
du wirst	
er	
sie } wird	gefallen sein
es	
wir werden	
ihr werdet	
sie werden	

Future Subjunctive

ich werde ⎫
du werdest ⎪
er ⎫ ⎪
sie ⎬ werde ⎬ fallen
es ⎭ ⎪
wir werden ⎪
ihr werdet ⎪
sie werden ⎭

Future Perfect Subjunctive

ich werde ⎫
du werdest ⎪
er ⎫ ⎪
sie ⎬ werde ⎬ gefallen
es ⎭ ⎪ sein
wir werden ⎪
ihr werdet ⎪
sie werden ⎭

CONDITIONAL

Simple
I should fall, etc.

ich würde ⎫
du würdest ⎪
er ⎫ ⎪
sie ⎬ würde ⎬ fallen
es ⎭ ⎪
wir würden ⎪
ihr würdet ⎪
sie würden ⎭

Compound
I should have fallen, etc.

ich würde ⎫
du würdest ⎪
er ⎫ ⎪
sie ⎬ würde ⎬ gefallen
es ⎭ ⎪ sein
wir würden ⎪
ihr würdet ⎪
sie würden ⎭

Better: ich wäre gefallen, etc.
See p. 159, note 1, and p. 155.

IMPERATIVE
fall(e)! fall!
fallt! fall!
fallen Sie! fall!

PARTICIPLES
Pres., **fallend,** falling
Past, **gefallen,** fallen

6. PASSIVE VOICE

INFINITIVES
Pres., **gelobt werden,** to be   *Perf.,* **gelobt worden sein,** to
praised   have been praised

PRESENT	IMPERFECT
I am praised, etc.	I was praised, etc.

Indicative

ich	werde		ich	wurde	
du	wirst		du	wurdest	
er			er		
sie	wird	gelobt	sie	wurde	gelobt
es			es		
wir	werden		wir	wurden	
ihr	werdet		ihr	wurdet	
sie	werden		sie	wurden	

Subjunctive

ich	werde		ich	würde	
du	werdest		du	würdest	
er			er		
sie	werde	gelobt	sie	würde	gelobt
es			es		
wir	werden		wir	würden	
ihr	werdet		ihr	würdet	
sie	werden		sie	würden	

PERFECT	PLUPERFECT
I have been praised, etc.	I had been praised, etc.

Indicative

ich	bin		ich	war	
du	bist		du	warst	
er			er		
sie	ist	gelobt worden	sie	war	gelobt worden
es			es		
wir	sind		wir	waren	
ihr	seid		ihr	wart	
sie	sind		sie	waren	

Subjunctive

ich	sei		ich	wäre	
du	sei(e)st	gelobt worden	du	wär(e)st	gelobt worden
er			er		
sie	sei		sie	wäre	
es			es		

Perfect Subjunctive (*contd.*)   *Pluperfect Subjunctive* (*contd.*)

wir seien		wir wären	
ihr sei(e)t	gelobt	ihr wär(e)t	gelobt
sie seien	worden	sie wären	worden

FUTURE   FUTURE PERFECT

I shall be praised, etc.   I shall have been praised, etc.

Indicative   *Indicative*

ich werde		ich werde	
du wirst		du wirst	
er		er	
sie } wird	gelobt	sie } wird	gelobt
es	werden	es	worden
wir werden		wir werden	sein
ihr werdet		ihr werdet	
sie werden		sie werden	

Subjunctive   *Subjunctive*

ich werde		ich werde	
du werdest		du werdest	
er		er	
sie } werde	gelobt	sie } werde	gelobt
es	werden	es	worden
wir werden		wir werden	sein
ihr werdet		ihr werdet	
sie werden		sie werden	

CONDITIONAL

Simple   *Compound*

I should be praised, etc.   I should have been praised, etc.

ich würde		ich würde	
du würdest		du würdest	
er		er	
sie } würde	gelobt	sie } würde	gelobt
es	werden	es	worden
wir würden		wir würden	sein
ihr würdet		ihr würdet	
sie würden		sie würden	

Better: ich wäre gelobt worden,
etc. See p. 159, note 1, and pp.
157-158

IMPERATIVE

werde gelobt! be praised!
werdet gelobt! be praised!
werden Sie gelobt! be praised!

PARTICIPLES

Future, **zu lobend,** to be praised (as adjective only)
Past,   **gelobt worden,** been praised

The prefix **ge-** of **geworden** is dropped throughout in the passive.

NOTE: 1. The imperfect subjunctive and pluperfect subjunctive are usually substituted for the conditional.

2. The future perfect, compound conditional, and perfect infinitive rarely occur.

162. Word Order in Principal Clauses

	Verb	
Er	**ist**	**heute nicht krank.**
Der Vater des Schülers	**war**	**hier.**
Hier	**ist**	**der Vater des Schülers.**
Im Sommer	**sind**	**die Bäume grün.**
Das Kind	**hat**	**heute nicht viel gespielt.**
Heute	**ist**	**sie nicht aus dem Haus gegangen.**

1. In principal clauses making a statement, the finite verb is the second idea (not necessarily the second word).

2. Any member other than the verb may occupy the first place, except in the case of simple interrogative sentences (§166) and imperative sentences (§238).

3. When any member other than the subject precedes the verb, the subject, with its attributes and enlargements, is placed after the verb, and occupies the third place.

4. In compound tenses the auxiliary is the main verb, and the past participle comes last in the perfect and pluperfect.

NOTE: The rules of word order are often disregarded in verse.

163. Word Order in Dependent Clauses

Ich arbeite nicht, weil ich müde bin.
I am not working, because I am tired.

Ich hoffe, daß er uns besuchen wird.
I hope that he will visit us.

Ich glaube, daß er die Arbeit bis morgen beendet haben wird.
I think that he will have finished the work by tomorrow.

Da ich müde bin, arbeite ich nicht.
As I am tired I am not working.

1. The finite verb comes last in a dependent clause.

2. In compound tenses, the participle and infinitive immediately precede the verb, i.e. the auxiliary.

3. If both participle and infinitive occur, the participle precedes the infinitive.

4. The place of the subject in a dependent clause is usually the same as in English.

5. The dependent clause is always separated from the principal clause by a comma.

6. When a dependent clause precedes the principal clause, the subject of the latter is placed after the verb.

164. The Indicative Mood

The indicative is the mood of reality and direct statement or question—i.e., it states fact(s) or asks questions of fact.

165. Present Indicative of **machen,** 'to make'

ich mache	I make, am making
du machst	you make (*familiar singular*)
er ⎫	he ⎫
sie ⎬ **macht**	she ⎬ makes
es ⎭	it ⎭
wir machen	we make
ihr macht	you make (*familiar plural*)
Sie machen	you make (*formal*)
sie machen	they make

Examples of the use of the Present Indicative:

Ich mache einen Papierhut.	I am making a paper hat.
Spielen sie Ball?	Do they play ball?
Wir kaufen einen Ring.	We buy a ring.
Du arbeitest.	You are working.
Regnet es?	Is it raining?

1. There are no auxiliary forms in German corresponding to the English 'I am making', 'Does he play?' etc.

2. Most verbs form the present indicative like **machen,** but when the infinitive stem (see §194) ends in **-t** or **-d,** or consonants after which **t** cannot be pronounced, the second person singular ends in **-est,** and the third person singular and the second person plural (**ihr** form) in **-et** (see §§195, 196,1).

166. The Interrogative

bin	**ich?**	am I?		**rauche**	**ich?**	do I smoke?	
bist	**du?**	are you?		**rauchst**	**du?**	do you smoke?	
ist	**er?** **sie?** **es?**	is	he? she? it?	**raucht**	**er?** **sie?** **es?**	does	he smoke? she smoke? it smoke?
sind	**wir?**	are we?		**rauchen**	**wir?**	do we smoke?	
seid	**ihr?**	are you?		**raucht**	**ihr?**	do you smoke?	
sind	**Sie?**	are you?		**rauchen**	**Sie?**	do you smoke?	
sind	**sie?**	are they?		**rauchen**	**sie?**	do they smoke?	

1. The interrogative is formed by inversion.

2. Besides meaning 'do I smoke?' **rauche ich?** also means 'am I smoking?' The continuous form 'am -ing' and the form 'do . . . ' have no equivalent in German, and the present tense, as exemplified above, is used in German for both.

167. The Negative

Ich rauche nicht.
I do not smoke *or* I am not smoking.

Ich rauchte nicht.
I did not smoke *or* I was not smoking.

Ich werde nicht rauchen.
I shall not smoke.

Ich habe nicht geraucht.
I have not smoked.

The negative is formed with **nicht,** which follows a finite verb or an auxiliary, but precedes an infinitive or past participle.

168. The Present Tense

1. This tense answers to all the English forms of the same tense (*e.g.*, **ich lobe**='I praise', 'I am praising', 'I do praise'), and is used to denote action now going on, or to state a general fact or custom.

2. It is used for the imperfect to give greater vividness to historical narrative; this is known as the 'historic present':

Er ging nichtsahnend durch den Wald. Plötzlich *sieht* er den Bären. Er *hebt* sein Gewehr und *schießt*. Der Bär war sofort tot.
He was walking unsuspecting through the forest. Suddenly he *sees* the bear. He *raises* his rifle and *shoots*. The bear was dead at once.

3. It is also used to denote what has happened *and still continues*, especially with **schon, seit,** and **seitdem:**

Wie lange ist er schon krank?
How long has he been ill?

Seit zwei Jahren lernen wir Deutsch.
We have been learning German for two years.

Seitdem er an seinem Buch schreibt, hat er überhaupt keine Zeit mehr für seine Freunde.
Since he has been working on his book he has had no time at all for his friends.

4. It is often used for the future, as sometimes in English:

Ich komme nächste Woche wieder.
I'll come again next week.

Meine Fahrprüfung ist morgen.
My driving test is tomorrow.

169. Weak Imperfects

Imperfect Indicative of **machen**, 'to make'

ich **machte**	I made, was	**machte ich?**	was I making?,
du **machtest**	making, did	**machtest du?**	did I make?
er ⎫	make	**machte er?**	
sie ⎬ **machte**		**machte sie?**	
es ⎭		**machte es?**	
wir **machten**		**machten wir?**	
ihr **machtet**		**machtet ihr?**	
Sie **machten**		**machten Sie?**	
sie **machten**		**machten sie?**	

A large number of verbs (called 'weak') form the imperfect indicative like **machen**, but infinitive stems ending in **-t, -d,** or consonants after which **t** cannot be pronounced, insert **e** between stem and ending (**arbeitete**, 'worked', **regnete**, 'rained', etc.).

170. Strong Imperfects

singen, 'to sing'	**bleiben**, 'to remain'	**tun**, 'to do'
I sang, etc.	I remained, etc.	I did, etc.
ich **sang**	ich **blieb**	ich **tat**
du **sangst**	du **bliebst**	du **tat(e)st**
er ⎫	er ⎫	er ⎫
sie ⎬ **sang**	sie ⎬ **blieb**	sie ⎬ **tat**
es ⎭	es ⎭	es ⎭
wir **sangen**	wir **blieben**	wir **taten**
ihr **sangt**	ihr **bliebt**	ihr **tatet**
Sie **sangen**	Sie **blieben**	Sie **taten**
sie **sangen**	sie **blieben**	sie **taten**

Many verbs (called 'strong') form the imperfect indicative by changing the stem vowel, without adding a tense ending in the 1st and 3rd person singular.

171. The Imperfect Tense

1. This is the past tense of historical narrative; it also denotes customary, repeated, or simultaneous action, answering to the English forms 'was doing', 'used to do', etc.:

In sechs Tagen schuf Gott die Welt und ruhte am siebenten.
In six days God created the world, and rested on the seventh.

Als Student ging er fast jeden Tag aus.
As a student he used to go out almost every day.

Sie beobachtete ihn, während er sprach.
She was watching him while he was speaking.
She was watching him while he spoke.
She watched him while he was speaking.
She watched him while he spoke.

2. 'Would', of customary, habitual or repeated action, must be rendered by the imperfect: **Er sagte oft...,** 'He would often say. . .'

3. It is used with **schon** and **seit** to denote what had happened and still continued:

Er war schon drei Tage hier, als ich ankam.
He had been here three days when I arrived.

Er hatte das Auto erst seit drei Monaten, als ihm der erste Unfall passierte.
He had had the car only three months when his first accident occurred.

172. Perfect Indicative of **haben, spielen**

I have had (have played, have been playing), etc.

ich habe gehabt (gespielt)
du hast gehabt (gespielt)
er
sie } hat gehabt (gespielt)
es
wir haben gehabt (gespielt)
ihr habt gehabt (gespielt)
Sie haben gehabt (gespielt)
sie haben gehabt (gespielt)

1. Verbs conjugated with **haben** form this tense by adding the past participle to the present of **haben,** as auxiliary.

2. The past participle of weak verbs is usually formed by prefixing **ge-** and adding **-t** (or **-et** after **d, t,** etc.; see §195) to the stem—*e.g.*, **spiel-en, ge-spiel-t; arbeit-en, ge-arbeit-et.** For exceptions see §213.

173. The Perfect Tense

1. This tense indicates an event in past time, continuing up to, but not including, the present:

Ich habe meine Uhr verloren.
I have lost my watch.

Es ist wärmer geworden.
It has become warmer.

2. It often answers to the English simple past tense, especially when referring to an action or state that is complete and that has happened or been in the recent past, or to an event as a separate and independent fact:

Was habt ihr gestern gemacht?
What did you do yesterday?

Wir sind gestern im Kino gewesen.
We went to the cinema yesterday.

Kolumbus hat Amerika entdeckt.
Columbus discovered America.

3. The perfect may replace the German future perfect, as the present may the future:

Ich komme, sobald ich das Kind zu Bett gebracht habe.
I shall come as soon as I have put the child to bed.

In zwei Wochen hast du die Arbeit beendet.
In two weeks you will have finished the work.

4. The perfect is used if a supposition referring to a past event is expressed:

Er hat sich doch nicht etwa ein Bein gebrochen?
You don't mean he has broken a leg, do you?

Sie haben wohl schon ihr Haus verkauft?
I suppose they've already sold their house?

Er ist doch nicht einfach davongerannt, als Sie mit ihm sprechen wollten?
But he didn't just run away when you were going to speak to him?

NOTE: The perfect tense is particularly used in speech. Compare **Wir haben keinen Parkplatz gefunden, und da sind wir stundenlang umhergefahren,** 'We didn't find a car-park, and there we were, driving around for hours', with the less colloquial, more formal **Da wir keinen Parkplatz fanden, sind wir stundenlang umhergefahren.**

174. Pluperfect Indicative of **haben, loben**

I had had (had praised, had been praising), etc.

ich hatte   gehabt (gelobt)
du hattest gehabt (gelobt)
er ⎫
sie ⎬ hatte gehabt (gelobt)
es ⎭
wir hatten gehabt (gelobt)
ihr hattet gehabt (gelobt)
Sie hatten gehabt (gelobt)
sie hatten gehabt (gelobt)

Verbs conjugated with **haben** form this tense by adding the past participle to the imperfect of **haben,** as auxiliary.

175. The Pluperfect Tense

This tense is used of a past action completed before another had begun:

Sie hatten das Haus schon wieder verkauft, als ich sie besuchte.
They had already resold the house when I paid them a visit.

Es war schon geschehen, als ich kam.
It had already happened when I came.

176. Future Indicative of **haben, machen**

I shall have (make), etc.

ich werde   haben (machen)
du wirst   haben (machen)
er
sie } wird   haben (machen)
es
wir werden haben (machen)
ihr werdet haben (machen)
Sie werden haben (machen)
sie werden haben (machen)

This tense is formed by adding the infinitive to the present indicative of **werden,** as auxiliary.

177. The Future Tense

This tense corresponds in general to the English future, and is used to denote probability or conjecture:

Er wird heute abend kommen.
He will come this evening.

Er wird wohl bald hier sein.
He will probably be here soon.

178. Future Perfect of **haben, machen**

I shall have had (made), etc.

ich werde   gehabt (gemacht) haben
du wirst   gehabt (gemacht) haben
er
sie } wird   gehabt (gemacht) haben
es
wir werden gehabt (gemacht) haben
ihr werdet gehabt (gemacht) haben
Sie werden gehabt (gemacht) haben
sie werden gehabt (gemacht) haben

This tense is formed by inserting the past participle of the verb before the infinitive of the future of the auxiliary.

179. The Future Perfect

This tense corresponds to the English future perfect, but also expresses probability, etc.:

Ich werde meine Arbeit beendet haben, ehe sie kommen.
I shall have finished my work before they come.

Sie werden wohl schon angekommen sein.
I expect they have already arrived.

Was hast du gestern gemacht?—Was werde ich schon gemacht haben? Natürlich habe ich gearbeitet.
What did you do yesterday?—What do you think I did? I worked, of course.

180. The Simple Conditional

I should have,   make,   be,   fall

ich würde			
du würdest			
er			
sie } würde	haben	machen	sein
es	(*better:* ich		(*better:*
wir würden	hätte, etc.)		ich wäre,
ihr würdet			etc.)
Sie würden			fallen
sie würden			

The simple conditional of all verbs is formed by adding their infinitive to the imperfect subjunctive of **werden,** though in the case of the verbs **haben** and **sein** the shorter forms **ich hätte, ich wäre,** are much to be preferred—see §161, note 1 (p. 159).

181. The Compound Conditional with **haben**

I should have had (made), you would, etc.

ich würde gehabt (gemacht) haben
du würdest gehabt (gemacht) haben
er würde gehabt (gemacht) haben, etc.

The compound conditional of a verb conjugated with **haben**
is formed by adding its past participle to the simple conditional
of **haben** (for word order, compare §192), though in practice the
shorter forms **ich hätte gehabt (gemacht)**, etc., are almost invariably used in preference—see §161, note 1 (p. 159).

182. The Compound Conditional with **sein**
I should have been (fallen), you would, etc.

ich würde   gewesen (gefallen) sein
du würdest gewesen (gefallen) sein
er würde   gewesen (gefallen) sein, etc.

The compound conditional of a verb conjugated with **sein**
(see §217) is formed by adding its past participle to the simple
conditional of **sein** (for word order, compare §192), though in
practice the shorter forms **ich wäre gewesen (gefallen)**, etc., are
almost invariably used in preference—see §161, note 1 (p. 159).

183. Conditional Sentences

Er wird kommen, wenn er kann.	He will come if he can.
Wenn ich Geld hätte, (so) würde ich ein Haus kaufen.	If I had money I should buy a house.
Hätte ich Zeit, so würde ich es tun.	If I had (Had I) time I should do it.
Wenn ich Geld hätte, könnte ich ein Haus kaufen.	If I had money I could buy a house.
Ich hätte ein Haus gekauft, wenn ich Geld gehabt hätte.	I should have bought a house if I had had money.
Hätte ich Zeit gehabt, (so) wäre ich gekommen.	If I had had (Had I had) time I should have come.

1. Conditional sentences regularly consist of two parts: the
condition and the result; and either part may come first.

2. The subjunctive mood is required in the imperfect or pluperfect of the 'if' clause, the result being then expressed by the
conditional; with other tenses the verb is in the indicative in both
clauses (see first example above).

3. The imperfect or pluperfect subjunctive usually replaces
the conditional in the result clause, whether the latter precedes
or follows.

NOTE: The shorter forms are used to avoid complicated constructions, as for example in the modal auxiliaries.

4. When the 'if' clause precedes, the subject of the result clause is placed after the verb (as in the second example above), the particle **so** being sometimes inserted before the verb, but not translated into English.

5. **Wenn,** = 'if', may be omitted when the condition precedes the result, in which case the verb begins the sentence, and the result clause is usually introduced by **so**.

6. There is a growing tendency in modern German to use the simple conditional instead of the imperfect subjunctive and the compound conditional instead of the pluperfect subjunctive in both principal and dependent clauses, particularly if the subjunctive forms are old-fashioned or unusual in speech—*e.g.*, **flöhe** (**fliehen**), **kennte** (**kennen**), etc.—or if they are the same as the indicative forms. But two **würde**-forms together are regarded as bad style, as in **Wenn ich ihn kennen würde, würde ich ihn danach fragen** (better: **Wenn ich ihn kennen würde, könnte ich ihn danach fragen**).

The use of the conditional instead of the subjunctive is correct in such sentences as:

An deiner Stelle würde ich ihm nicht das Geld geben.

(instead of: ... **gäbe ich ihm nicht das Geld.**)

If I were you I should not give him the money.

Es sieht nicht so aus, als würde es bald regnen.

(instead of: ... **als regnete es bald.**)

It does not look as though it is going to rain soon.

184. The Infinitive

The infinitive expresses the idea or action or state of a verb without reference to person or number. The word is more commonly used to denote that part of the verb which in English is characterized by the presence of the preposition 'to', as in 'to be', 'to have'. In German the infinitive form nearly always ends in -en (*e.g.* **singen**, **telephonieren**), though a few end in -n (*e.g.* **sein**, 'to be', **dauern**, 'to last'). All these infinitives mentioned above are *present* infinitives; there also exists the *perfect* infinitive—*e.g.* 'to have been', 'to have had', formed in German by prefixing the past participle to the present infinitive: **gewesen (zu) sein, gehabt (zu) haben:**

Present Infinitive	*Perfect Infinitive*
(zu) haben, to have	**gehabt (zu) haben,** to have had
(zu) sein, to be	**gewesen (zu) sein,** to have been
(zu) werden, to become	**geworden (zu) sein,** to have become
(zu) machen, to make	**gemacht (zu) haben,** to have made

185. Infinitive after Verbs

Ich beginne zu arbeiten.	I begin to work.
Ich beginne, meine Schularbeit zu machen.	I begin to do my homework.
Er beginnt, schnell zu laufen.	He begins to run quickly.
Ich habe Lust zu lesen.	I feel like reading (I want *or* wish to read).
Wir haben Lust, einen Spaziergang zu machen.	We feel like going for a walk.

1. Many verbs and nouns take an infinitive with **zu** to complete their meaning.

2. The infinitive comes at the end of its clause.

NOTE: There is a comma before the infinitive clause if the infinitive is preceded by an object or adverb.

186. Infinitive with zu

This form usually corresponds to the English infinitive with 'to', and is used as follows:

1. After verbs requiring an infinitive complement, except those mentioned in §188:

Es fängt an zu regnen.
It is beginning to rain.

Er scheint reich zu sein.
He seems to be rich.

Ich habe viel zu tun.
I have a great deal to do.

Sie entschloß sich, den Abwasch stehen zu lassen.
She decided to leave the washing-up.

Er beabsichtigt, seine Stellung aufzugeben. (see §201, 3)
He intends to give up his job.

Du brauchst nicht zu Fuß zu gehen.
You don't have to go on foot.

NOTE: 1. With most of such verbs a **daß** clause may replace the infinitive, and must do so unless the subject of the two clauses is the same: **Er glaubt, recht zu haben** (*or* **daß er recht hat**), 'He thinks he is right'; **Er wünscht zu kommen,** 'He wishes to come'; **Er wünscht, daß ich komme,** 'He wishes me to come'; observe from the last example that the English construction of the accusative with infinitive is inadmissible in German.

2. Sagen, 'to tell', requires a clause with **sollen: Sagen Sie ihm, daß er kommen soll,** *or* **Sagen Sie ihm, er soll kommen,** 'Tell him to come'.

2. After verbs, as adverbial complement denoting purpose, usually preceded by **um,** which heads the infinitive clause:

Er kam, um mich zu warnen.
He came to warn me.

Sie tat das nur, um dich zu ärgern.
She only did that to annoy you.

3. After nouns, as adjectival complement:

Er hat Lust zu bleiben.
He has a mind to stay.

Er hat den Wunsch, auszuwandern. (see §201, 3)
He wants to emigrate.

Es macht Spaß, Tennis zu spielen.
It is fun playing tennis.

4. After adjectives, as adverbial complement:

Ich bin bereit, euch zu helfen.
I am ready to help you.

NOTE: Where **zu** (=‘too’) precedes the adjective, **um** may be used: **Er ist zu stolz, um zu betteln** *or* **Er ist zu stolz zu betteln,** 'He is too proud to beg'.

5. After **sein, stehen, bleiben,** with passive force:

Es ist zu bedauern.
It is to be regretted.

Es bleibt noch viel zu tun.
Much remains to be done.

Es steht zu erwarten, daß das Land wirtschaftlich boykottiert wird.
It is to be expected that the country will be economically
boycotted.

See also §330.

NOTE: Observe the following analogous idiom with **haben: Ich
habe einen Brief zu schreiben,** 'I have a letter to write'.

187. Infinitive of Purpose

Ich fahre in die Stadt, um ein Buch zu kaufen.
I am going into (the) town (in order) to buy a book.

Wir kaufen ein Auto, um damit in (die) Ferien zu fahren.
We are buying a car to go on holiday with.

1. Purpose is often expressed by an infinitive with **zu,**
governed by **um.**

2. **Zu** and the infinitive stand at the end of the dependent
clause.

188. Infinitive without **zu**

This form is used as follows:

1. With **werden** to form the future and conditional tenses, and
with the modal auxiliaries **dürfen, können, lassen,** etc. (§227).

2. With the verbs **bleiben, fühlen, heißen, helfen, hören, lehren,
lernen, machen, sehen:**

Er blieb stehen.
He remained standing.

Er fühlte die Kälte größer werden.
He felt the cold becoming more intense.

Sie hieß ihn gehen (*literary*).
She bade him go.

Ich helfe ihm aufräumen.
I am helping him to tidy up.

Er hörte sie die Tür zuschlagen.
He heard her slam the door.

Sie lehrte die Kinder schreiben.
She taught the children to write.

Sie lernt Klavier spielen.
She is learning to play the piano.

Die zugezogenen Vorhänge sollten die Leute glauben machen, daß niemand zu Hause sei.
The drawn curtains were meant to make people believe that there was no one at home.

Ich habe das Unglück kommen sehen.
I saw the accident coming.

NOTE: **Helfen, lehren, lernen** also take an infinitive with **zu**, especially with a compound tense: **Ich habe gelernt zu gehorchen**, 'I have learnt to obey'.

3. In certain phrases with **gehen** and other verbs of motion:

Ich gehe spazieren.
I am going for a walk.

Morgen gehen wir fischen.
We are going fishing tomorrow.

Ich möchte heute früher schlafen gehen.
I should like to go to bed earlier today.

Er legte sich schlafen.
He went to bed.

Liegen, stehen, wohnen, are used as infinitives without **zu**, together with the auxiliary **haben**:

Wir haben noch eine alte Kelter im Keller stehen.
We still have an old wine-press (standing) in the cellar.

Er hat seine Familie in Berlin wohnen.
He's got his family living in Berlin.

Sie haben die Weinflaschen im Keller liegen.
You have the wine-bottles in the cellar.

189. Substantival Infinitive

1. Any infinitive may be used in the singular as a neuter noun of the **Maler** model (§34, V), and takes a capital letter:

Sein lautes Reden ist lästig.
His loud talking is annoying.

Das Wasser war zum Schwimmen zu kalt.
The water was too cold for swimming.

NOTE: Such an infinitive has the force of the English form in '-ing', denoting an act—*e.g.*, **das Lesen,** '(the act of) reading', or of an English noun—*e.g.*, **das Leben,** 'life'.

2. This infinitive (with or without adjuncts) often stands as the subject of a verb, preferably with **zu,** which must be used when **es** precedes the principal verb:

Zuzuhören machte ihm großen Spaß.
Listening gave him great enjoyment.

Einen wirklichen Freund zu finden ist nicht so leicht.
To find a real friend is not so easy.

Es ist schön, dich wiederzusehen.
It is nice to see you again.

190. Interrogative Infinitive

The English infinitive in indirect questions must be replaced in German by a finite clause:

Ich weiß, was ich tun soll.
I know what to do.

Sage mir, wo ich stehen soll.
Tell me where to stand.

191. Elliptical Infinitive

1. The infinitive is used, as in English, in various elliptical constructions:

Warum ihn stören?
Why disturb him?

Wozu sich aufregen?
Why get excited?

Danach zu urteilen.
To judge by that.

2. For the elliptical infinitive with imperative force, see
§241, 3.

192. Position of Infinitive

Wir werden Zeit haben.
We shall have time.

Er wird Zeit gehabt haben.
He will have had time.

In einem Jahr wird er noch immer kein Auto gekauft haben.
In a year he will still not have bought a car.

In these tenses the infinitive comes at the end, preceded by
the past participle if both occur.

193. Principal Parts

The 'principal parts' of a verb are: the infinitive, the imperfect indicative (shown in the third person singular), and the
past participle:

	Infinitive	Imperfect Indicative	Past Participle
Weak Verb:	**machen**	**machte**	**gemacht**
Strong Verb:	**singen**	**sang**	**gesungen**

From the principal parts may be inferred the various forms
of the stem, which is regularly changeable only in strong verbs.

194. Verb Stems

*mach*en (to make)   *rechn*en (to reckon)
*red*en (to speak)   *ruder*n (to row)
        *wechsel*n (to (ex)change)
        *sing*en   (to sing)

The stem of a verb is what is left when the ending **-en** or **-n** is dropped from the infinitive.

195. Stems ending in **-d, -t,** etc.

Present Indicative

binden	bitten	fechten	raten	beißen
to bind	to beg	to fight	to advise	to bite
ich binde	bitte	fechte	rate	beiße
du bindest	bittest	fichtst	rätst	beißt
er bindet	bittet	ficht	rät	beißt
wir binden	bitten	fechten	raten	beißen
ihr bindet	bittet	fechtet	ratet	beißt
sie binden	bitten	fechten	raten	beißen

1. Stems ending in **-d, -t,** without vowel change in the present indicative, retain **-e** before **-st, -t.**

2. Stems ending in **-d, -t,** with vowel change, drop **-e** of the ending in the second person singular and **-et** in the third; in other forms they retain the **-e** and **-et.**

3. Stems ending in sibilants usually drop **-es** of the second person singular.

196. Special Forms of Weak Verbs

1. Verb stems ending in **-d, -t** (*e.g.*, **reden, arbeiten**), or in any combination of consonants after which **-t** or **-st** cannot be pronounced (*e.g.*, **atmen, rechnen**), retain **e** of the ending throughout:

> **reden,** 'to speak': **reden, redete, geredet.**

Present Indicative

ich rede	wir reden
du redest	ihr redet
er ⎫	
sie ⎬ redet	sie reden
es ⎭	

2. Verb stems ending in **-el** drop **e** of the stem in the first person singular present indicative, and in the second person singular imperative; verb stems in **-el** and **-er** drop **e** of the ending **-en**.

tadeln, 'to blame': **tadeln, tadelte, getadelt.**
bewundern, 'to admire': **bewundern, bewunderte, bewundert.**

Present Indicative		*Imperative*	
ich tadle	wir tadeln		
du tadelst	ihr tadelt	tadle!	tadelt!
er sie es } tadelt	sie tadeln		

Formal: **Sie tadeln**   **tadeln Sie!**

Present Indicative

ich bewundere	wir bewundern
du bewunderst	ihr bewundert
er sie es } bewundert	sie bewundern

NOTE: Stems in **-el** drop **-e** of the stem in the present subjunctive.

3. Verb stems ending in a sibilant (**s, sch, ß, x, tz, z**) may insert **e** or **es** in the ending of the second person singular present indicative, but these forms are nowadays always spoken and often written **du tanzt, du reist,** etc.

197. Irregular Weak Verbs

Infinitive	*Imperfect Indicative*	*Imperfect Subjunctive*	*Past Participle*
brennen, to burn	**brannte**	**brennte**	**gebrannt**
kennen, to know	**kannte**	**kennte**	**gekannt**
nennen, to name	**nannte**	**nennte**	**genannt**
rennen, to run	**rannte**	**rennte**	**gerannt**
senden, to send; to broadcast	**sandte** **sendete** }	**sendete**	**gesandt** **gesendet** }

wenden, to turn	**wandte** ⎫ **wendete** ⎭	**wendete**	**gewandt** ⎫ **gewendet** ⎭
bringen, to bring	**brachte**	**brächte**	**gebracht**
denken, to think	**dachte**	**dächte**	**gedacht**

1. Note the change of the stem vowel to **a** in the imperfect indicative and past participle.

2. The last two verbs have also a consonant change, and umlaut in the imperfect subjunctive.

3. Otherwise these verbs are conjugated regularly.

NOTE: 1. The regular weak form of **senden** is always used when the sense is 'to broadcast'.

2. The regular weak form of **wenden** is more commonly used in literal than in figurative senses—*e.g.*, **Er wendete das Auto,** 'He turned the car round'.

198. The Verb wissen

Infinitive	Present Indicative	Imperfect Indicative
wissen, to know	**ich weiß**	**ich wußte**
	du weißt	**du wußtest**
	er weiß	**er wußte**
	wir wissen	**wir wußten**
	ihr wißt	**ihr wußtet**
	sie wissen	**sie wußten**

Imperfect Subjunctive	Past Participle
ich wüßte	**gewußt**

1. Note that this verb is irregular in the present singular.

2. **Wissen** is like the irregular weak verbs mentioned in §197 in that it has the characteristic stem-vowel change of the strong conjugation and the typical endings of the weak. In structure, though not in function, it is identical to the modal auxiliaries (§225).

NOTE: **Wissen** means 'to know (something as a fact)' whereas **kennen** means 'to know' in the sense of 'to be acquainted with (someone or something)', 'to have a good knowledge of'—*e.g.* **Ich weiß, was ich tun soll,** 'I know what to do', but **Ich kenne ihn seit Jahren,** 'I have known him for years', **Sie kennt das klassische Altertum,** 'She has a good knowledge of classical antiquity'.

199. Vowel Changes of Present Stem

sprechen, to speak

Pres. Indic.

ich spreche
du sprichst
er ⎫
sie ⎬ spricht
es ⎭
wir sprechen
ihr sprecht
sie sprechen

Formal:
Sie sprechen

stehlen, to steal

Pres. Indic.

ich stehle
du stiehlst
er ⎫
sie ⎬ stiehlt
es ⎭
wir stehlen
ihr stehlt
sie stehlen

Formal:
Sie stehlen

fallen, to fall

Pres. Indic.

ich falle
du fällst
er ⎫
sie ⎬ fällt
es ⎭
wir fallen
ihr fallt
sie fallen

Formal:
Sie fallen

stoßen, to push

Pres. Indic.

ich stoße
du stöß(es)t
er ⎫
sie ⎬ stößt
es ⎭
wir stoßen
ihr stoßt
sie stoßen

Formal:
Sie stoßen

Imperative

sprich!	stiehl!	fall! *or* falle!	stoß! *or* stoße!
sprecht!	stehlt!	fallt!	stoßt!
sprechen Sie!	stehlen Sie!	fallen Sie!	stoßen Sie!

1. Many strong verbs change short **e** of the infinitive stem vowel to **i,** and long **e** to **ie,** in the 2nd and 3rd persons singular present indicative and the 2nd person singular imperative, and also drop **-e** of the latter.

2. Most strong verbs with **a,** some with **o,** of the infinitive stem take umlaut in the 2nd and 3rd persons singular of the present indicative, but not in the imperative.

3. Hence the principal parts of such verbs are as follows:

Infin.	*Impf. Ind.*	*Past Part.*	2 *Sg.,* 3 *Sg. Pr. Ind.*	*Imperative*
geben	gab	gegeben	gibst, gibt	gib!
sprechen	sprach	gesprochen	sprichst, spricht	sprich!
sehen	sah	gesehen	siehst, sieht	sieh(e)!
stehlen	stahl	gestohlen	stiehlst, stiehlt	stiehl!
fallen	fiel	gefallen	fällst, fällt	fall(e)!
schlagen	schlug	geschlagen	schlägst, schlägt	schlag(e)!
stoßen	stieß	gestoßen	stöß(es)t, stößt	stoß(e)!

200. Compound Verbs

A compound verb is made up in German of a simple verb preceded by a separable prefix (*e.g.* ˈausgehen, 'to go out'—see §201) or an inseparable prefix (*e.g.* beˈzahlen, 'to pay'—see §202), by the adverbial prefixes **hin, her** (*e.g.,* ˈhingehen, 'to go there', ˈherkommen, 'to come from'—see §205), or these prefixes added to another prefix (*e.g.* hinˈeingehen, 'to go in', her ˈauskommen, 'to come out'), by other double prefixes (*e.g.* vorˈaussagen, 'to forecast'—see §207), or, less commonly, by a noun (*e.g.* ˈteilnehmen, 'to take part') or an adjective (*e.g.* ˈfreisprechen, 'to acquit'). Compound verbs are conjugated like the simple verbs from which they are derived.

201. Separable Prefixes

ˈAusgehen, ˈabreisen.	To go out, to set out.
ˈZumachen, ˈaufmachen.	To close, to open.
Wir reisen morgen ab.	We are leaving tomorrow.
Machen Sie die Tür zu!	Close the door!
Ich wünsche ˈauszugehen.	I wish to go out.
Er wird morgen ˈfortgehen.	He will go away tomorrow.
Wer hat die Tür ˈaufgemacht?	Who opened the door?

1. Certain prepositions and adverbs (such as **aus, mit, nach, fort**) are much used as prefixes to verbs, and are always stressed.

2. In the simple tenses these particles come at the end of principal clauses (including direct questions and commands).

3. They precede and are written as one word with the infinitive (with or without **zu**) and the past participle, wherever these occur.

202. Inseparable Prefixes

1. The prefixes **be-, emp-, ent-, er-, ge-, ver-, wider-, zer-,** are always inseparable and unstressed.

2. Verbs with these prefixes omit the **ge-** of the past participle.

Examples:

(*a*) **be-: betrachten,** to look at:

Er hat das Bild betrachtet.
He has looked at the picture.

(*b*) **emp-: empfehlen,** to recommend:

Wir haben ihnen das Buch empfohlen.
We have recommended the book to them.

(*c*) **ent-: entkommen** (+ *dative*), to escape:

Du bist der Gefahr entkommen.
You have escaped the danger.

(*d*) **er-: erzählen,** to tell:

Ich habe ihm die Geschichte erzählt.
I have told him the story.

(*e*) **ge-: gefallen** (+ *dative*), to please:

Der Film hat mir gefallen.
I liked the film.

(*f*) **ver-: verlieren,** to lose:

Er hat sein Taschentuch verloren.
He has lost his handkerchief.

(g) **wider-: widersprechen** (+ *dative*), to contradict:

Du hast dir selbst widersprochen.
You have contradicted yourself.

(h) **zer-: zerbrechen,** to break (to pieces):

Sie hat die Vase zerbrochen.
She has broken the vase.

203. Prefixes of Compound Verbs

1. The prefixes of compound verbs are either stressed or unstressed—i.e., the principal stress falls either on the prefix or on the verb stem:

ˈAusgehen; verˈgehen. To go out; to pass away.

2. Unstressed prefixes are inseparable (see §202):

Ich verˈspreche es. I promise.

3. Stressed prefixes are separable (for word order, see §201):

Ich gehe heute aus. I am going out today.
Karl ist eben ˈausgegangen. Karl has just gone out.
Kommen Sie doch herein! *Do* come in.

NOTE: The difficulties of detail explained in the following paragraphs depend upon the principles stated above.

204. Prefixes of Separable Verbs

1. As in English, prepositions, in addition to their ordinary function, are used to form compound verbs: 'He put coal *on the fire*' (preposition); 'He *put* coal *on*' (compound verb). It should be noted that whereas the verb + preposition are never written as one word in English they are in German in the infinitive and participles and in dependent clauses: **Er ging hinein** (as in English: 'He went in') but **Er ist hineingegangen; Er will hineingehen; Als er hineinging, ...**

2. There are numerous prefixes of separable verbs—*e.g.*, **ab-, an-, auf-, aus-, ein-, nieder-, über-, um-, unter-, vor-**—denoting motion in a very general way. But their meanings,

which sometimes are highly idiomatic, are best illustrated by
examples:

(*a*) ab-

Wir reisen morgen ab.
We leave tomorrow.

Er hebt 50 DM von der Bank ab.
He draws 50 DM from the bank.

Sie lehnen den Vorschlag ab.
They reject the proposition.

Der Bergsteiger stürzte ab.
The mountaineer fell headlong.

Sie nimmt ständig ab.
She constantly loses weight.

Ein Lastwagen schleppte das Auto ab.
A lorry towed the car away.

(*b*) an-

Sie kamen früh morgens in London an.
They arrived in London early in the morning.

Ich nehme Ihr Angebot dankend an.
I gratefully accept your offer.

Er bot ihr eine Zigarette an.
He offered her a cigarette.

Der Tag bricht an.
Day is dawning.

Das geht mich nichts an.
That is no concern of mine.

Starker Tee regt an.
Strong tea acts as a stimulant.

(*c*) auf-

Er gibt die Hoffnung nicht auf.
He is not giving up hope.

Hatte er einen Hut auf?
Did he have a hat on?

Er räumt sein Zimmer auf.
He is tidying up his room.

Er sah von seinem Buch auf.
He looked up from his book.

Sie schrieb die Geschichte auf.
She wrote the story down.

Er forderte sie zum Tanz auf.
He asked her to dance with him.

(*d*) aus-

Sie breiteten die Landkarte aus.
They spread the map out.

Er brach aus dem Gefängnis aus.
He broke out of prison.

Sie gruben den Schatz aus.
They dug up the treasure.

Er suchte sich den größten Apfel aus.
He picked out the largest apple.

Sie machten aus, sich in zehn Jahren zu treffen.
They agreed to meet in ten years.

Sie lachten ihn aus.
They laughed at him.

(*e*) ein-

Er steckte die Prospekte ein.
He put the prospectuses into his pocket.

Sie kaufte die Lebensmittel ein.
She bought the provisions.

Er mischte sich in ihren Streit ein.
He interfered in their quarrel.

Er schlief im Konzert ein.
He fell asleep at the concert.

Das Haus stürzte ein.
The house collapsed.

Die Wasserleitung friert im Winter ein.
The water pipes freeze in the winter.

(*f*) **nieder-**

Er legte sich nieder und schlief ein.
He lay down and fell asleep.

Sie kniete nieder.
She knelt down.

Er streckte ihn mit einem Schuß nieder.
He brought him down with one shot.

Die Nachricht hat ihn niedergeschmettert.
The news has shattered him.

Die Menge schrie ihn nieder, und er konnte nicht weitersprechen.
The crowd shouted him down and he was unable to continue.

Er stieg die Leiter nieder.
He climbed down the ladder.

(*g*) **über-**

Die Milch kochte über.
The milk boiled over.

Das Wasser floß über.
The water overflowed.

Das Feuer griff auf die umliegenden Häuser über.
The fire spread to the neighbouring houses.

(*h*) **um-**

Sie warf das Glas um.
She upset the glass.

Nach zwei Stunden kehrten sie um.
After two hours they went back.

Er grub den Garten um.
He dug the garden.

(i) unter-

Die Sonne geht unter.
The sun is setting.

Der Regen zwang ihn, sich unterzustellen.
The rain compelled him to take cover.

Er tauchte in der Menge unter, so daß die Polizei ihn nicht fand.
He disappeared into the crowd so that the police did not find
him.

(j) vor-

Es kommt oft vor, daß Leute ihr Gedächtnis verlieren.
It often happens that people lose their memory.

Er zeigte seinen Ausweis vor.
He produced his passport.

Er ist mir noch nicht vorgestellt worden.
He hasn't been introduced to me yet.

205. Her, hin

1. The prefixes **her** ('hither') and **hin** ('thither') indicate
direction, **her** towards the speaker or point of reference, etc.,
hin away from the speaker or point of reference, etc.:

Kommen Sie bitte her. (*herkommen*)
Come here, please.

Morgen gehen wir ins Konzert. Gehst du auch hin? (*hingehen*)
Tomorrow we are going to the concert. Are you going too?

2. **Aus-, vor-,** and also **ab-** in the sense of 'down', require
her- or **hin-** prefixed, when a starting-point is implied but not

specified; the others (**an-, auf-,** etc.), when a destination is implied but not specified:

Er sah zum Fenster hinaus.
He looked out of the window.

Er zog ein Buch hervor.
He produced a book.

Sie stiegen ins Tal hinab.
They climbed down into the valley.

Sie ging die Treppe hinunter.
She went down the stairs.

Er ist heraufgekommen.
He has come up(stairs).

3. When the starting-point or destination is specified, these compound prefixes are used if the preposition and prefix do not correspond:

Wir fuhren oft nach Frankreich hinüber.
We often crossed over to France.

Die Katze kroch unter dem Bett hervor.
The cat crept out from under the bed.

4. When preposition and prefix correspond, the compound prefix may be used:

Wir gingen um die Stadtmauer herum.
We walked round the town wall.

Er ging aus dem Zimmer (hinaus), als ich eintrat.
He went out of the room when I entered.

5. **Her** and **hin** are required with certain adverbs when motion and a starting-point or destination are implied:

(*a*) **Woher kommst du?** (*colloquial:* **Wo kommst du her?**)
Where do you come from?

Woher hast du das Geld? (*colloquial:* **Wo hast du das Geld her?**)
Where did you get the money from?

(b) **Wohin gehst du?** (*colloquial:* **Wo gehst du hin?**)
Where are you going?

Wohin schickst du das Paket? (*colloquial:* **Wo schickst du das Paket hin?**)
Where are you sending that parcel to?

(c) **Komm jetzt hierher!**
Come here now!

Bis hierher und nicht weiter!
Thus far and no further!

(d) **Ich möchte zur Oper. Wie komme ich am besten dahin** (*or* **dorthin**)?
I should like to go to the opera. Which is the best way of getting there?

Wie lange fahren wir (bis) dahin (*or* **dorthin**)?
How long does it take to get there?

206. Quasi-Prefixes

1. Besides the ordinary verb-prefixes, many words and phrases in common use have practically the function of separable prefixes, and follow the same rules of word order—*i.e.*, in simple sentences they come at the end of principal clauses.

2. Such are nouns as objects, with or without prepositions:

Auf seine Gesundheit ¹achtgeben.
To take good care of one's health.

Gib auf die Stufe acht!
Mind the step!

Nimm dich in acht!
Look out! Mind yourself!

NOTE: Whether a noun so used is written with a capital letter and separated from the verb usually depends on its own importance in the sentence, and also on whether the thing or idea it expresses is fully conceivable, as in **Auto fahren**, 'to drive a car', **Karten spielen**, 'to play cards', **Klavier spielen**, 'to play the piano', **Ski laufen**, 'to ski'. Some verbs have a small initial letter when the noun and verb are written as one word but a capital when separated—*e.g.*, ˈ**radfahren**, 'to cycle': **Er fährt Rad; maschinenschreiben**, 'to type': **sie schreibt Maschine**. Sometimes there is an option between the two forms, as in **Dank sagen**, ˈ**danksagen**.

3. So also certain adjectives:

Lassen Sie mich los!
Let me go!

Er wurde freigesprochen.
He was acquitted.

Er muß sein Zimmer allein saubermachen.
He has to clean his room on his own.

NOTE: 1. Some adjective-prefixes are inseparable, even when stressed, and retain the prefix **ge-**: **Er fing an zu** ˈ**weissagen**, 'He began to prophesy'; **Sie hat sich ge**ˈ**rechtfertigt**, 'She has justified herself'.

2. **Voll**, except in the literal sense of 'full' (*e.g.* **Er hat das Glas** ˈ**vollgefüllt**, 'He has filled the glass'), is unstressed and inseparable: **Er hat das Werk voll**ˈ**endet**, 'He has completed the work'; **Er voll**ˈ**führte einen doppelten Salto**, 'He performed a double somersault'.

4. So also certain verbs
(*a*) if they create a completely new meaning with another verb:

Man sollte sich nicht gehenlassen.
One shouldn't get into slovenly ways.

Er fürchtet, in diesem Jahr sitzenzubleiben.
He is afraid that he will not be moved up to the next class this
year.

(*b*) if they unite to form an integrated whole:

Ich möchte ihn gern kennenlernen.
I should like to make his acquaintance.

Es ist gesund, viel spazierenzugehen.
It is healthy to go for lots of walks.

207. Double Prefixes

1. Separable + separable; both separable:

Er hat das Unwetter vor'ausgesagt.⎫ He forecast the thunder-
Er sagte das Unwetter voraus. ⎭   storm.

2. Separable + inseparable; the former alone separable:

Ich habe die alten Briefe 'aufbewahrt.⎫ I kept the old
Ich bewahrte die alten Briefe auf. ⎭   letters.

Sein Anspruch wurde 'anerkannt.⎫
Man erkannte seinen Anspruch an.⎭ His claim was allowed.

3. Inseparable + separable; both inseparable:

Ich be'absichtige, meine Stellung aufzugeben.
I intend to give up my job.

Sie ver'anstalteten ein großes Fest.
They organized a big celebration.

208. Verbal Prefixes with Varying Stress

1. The prefixes **durch-, über-, um-, unter-,** are sometimes
stressed (separable), and sometimes unstressed (inseparable).
2. Some of these compounds are used both separably and
inseparably, usually with different meaning:

Er ist hier 'durchgereist.
He passed through here.

Er hat das Land durch'reist.
He has travelled all over the country.

Er warf sich den Mantel über.
He threw the coat over his shoulders.

Er über'warf sich mit seinen Freunden.
He fell out with his friends.

In dem Schloß geht ein Gespenst um.
A ghost haunts the castle.

Er um'ging die Schwierigkeiten.
He evaded the difficulties.

3. Some exist only as inseparable verbs:

Er durch'querte das Gebiet zu Fuß.
He crossed the region on foot.

Ich über'lasse das Ihnen.
I leave that to you.

Unter'brechen Sie mich nicht!
Don't interrupt me.

4. Others exist only as separable verbs:

Er ist 'umgekehrt.
He has turned back.

Der Kessel kocht 'über.
The kettle is boiling over.

5. The prefix **miß–**.

(*a*) **Miß–** is usually inseparable and unstressed. Examples:
miß'billigen (miß'billigte, miß'billigt), 'to disapprove of',
miß'brauchen, 'to misuse, abuse', **miß'fallen (miß'fiel, miß'fallen)**
(+ *dat.*), 'to displease', **miß'glücken** (+ *sein*), 'to fail', (**jemandem
etwas) miß'gönnen,** 'to begrudge (someone something)', **miß-
'handeln,** 'to ill-treat', **miß'hören,** 'to mishear', **miß'lingen (miß-
'lang, miß'lungen)** (+ *sein*), 'to be unsuccessful, go wrong, fail',
miß'raten (miß'riet, miß'raten), 'to turn out badly', **miß'trauen,**
'to distrust'.

(*b*) When in emphatic contrast to the sense of the verb, **miß-** is stressed and of mixed conjugation. Examples: **ˈmißachten** (**ˈmißachtete, ˈmißgeachtet,** occasionally **geˈmißachtet**), 'to show contempt for', BUT: **mißˈachten (mißˈachtete, mißˈachtet),** 'to disregard'; **ˈmißbilden (ˈmißbildete, ˈmißgebildet),** 'to misshape, deform'; **ˈmißdeuten (ˈmißdeutete, ˈmißgedeutet,** occasionally **geˈmißdeutet),** 'to put an unfavourable interpretation on, to misinterpret deliberately', BUT: **mißˈdeuten (mißˈdeutete, mißˈdeutet),** 'to misconstrue, misinterpret accidentally'; **ˈmißstimmen** (**ˈmißstimmte, ˈmißgestimmt),** 'to put in a bad mood'.

(*c*) With verbs having prefixes or ending in **-ieren, miß-** is inseparable and stressed. Examples: **ˈmißverstehen (ˈmißverstand, ˈmißverstanden),** 'to misunderstand', **ˈmißkalkulieren (ˈmiß-kalkulierte, ˈmißkalkuliert),** 'to miscalculate'.

NOTE: 1. The inseparable transitive compound is often replaced by the simple verb + the prefix as preposition: **Er durchschritt das Tor** or **Er schritt durch das Tor,** 'He passed through the gate'.

2. **Hinter-** as a prefix is inseparable; **wieder-** is inseparable only in **wiederˈholen,** 'to repeat': **Er hat mich hinterˈgangen,** 'He has deceived me'; **Er hinterˈließ nichts,** 'He left nothing (in his will)'; **Ich habe es wiederˈholt,** 'I repeated it'.

209. Participles

A participle is a part of a verb that often has characteristics of both a verb and an adjective. In English there are two kinds of participles—the *present* participle and the *past* participle; in German there are three kinds, the *present*, the *past*, and the *future passive* participles.

210. The Present Participle

In English the present participle of all verbs ends in '-ing' and in German in **-end**:

> **habend,** having
> **machend,** making
> **eilend,** hurrying
> **singend,** singing

211. The Past Participle

In English the past participle usually ends in '-ed', '-d', '-t', -n', or '-en' (*e.g.* [I have] played, saved, spent, known, written). In German the past participle is usually formed, in the case of weak verbs, by prefixing **ge-** to the stem and adding **-t** or **-et** (*e.g.* **ge-spiel-t**, from **spielen**, 'to play'; **ge-bad-et,** from **baden,** 'to bathe'), and in the case of strong verbs by prefixing **ge-** to the stem and adding **-en,** usually also with change of stem-vowel (*e.g.* **ge-sung-en,** from **singen,** 'to sing'):

Past Participles

Weak: **gemacht,** made
geeilt, hurried
gelobt, praised
gearbeitet, worked
gedauert, lasted

Strong: **gesungen,** sung (from **singen**)
gelaufen, run (from **laufen**)
geschrieben, written (from **schreiben**)
getan, done (from **tun**)
gerochen, smelt (from **riechen**)

212. Future Passive Participle

It has the form of the present participle preceded by **zu,** is formed from transitive verbs only, and is always used attributively:

Eine ernstzunehmende Angelegenheit.
A matter to be taken seriously.

Sie stellte alle abzuwaschenden Teller zusammen.
She put together all the plates (that were) to be washed up.

213. Omission of **ge-**

Foreign verbs ending in **-ieren** and verbs with inseparable prefixes (see §202) omit the prefix **ge-** of the past participle:

studieren, to study	**studiert**
komplizieren, to complicate	**kompliziert**
quadrieren, to square	**quadriert**
bezahlen, to pay	**bezahlt**
entdecken, to discover	**entdeckt**
vergessen, to forget	**vergessen**

214. Uses of Present and Past Participles

1. The following participles may be used adjectivally:

(*a*)   all present participles—*e.g.:*
Das schlafende Kind.
The sleeping child.

Der fliegende Holländer.
The Flying Dutchman.

Jeder denkende Mensch.
Every thinking person.

(*b*)   the past participle of transitive verbs—*e.g.:*
Das verkaufte Haus.
The house which was (has been) sold.

Die verabscheute Medizin.
The abhorred medicine.

Seine ausgestreckten Arme.
His outstretched arms.

(*c*)   the past participles of those intransitive verbs conjugated with **sein** which have a perfective meaning
(i.e., which express or imply the notion of completion)
—*e.g.:*
Der Großvater ist gestorben/der gestorbene Großvater.
The grandfather has died/the dead grandfather.

Die Blumen sind verblüht/die verblühten Blumen.
The flowers have withered/the withered flowers.

When used as adjectives, past participles are variable or
invariable like ordinary adjectives.

NOTE: 1. The present participle cannot be used predicatively in German.

2. Some present and past participles are almost exclusively used as adjectives—for example, **Ein betrunkener Mann,** 'A drunk man'; **Er findet es schwer, eine geeignete Stellung zu bekommen,** 'He is finding it difficult to obtain a suitable job'; **Ein reizendes Mädchen,** 'A charming girl'; **Die besorgten Eltern,** 'The anxious parents'; **Ein erfahrener Lehrer,** 'An experienced teacher'; **Ein spannendes Buch,** 'An exciting book'.

2. Like other adjectives, they may be used substantivally (§148):

Der Reisende, the traveller.
Die Verwandten, the relatives.

3. They are also used as adverbs:

Er ist bedeutend größer als ich.
He is considerably taller than I.

Der Politiker hat ausgezeichnet gesprochen.
The politician spoke excellently.

Sie arbeiten angestrengt.
They are working strenuously.

See also §250, 2.

NOTE: For appositive participle, see §159.

4. The participle must follow all its adjuncts, and come at the end of the phrase:

Über seine Unbekümmertheit entsetzt, nannte sie ihn einen Taugenichts.
Appalled at his lack of concern, she called him a good-for-nothing.

Von allen Seiten umringt, gab der Schauspieler Autogramme.
Surrounded on all sides, the actor was giving autographs.

215. Past Participle Idioms

1. The *past* participle is used after **kommen** to denote the manner of the action, where English uses the present participle:

Er kam gelaufen.   He came running.

2. It occurs in absolute constructions, with or without a substantive (usually in the accusative):

Meinen Bruder ausgenommen,... My brother excepted...
Wie gewonnen, so zerronnen. Easy come, easy go.

NOTE: For the imperative use, see §241, 4.

216. The Adjectival Participle

1. The English present participle with the force of a relative clause is rendered in German by a relative clause:

Die Frau, die dort drüben steht, ist die Mutter meiner Freundin.
The woman standing over there is my friend's mother.

2. A German participle used attributively very commonly replaces the construction employed in the example above:

Die dort drüben stehende Frau ist die Mutter meiner Freundin.

Attributive participles and adjectives immediately precede the substantive qualified. This construction has long been very common in journalism and is also often found in literature. Examples:

(*a*) **Die Stadt Algier liegt an der Westseite einer geräumigen, von Kap Pescada im Westen und Kap Matifu im Osten begrenzten, nach Norden geöffneten herrlichen Bucht.**
    The city of Algiers lies on the west side of a spacious and magnificent bay, bounded by Cape Pescada on the west and Cape Matifu on the east, and open towards the north.

(*b*) **"Hier saßen wir nun nach der Abendmahlzeit im anfänglich von keinem Gespräch unterbrochenen Genusse des still zu unseren Füßen ruhenden Sees ..."** (J. V. Widmann, *Feuilletons*).
    Here we sat now, after the evening meal, enjoying the pleasure, which was at first uninterrupted by any conversation, of the lake reposing peacefully at our feet.

217. Verbs conjugated with **sein**

The following classes of verbs are conjugated with **sein** as an auxiliary of tense:

1. The two verbs of rest:

sein, to be   **bleiben,** to remain

2. Verbs of motion, such as:

begegnen, to meet	**fallen,** to fall	**kommen,** to come
eilen, to hurry	**folgen,** to follow	**laufen,** to run
erscheinen, to appear	**gehen,** to go	**verschwinden,** to
fahren, to drive, etc.		disappear

Some of these verbs also admit **haben** when a direct object is present or implied. Compare the following sentences, in which the first of each pair is intransitive, and therefore conjugated with **sein,** while the second of each pair is transitive, and therefore conjugated with **haben:**

Er ist den ganzen Tag lang gefahren.
He has been driving the whole day.

Er hat seinen Wagen den ganzen Tag lang gefahren.
He has been driving his car the whole day.

Er ist eine Stunde lang gelaufen.
He ran for an hour.

Er hat die Hundertmeter (= den Hundertmeterlauf) gelaufen.
He ran the hundred metres (= the hundred metres race).

3. Intransitive verbs expressing a change of condition, such as:

aufwachen, to wake up	**schmelzen,** to melt
einschlafen, to fall asleep	**sterben,** to die
erkranken, to fall ill	**wachsen,** to grow
genesen, to recover	**werden,** to become

4. The following impersonal verbs (cf. §218):

gelingen, to succeed	**geschehen,** to happen
mißlingen, to fail	**glücken,** to succeed

218. Impersonal Verbs

Es friert (schneit, regnet).	It is freezing (snowing, raining).
Es klopft.	Someone is knocking.
Plötzlich raschelte es im Gebüsch.	Suddenly there was a rustling in the bushes.
Es kracht in meinem Radio.	My radio is crackling.
Wie geht's dir?	How are you?
Was gibt's?	What's up? What's the matter?
Es tut mir leid.	I am sorry.
Es freut mich (or Mich freut), daß es dir besser geht.	I am glad that you are feeling better.
Es ärgert mich (or Mich ärgert), daß ich den Film versäumt habe.	I am annoyed at having missed the film.
Es überrascht mich (or Mich überrascht), dich hier zu treffen.	I am surprised at meeting you here.
Mich friert (hungert, dürstet).	I am cold (hungry, thirsty).
Er sagte, daß ihn hungere (or Er sagte, es hungere ihn).	He said he was hungry.

1. Impersonal verbs are used only in the third person singular with **es** as subject.

2. Many verbs are used impersonally with a special sense.

3. Those denoting bodily or mental affection drop **es** if the object precedes the verb of a principal clause, and also in dependent clauses—i.e., unless the word **es** begins the sentence or clause.

219. Agreement of Verb and Subject

`1. This agreement is, in general, the same in German as in English; for exceptions, see below.

2. With several subjects, the verb may agree with the nearest singular subject, especially if the subjects follow the verb, or are grouped together:

An ihm ist Hopfen und Malz verloren.
He is a dead loss.

Geld und Gut ist hin.
Money and wealth are gone.

3. The singular of the auxiliary verb is used if there is an enumeration of subordinate clauses with different past participles:

Er sah, daß das Zimmer aufgeräumt, das Geschirr abgewaschen und der Papierkorb ausgeleert war.
He saw that the room had been tidied up, the dishes washed and the waste-paper basket emptied.

4. The singular of a verb may be used if the subjects are preceded by an indefinite adjective such as **kein, jeder**:

Jeder Junge und jedes Mädchen hat ein Buch bekommen.
Every boy and every girl have received a book.

5. (a) The agreement of a verb with a collective is in general the same as in English, with similar uncertainty and fluctuation:

Von den Großmächten wurde(n) eine Reihe (von) Atombombentests durchgeführt.
A series of atom bomb tests was (were) carried out by the Great Powers.

Eine Anzahl Leute (or von Leuten) war(en) im Saal versammelt.
A number of people were assembled in the hall.

Similarly with: **eine Bande** ('a band, gang'), **eine Gruppe** ('a group'), **eine Handvoll** ('a handful'), **ein Kreis** (*m.*) ('a circle'), **eine Masse** ('a mass'), **eine Menge** ('a crowd'), **eine Schar** ('a flock, crowd'), etc.

(b) Group-terms relating to animals and birds are always used with the singular in German—*e.g.*, **Eine Herde Schafe weidete auf der Wiese**, 'A flock of sheep *were* grazing in the meadow'.

220. Reflexive Verbs

A reflexive verb is a verb which in English is always transitive in form, the object invariably being a reflexive pronoun—*e.g.* 'He *washed himself*', 'They *hurt themselves*', '*Help yourself!*'— the action passing back to the doer. In German, reflexive verbs usually have the object in the accusative, but sometimes in the dative with the remote object in the accusative (see §222, 1, 2). In the past tenses they are always conjugated with **haben**—*e.g.* **sie hatte sich erkältet**, 'she had caught a cold'. Reflexive verbs are more often used in German than in English.

221. Reflexive Verbs

sich freuen, 'to be glad'

Present Indicative
ich freue mich
du freust dich
er freut sich
wir freuen uns
ihr freut euch
Sie freuen sich
sie freuen sich

Perfect Indicative
ich habe mich gefreut
du hast dich gefreut
er hat sich gefreut
wir haben uns gefreut
ihr habt euch gefreut
Sie haben sich gefreut
sie haben sich gefreut

sich vorstellen, 'to imagine'

Present Indicative
ich stelle mir vor
du stellst dir vor
er stellt sich vor
wir stellen uns vor
ihr stellt euch vor
Sie stellen sich vor
sie stellen sich vor

Perfect Indicative
ich habe mir vorgestellt
du hast dir vorgestellt
er hat sich vorgestellt
wir haben uns vorgestellt
ihr habt euch vorgestellt
Sie haben sich vorgestellt
sie haben sich vorgestellt

1. The pronouns of the 1st and 2nd persons have no special form for reflexive action, but those of the 3rd person (also the formal **Sie**) have the form **sich** for both accusative and dative of all genders and both numbers. See also §109.

2. Transitive verbs in English are frequently also used intransitively; such verbs are usually reflexive in German:

Das Wetter hat sich geändert.
The weather has changed.

Die Tür öffnete sich.
The door opened.

3. Intransitive reflexive verbs take the accusative pronoun. The action refers to the subject only:

Ich beeile mich.	**Du freust dich.**
I hurry.	You are glad.

4. Reflexive verbs with transitive meaning take the dative reflexive pronoun. The action is directed towards an object (but with reference to the subject):

Ich wünsche mir ein Haus.
I'd like to have a house (i.e., for myself).

For word order of reflexive pronouns, see §110.

222. Government of Reflexives

1. The reflexive object is usually in the accusative, the remote object being in the dative or the genitive, or governed by a preposition:

Die Festung hat sich (*acc.*) **dem Feind** (*dat.*) **übergeben.**
The stronghold has surrendered to the enemy.

Erbarme dich (*acc.*) **der Armen** (*gen.*)!
Take pity on the poor.

Kümmere dich um deine eigenen Angelegenheiten!
Mind your own business!

Begnügen Sie sich damit!
Content yourself with that.

Ärgern Sie sich nicht darüber!
Don't be cross about it.

2. The reflexive object is sometimes in the dative and the remote object in the accusative:

Das (*acc.*) **kann ich mir** (*dat.*) **denken.**
I can imagine that.

Stell dir (*dat.*) **das** (*acc.*) **vor!**
Fancy that!

3. The majority of reflexive verbs govern the accusative case—*e.g.*:

sich ausruhen, to rest (**ich ruhe** *mich* **aus**)
sich ausschweigen, to remain silent
sich baden, to have a bath
sich beeilen, to hurry
sich befinden, to be (situated)
sich entfernen, to move away, withdraw
sich entkleiden, to undress
sich erholen, to recover (one's health)
sich erkälten, to catch a cold
sich freuen, to be glad
sich hinlegen, to lie down
sich irren, to be mistaken
sich setzen, to sit down
sich waschen, to wash (oneself)
sich wundern, to be surprised

4. Reflexive verbs governing the dative include the following, with examples in parenthesis:

sich (dem Feind) ergeben, to surrender to (the enemy)
sich (einer Stadt) nähern, to approach (a town)
sich (den Bedingungen) unterwerfen, to submit to (the terms)
sich (dem Krieg) widersetzen, to oppose (the war)
sich (der Kunst) widmen, to devote oneself to (art)

5. Many reflexive verbs used to govern the genitive, but now use alternative constructions—for example, **sich erinnern +** *gen.* ('to remember') has become rare and has been replaced by **sich erinnern an +** *acc.* The commonest of the dwindling number of reflexive verbs still used with the genitive are as follows, with examples in parenthesis:

sich (einer Sache) annehmen, to attend to (a matter)
sich (jemandes) bedienen, to make use of (someone)
sich (seines Rechtes) begeben, to renounce (one's right)
sich (einer Sache) bemächtigen, to take possession of (a thing)
sich (des Alkohols) enthalten, to abstain from (alcohol)

6. Among the commonest of the large number of reflexive verbs which govern a preposition are:

sich ärgern über (+*acc.*), to be cross about
sich bedanken für (+*acc.*), to thank for
sich beklagen über (+*acc.*), to complain about
sich beschränken auf (+*acc.*), to confine oneself to
sich entschuldigen bei (+*dat.*), to apologize to
sich erfreuen an (+*dat.*), to enjoy
sich erinnern an (+*acc.*), to remember
sich freuen auf (+*acc.*), to look forward to
sich freuen über (+*acc.*), to be pleased about
sich fürchten vor (+*dat.*), to be frightened of
sich gewöhnen an (+*acc.*), to get used to
sich mischen in (+*acc.*), to meddle with
sich mischen unter (+*acc.*), to mingle with
sich rächen an (+*dat.*), to avenge oneself on
sich richten nach (+*dat.*), to conform to
sich sehnen nach (+*dat.*), to long for
sich stützen auf (+*acc.*), to rely upon
sich unterhalten über (+*acc.*), to talk about
sich verlassen auf (+*acc.*), to rely on
sich verlieben in (+*acc.*), to fall in love with
sich wundern über (+*acc.*), to be surprised at

223. Reciprocal Action

1. Reflexive pronouns are used in the plural to express reciprocal action; but in the case of ambiguity, or for the sake of good style, the invariable reciprocal pronoun **einander** ('each other', 'one another') replaces them for all persons. In the last example below (at the top of p. 205), the first verb is genuinely reflexive and so **sich** is used, whereas the second denotes a mutual (reciprocal) action and can therefore be expressed optionally by **sich** or **einander**:

Sie werden sich wiedersehen.
They will see each other again.

Wir begegneten uns (*dat.*).
We met each other.

Wir küßten uns.
We kissed.

Sie trafen sich und gaben einander (*or* sich) die Hand.
They met and shook hands.

2. Sometimes the adverb **gegenseitig**, 'mutually', 'reciprocally', is used to reinforce **sich** in the sense of 'each other', 'one another':

Wir müssen uns gegenseitig vertrauen.
We must trust each other (*or* one another).

Sie haben sich gegenseitig vernichtet.
They have destroyed each other (*or* one another).

224. Modal Auxiliaries

The verbs **dürfen, können, mögen, müssen, sollen, wollen** (whose primary meanings are given in §226), with the verb **lassen**, 'to let', are called 'modal auxiliaries' (often abbreviated to 'modals'), or 'auxiliaries of mood', since they form constructions equivalent to various moods.

225. Conjugation of Modal Auxiliaries

PRINCIPAL PARTS

Infinitive	*Imperfect Indicative*	*Past Participle*
dürfen	durfte	gedurft
können	konnte	gekonnt
mögen	mochte	gemocht
müssen	mußte	gemußt
sollen	sollte	gesollt
wollen	wollte	gewollt

The imperfect indicative and past participle have the weak endings **-te, -t**, without umlaut.

NOTE: The imperative is lacking in all, except **wollen (wolle!** etc.).

Present Indicative

ich darf	kann	mag	muß	soll	will
du darfst	kannst	magst	mußt	sollst	willst
er darf	kann	mag	muß	soll	will
wir dürfen	können	mögen	müssen	sollen	wollen
ihr dürft	könnt	mögt	müßt	sollt	wollt
sie dürfen	können	mögen	müssen	sollen	wollen

1. Note the vowel change in the singular (except **sollen**) and the absence of personal endings in the first and third persons singular.

2. The plural is formed regularly from the infinitive stem.

Subjunctive

Present: **ich dürfe,**	**könne,**	**möge,**	**müsse,**	**solle,**	**wolle**
etc.	etc.	etc.	etc.	etc.	etc.
Imperf.: **ich dürfte,**	**könnte,**	**möchte,**	**müßte,**	**sollte,**	**wollte**
etc.	etc.	etc.	etc.	etc.	etc.

Continue the examples with regular subjunctive endings (see §161, 2).

Note the absence of umlaut in **sollte** and **wollte**.

Compound Tenses

Perf. Ind.:	**ich habe,**	**du hast,** etc.	**gedurft,** etc.
Perf. Subj.:	**ich habe,**	**du habest,** etc.	**gedurft,** etc.
Plupf. Ind.:	**ich hatte,**	**du hattest,** etc.	**gedurft,** etc.
Plupf. Subj.:	**ich hätte,**	**du hättest,** etc.	**gedurft,** etc.
Fut. Ind.:	**ich werde,**	**du wirst,** etc.	**dürfen,** etc.
Fut. Subj.:	**ich werde,**	**du werdest,** etc.	**dürfen,** etc.
Fut. Perf. Ind.:	**ich werde,**	**du wirst,** etc.	**gedurft,** etc., **haben**
Fut. Perf. Subj.:	**ich werde,**	**du werdest,** etc.	**gedurft,** etc., **haben**
Simp. Condl.:	**ich würde,**	**du würdest,** etc.	**dürfen,** etc.
Comp. Condl.:	**ich würde,**	**du würdest,** etc.	**gedurft,** etc., **haben**

226. Primary Meanings of Modal Auxiliaries

The following paragraphs contain examples of the commoner uses of modals; for the construction of the compound tenses and the more idiomatic distinctions, see §230:

1. **dürfen** (*permission, concession*):

Darf ich Sie um Feuer bitten?
May I ask you for a light?

Wir dürfen bis Mitternacht aufbleiben.
We are allowed to stay up until midnight.

2. **können** (*ability, possibility*):

Er konnte nicht schwimmen.
He could not swim.

Das kann schon sein.
That may well be so.

Können Sie Deutsch?
Do you know German?

3. **mögen** (*preference, concession*):

Er mochte Süßigkeiten nie gern.
He never liked sweets.

Er möchte (gern) bleiben.
He would like to stay.

Er mag bleiben.
He may (= Let him) stay.

4. **müssen** (*necessity, obligation*):

Wir müssen alle sterben.
We must all die.

Ich muß morgen um 7 Uhr aufstehen.
I must get up tomorrow at 7 o'clock.

5. **sollen** (*obligation, duty*):

Ich soll morgen abreisen.
I am to start on my way tomorrow.

Soll ich bleiben?
Shall I (= Am I to) stay?

Das sollte er nicht tun.
He ought not to do that.

In the first person **sollen** = 'am to', etc., in statements, and in questions 'shall' or 'am to', etc.

NOTE: The obligation is that imposed by the will of someone else.

6. **wollen** (*resolution, intention*):

Er will nicht warten.
He is unwilling to wait.

Ich will morgen endlich den Brief schreiben.
I intend to write the letter tomorrow at long last.

7. **lassen** (*with imperative force, see* §239):

Lassen Sie mich bleiben!
Let me stay.

227. Remarks on Modal Auxiliaries

1. All modal auxiliaries govern an infinitive without **zu**:

Ich kann lesen.
I can read.

Ich möchte gehen.
I should like to go.

Lassen Sie uns gehen!
Let us go.

2. Unlike their English counterparts, which are defective and so have to resort to paraphrase ('I *can* do it' but 'I have not *been able to* do it'), these verbs have an infinitive and past participle, and are therefore capable of forming a complete set of tenses:

Ich werde arbeiten müssen.
I shall have to work.

Er wird nicht kommen können.
He will not be able to come.

3. After a governed infinitive, in the compound tenses, the past participle takes the form of an infinitive:

Er hat nicht spielen können.
He was unable to play.

Er hat es schicken lassen.
He had it sent (caused it to be sent).

NOTE: The verbs **hören, sehen,** and **helfen** (and, in literary language, **heißen,** 'to bid, command') also share this peculiarity: **Ich habe ihn kommen hören (sehen),** 'I heard (saw) him come'; **Ich habe ihr aussteigen helfen,** 'I helped her to alight'.

4. They may also be used independently (without a governed infinitive), and even as transitive verbs, and have then the regular forms of the past participle in compound tenses:

Er hat nicht gewollt.	He did not want to.
Ich habe Wein noch nie gemocht.	I have never liked wine.

5. Owing to the defective conjugation and limited meaning of the English modals, German modal constructions are variously rendered into English (see §§226, 228, 230).

6. The imperfect subjunctive is regularly used for the simple conditional:

Das dürfte genug sein.	That should (ought to) be enough.
Ich möchte es tun.	I should like to do it.

7. Distinguish carefully between 'could' (='was able'), **konnte** (*indicative*) and 'could' (='would be able'), **könnte** (*conditional*):

Er konnte es nicht tun, da er krank war.
He could not (was unable to) do it, as he was ill.

Er könnte es nicht tun, wenn er es auch wollte.
He could not (would not be able to) do it, even if he wanted to.

8. The infinitive of a verb of motion (especially **kommen, gehen**) is often omitted after the modals when an adverb or adverbial phrase denoting 'whither' is present:

Ich will herein.
I wish to come in.

Ich muß nach Hause.
I must go home.

Am Mittwoch muß ich zurück.
On Wednesday I must return.

Ich muß jetzt weg.
I have to go now.

Wir dürfen nicht in die Stadt.
We are not allowed (to go) into the town.

228. Compound Tenses of Modal Auxiliaries

1. The following condensed table illustrates the compound tense forms of the modal auxiliaries (including **lassen**) with a governed infinitive:

Perf. Indic.:   **ich habe**
   du hast
Perf. Subj.:   **ich habe**
   du habest ⎫ **spielen dürfen, können, mögen,** etc.
Plupf. Indic.:   **ich hatte**
Plupf. Subj.:   **ich hätte**

The past participle here has the form of an infinitive.

NOTE: The last form above replaces the compound conditional, which is not in use.

2. The following examples show the use of the pluperfect subjunctive as a shorter compound conditional:

Ich hätte es tun dürfen.   I should have been allowed to do it.

Ich hätte es tun können.   I could have done it.
Ich hätte es tun mögen.   I should have liked to do it.
Ich hätte es tun müssen.   I should have had to do it.
Ich hätte es tun sollen.   I ought to have done it.

3. These verbs have also another form of the perfect and the pluperfect, with the modal in a simple and the infinitive in a compound tense. The following parallel examples show the respective meanings of the two forms:

Er hat es nicht tun können.	He has been unable to do it.
Er kann es getan haben.	He may possibly have done it.
Er hat es nicht tun mögen.	He didn't like to do it.
Er mag es getan haben.	He may possibly have done it.
Er hat es tun müssen.	He has had to do it.
Er muß es getan haben.	He must have done it.
Er hat es tun wollen.	He meant to have done it.
Er will es getan haben.	He claims to have done it.
	(He maintains that he did it.)
Er hat es tun sollen.	He was supposed to do it.
Er soll es getan haben.	He is said to have done it.

229. Word Order

In a dependent clause with compound tense and governed infinitive, the auxiliary of tense (**haben** or **werden**) does not come last, but precedes both the participle and the governed infinitive:

Er sagte, daß er es nicht habe tun mögen.
He said that he had not liked to do it.

Wenn er hätte kommen wollen, wäre er auch gekommen.
If he had wanted to come he would have come.

Ich weiß nicht, ob ich werde kommen können.
I don't know whether I shall be able to come.

230. Idiomatic Uses of Modals

The following sections contain, for reference, examples of the idiomatic uses of the modal auxiliaries:

1. **dürfen:**
1. **Darf ich fragen, was er will?**
   May I ask what he wants?

2. **Du darfst den Ball behalten.**
   You may keep the ball.

3. **Hier darf man nicht rauchen.**
   Smoking is not allowed here.

4. **Es dürfte wahr sein.**
   It may well be true (is probably true).

5. **Ich darf wohl sagen, daß alle unsere Erwartungen weit übertroffen worden sind.**
   I can venture to say that all our expectations have been greatly exceeded.

6. **Das darf ich nicht.**
   I am not allowed to do that.

7. **Du darfst nicht zu spät nach Hause kommen.**
   You must not come home late.

8. **Sie darf nichts davon wissen.**
   She must not know anything about it.

1–3 indicate permission; 4 expresses reasonable supposition, with subjunctive; 5, modest assertion; 6 shows the absolute use; 7, 8, command, replacing **müssen** in certain negative phrases.

NOTE: **Dürfen** renders the English 'may', 'might', in questions, as in 1 above.

2. **können:**

1. **Ich hätte es tun können.**
   I could have done it.

2. **Ich könnte es getan haben.**
   I might have done it (= It is quite possible that I did it).

3. **Das kann sein.**
   That may be.

4. **Er kann die Lektion nicht.**
   He doesn't know the lesson.

5. **Ich habe nicht gekonnt.**
   I have not been able to.

1 denotes ability; 2, 3, possibility; 4, the transitive use; 5, absolute use.

3. mögen:

1. **Möge der Himmel das geben!** (*literary*)
 May Heaven grant that!

2. **Ich möchte gern hier bleiben.**
 I should like to stay here.

3. **Er hat nie arbeiten mögen.**
 He has never liked working.

4. **Ich hätte das sehen mögen.**
 I should like to have seen that.

5. **Ich mag dieses Buch nicht.**
 I don't like this book.

6. **Ich war wohl der einzige, der ihn mochte.**
 I was probably the only one who liked him.

7. **Er mag zehn Jahre alt sein.**
 He may be ten years old.

8. **Das mag sein.**
 That may be (but I doubt it).
 or That may well be (but even so. . .).

9. **Was du auch hören magst, sage nichts.**
 Whatever you (may) hear, say nothing.

10. **Wie dem auch sein mag.**
 Be that as it may.

1 denotes a wish; 2–4, preference or liking; 5, 6, transitive use, indicating a liking for something or someone; 7, 8, possibility or probability; 9, concession; 10, special idiom.

NOTE: The adverb **gern** further emphasizes the idea of liking or preference, as in the second example above.

4. müssen:

1. **Alle Menschen müssen sterben.**
 All men must die.

2. **Ich habe gehen müssen.**
I have had to go.

3. **Rom muß eine sehr schöne Stadt sein.**
Rome must be a very beautiful city.

4. **Im Frühling muß es dort herrlich sein.**
It must be marvellous there in the Spring.

5. **Ich habe gemußt.**
I have been obliged to.

1 denotes necessity; 2, compulsion by another person; 3, 4, inference; 5, absolute use.

NOTE: 'To be obliged, compelled', after a negative in simple tenses, is rendered either by **müssen: Du mußt nicht nach Hause gehen,** 'You don't *have* to go home' (cf. **du darfst nicht . . .** , no. 7 on p. 212), or by **brauchen: Er braucht nicht zu gehen,** 'He is not obliged to go', 'He doesn't have to go'.

5. sollen:

1. **Du sollst nicht töten.**
Thou shalt not kill.

2. **Er soll sofort herkommen!**
He is to come here at once!

3. **Er hätte gehen sollen.**
He ought to have gone.

4. **Ich weiß nicht, was ich sagen soll.**
I don't know what I should (ought to) say.

5. **Was soll geschehen?**
What is to be done?

6. **Was sollte ich tun?**
What was I to do?

7. **Er soll sehr reich sein.**
He is said to be very rich.

8. **Wenn er kommen sollte, . . .**
If he should (were to) come . . .

9. **Was soll das?**
What is the meaning of that? What's the (big) idea?

1, 2 denote command; 3, 4, duty or obligation; 5, 6, submission of the speaker's will; 7, statement not vouched for by the speaker; 8, conditional use; 9, special idiom.

6. wollen:

1. **Er will nicht gehorchen.**
He won't (refuses to) obey.

2. **Er will morgen abreisen.**
He intends to go tomorrow.

3. **Er wollte eben gehen.**
He was just about to go.

4. **Das Auto will einfach nicht starten.**
The car simply won't start.

5. **Er will in Indien gewesen sein.**
He claims that he has been in India.

6. **Ich will das Buch nicht.**
I don't want the book.

7. **Ich habe nicht gewollt.**
I didn't want to.

1 denotes exertion of will on the part of the subject; 2, intention; 3, 4, impending action or event; 5, assertion or claim not vouched for by the speaker; 6, transitive use; 7, absolute use.

7. lassen:

1. **Lassen Sie uns fortgehen!**
Let us go away.

2. **Man hat ihn reden lassen.**
He was allowed to speak.

3. **Der Professor ließ den Kandidaten durch die Prüfung fallen.**
The professor failed the candidate.

4. **Ich lasse mir einen Anzug machen.**
I have a suit made.

5. **Es läßt sich nicht leugnen.**
It cannot be denied.

6. **Das läßt sich leicht machen.**
That is easily done.

1, imperative use; 2, permission; 3, 4, causative use; 5, 6, impersonal reflexive use.

NOTE: After **lassen** the infinitive of transitive verbs has passive force, as in examples 4, 5, 6, above.

231. The Subjunctive Mood

The subjunctive is the mood of indirect statement and of supposed or unreal condition.

232. The Present and Imperfect Subjunctive of haben, sein, werden

Present		*Imperfect*	
I have, may have, etc.		I had, might have, etc.	
(see §235, 2)		(see §235, 2)	
ich habe	wir haben	ich hätte	wir hätten
du habest	ihr habet	du hättest	ihr hättet
er		er	
sie } habe	sie haben	sie } hätte	sie hätten
es		es	

I am, may be, etc.		I was, might be, etc.	
ich sei	wir seien	ich wäre	wir wären
du sei(e)st	ihr sei(e)t	du wär(e)st	ihr wär(e)t
er		er	
sie } sei	sie seien	sie } wäre	sie wären
es		es	

(The forms **seist, seit, wärst, wärt,** are more usual nowadays than **seiest, seiet, wärest, wäret.**)

I become, may become, etc.		I became, might become, etc.	
ich werde	wir werden	ich würde	wir würden
du werdest	ihr werdet	du würdest	ihr würdet
er		er	
sie } werde	sie werden	sie } würde	sie würden
es		es	

1. Note the persistent **e** of the present-tense endings; also the umlaut of the imperfect.

2. These tenses of **haben, sein,** and **werden** serve to form the compound tenses of other verbs (see §233).

233. Subjunctive of **machen** (Weak Verb) **sprechen, fallen** (Strong Verbs)

Present

I make, may make, etc.	I speak, may speak, etc.	I fall, may fall, etc.
ich mache	ich spreche	ich falle
du machest	du sprechest	du fallest
er ⎫ sie ⎬ mache es ⎭	er ⎫ sie ⎬ spreche es ⎭	er ⎫ sie ⎬ falle es ⎭
wir machen	wir sprechen	wir fallen
ihr machet	ihr sprechet	ihr fallet
sie machen	sie sprechen	sie fallen

Imperfect

I made, might make, etc.	I spoke, might speak, etc.	I fell, might fall, etc.
ich machte	ich spräche	ich fiele
du machtest	du sprächest	du fielest
er ⎫ sie ⎬ machte es ⎭	er ⎫ sie ⎬ spräche es ⎭	er ⎫ sie ⎬ fiele es ⎭
wir machten	wir sprächen	wir fielen
ihr machtet	ihr sprächet	ihr fielet
sie machten	sie sprächen	sie fielen

Perfect

I have (may have) made, spoken, etc.	I have (may have) fallen, etc.
ich habe gemacht, gesprochen	ich sei gefallen
du habest gemacht, gesprochen	du sei(e)st gefallen
er habe gemacht, gesprochen, etc.	er sei gefallen, etc.

Pluperfect

I had (might have) made, spoken, etc.	I had (might have) fallen, etc.
ich hätte gemacht, gesprochen **du hättest gemacht, gesprochen,** etc.	**ich wäre gefallen** **du wär(e)st gefallen**, etc.

Future

I shall make, speak, fall, etc.

ich werde machen, sprechen, fallen
du werdest machen, sprechen, fallen
er werde machen, sprechen, fallen, etc.

Future Perfect

I shall have made (spoken), etc.

ich werde gemacht (gesprochen) haben
du werdest gemacht (gesprochen) haben, etc.

I shall have fallen, etc.

ich werde gefallen sein,
du werdest gefallen sein, etc.

1. Note the persistent **e** of the endings.
2. The imperfect subjunctive of all regular weak verbs is the same as the imperfect indicative.
3. Strong verbs with **a, o, u** in the imperfect indicative stem take umlaut in the imperfect subjunctive (see §246).

NOTE: In some verbs the vowel of the imperfect subjunctive does not correspond to that of the imperfect indicative: **helfen**, 'to help', imperfect indicative **half**, imperfect subjunctive **hülfe**; some have double forms: **gewinnen**, 'to win', imperfect indicative **gewann**, imperfect subjunctive **gewänne** or **gewönne**; see Alphabetical List in §246. See also the irregular weak verbs listed in §197.

4. The compound tenses are formed by adding the past participle or the infinitive, or both, to the auxiliary, precisely as in the indicative (for word order, see §192).

234. The Use of the Subjunctive in Main Clauses

1. In main clauses the present subjunctive is used
(a) in the first and third persons, to express a wish or a hope:

Hoffen wir es!
Let us hope so!

Geheiligt sei dein Name!
Hallowed be Thy name!

Der Talisman bringe dir Glück! (*literary*)
May the talisman bring you good luck!

NOTE: The last example may also be expressed by using a modal
auxiliary—**Der Talisman möge dir Glück bringen!** or **Möge dir der
Talisman Glück bringen!**

(b) to replace the missing persons of the imperative (see
§238, 1):

Es lebe der König!
Long live the king!

2. The imperfect or pluperfect subjunctive is used to express
(a) possibility:

Er wäre ein ausgezeichneter Lehrer.
He would make an excellent teacher.

Mit diesem Auto könntest du an einem Rennen teilnehmen.
With this car you could take part in a race.

(b) doubt or a (sometimes rhetorical) question:

Was für einen Sinn hätte es, ihm noch mehr Geld zu geben?
What sense would there be in giving him even more
money?

(c) (i) a wish, (ii) the impossibility of fulfilment of a wish:

Ich hätte gern ein neues Kleid.
I should like to have a new dress.

Hätte er doch nicht diese ehrgeizige Frau geheiratet!
If only he hadn't married that ambitious woman!

(*d*) an imaginary situation (non-reality):

Fast hätte ich das Verkehrszeichen übersehen.
I nearly didn't notice the traffic signal.

Es wäre besser gewesen, das Haus zu verkaufen.
It would have been better to sell the house.

(*e*) conditional and qualified statements:

An deiner Stelle täte ich das nicht.
If I were you I should not do that.

Ohne die Unterstützung seiner Eltern hätte er nie sein Studium beendet.
Without the support of his parents he would never have completed his studies.

235. The Use of the Subjunctive in Dependent Clauses

1. The use of the subjunctive is more common with dependent than with main clauses. It is used, for example, to express purpose—especially after a past tense in the governing clause—with the conjunction **damit** (occasionally **daß**):

Wir gaben ihm eine Liste, damit er nichts vergäße.
We gave him a list so that he would not forget anything.

NOTE: 1. Although the above sentence is strictly correct, it is usual in modern German to avoid the subjunctive in such dependent clauses and to use the indicative instead. Thus the above sentence would nowadays use **vergaß** rather than **vergäße**.

2. If the subject is the same in the governing and dependent clauses the subjunctive is usually replaced by **um ... zu** + infinitive: **Er beeilte sich, um nicht zu spät zu kommen.**

2. The English forms with 'may' and 'might' in the tables in §232 only partially and occasionally represent the exact force of the German subjunctive:

Er sagte, daß er jetzt mehr Geld habe.
He said he now had more money.

Ich habe oft gewünscht, daß ich mehr Geld hätte.
I have often wished that I had (might have) more money.

236. Indirect Statements and Questions

Er sagt: „Ich bin müde."	He says: "I am tired."
Er sagt, daß er müde sei.	He says (that) he is tired.
Er sagte: „Ich bin müde."	He said: "I am tired."
Er sagte, daß er müde sei.	He said (that) he was tired.
Er fragte: „Wer ist da?"	He asked: "Who is there?"
Er fragte, wer da sei.	He asked who was there.
Ich fragte, ob er müde sei.	I asked if (whether) he was tired.
Sie sagten, daß sie niemals Fleisch äßen.	They said that they never ate meat.
Er sagte, er sei müde.	He said (that) he was tired.

1. Indirect statements and questions are dependent clauses, and have the word order of such clauses (§163)—but see 5, below.

2. The verb of the dependent clause is usually in the subjunctive if the verb of the governing clause is in a past tense, and, unlike English, normally retains the same tense which it would have if the statement or question were direct.

NOTE: 1. In North Germany, there is a distinct preference for the imperfect subjunctive in reported speech (*e.g.* **Er sagte, daß er müde wäre**); this construction, however, is not regarded as standard German.

2. The indicative is used in indirect statement (= reported speech) to express a fact as undisputed or as vouched for by the speaker— *e.g.* **Er sagt, daß er müde ist.**

3. Where the present subjunctive of a verb has no forms distinct from those of its present indicative, the imperfect subjunctive is used instead of the present, as in the last example but one above.

4. 'If' or 'whether' in indirect questions=**ob.**

5. The conjunction **daß** may be omitted in clauses of indirect statement, which then have the word order of a principal clause (verb second), as in the last example above. **Daß** cannot, however, be omitted if the verb in the main clause is in the negative.

237. The Imperative Mood

The imperative expresses command or entreaty.

238. The Imperative of **machen, singen**

mach! or **mache!** make!	**sing!** *or* **singe!** sing!
er mache!⎫ **mache er!**⎭ let him make!	**er singe!**⎫ **singe er!**⎭ let him sing!
machen wir! let us make!	**singen wir!** let us sing!
macht! make!	**singt!** sing!
machen sie! let them make!	**singen sie!** let them sing!
machen Sie! make!	**singen Sie!** sing!

1. The only true imperative forms are the second person singular and the second person plural; the remaining forms are present subjunctives used with imperative force.

2. The imperative of most verbs (weak and strong) is formed as above.

3. In the **du** form the **-e** is often omitted, especially in speech.

4. In modern usage, the spelling with an apostrophe in the **du** form (*mach'!*) is to be avoided.

5. The imperative of the **ihr** and **Sie** forms is identical with the corresponding forms in the present tense.

6. The pronoun of the third person singular more commonly precedes, but **Sie** always follows; the third person plural (= 'let them') is very rare.

NOTE: If contrast or emphasis is required in the second person, the pronouns **du** or **ihr** may be added after the imperative —*e.g.*, **Sprich du mit ihm!** '*You* speak to him!'; **Antwortet ihr ihm!** '*You* answer him!'

239. The Imperative with **lassen**

The imperative of the verb **lassen,** 'to let', is used as an auxiliary, with the force of an imperative, to replace the third person singular and plural and the first person plural, as follows:

laß	(2nd sing.)⎫	
laßt	(2nd plur.)⎬ **uns bleiben!** let us remain!
lassen Sie	(formal) ⎭	

240. **Sollen** as Imperative

In persons other than the first person, **sollen** is equivalent to an emphatic imperative (='shall' or 'are to', etc.), unless interrogative:

Du sollst nicht stehlen.	Thou shalt not steal.
Er soll kommen.	He is to (shall) come.

241. Substitutes for the Imperative

Besides the use of **lassen** and **sollen** with imperative force (§§239, 240), other substitutes for the imperative are:

1. the present (and occasionally the future) indicative:

Du bleibst! ⎫
Du wirst bleiben! ⎭
You stay! You'll stay!

Du bist jetzt still, Wolfgang!
Will you be quiet, Wolfgang!

Du gehst jetzt nicht weg!
You're not going away now!

2. the present passive:

Vor Taschendieben wird gewarnt!
Beware of pickpockets!
See §245, 2 (note 2).

3. (in exclamatory clauses) the infinitive:

Alle (*or* Alles) aussteigen!	**Nicht hinauslehnen!**
All change!	Do not lean out of the window!

4. (in exclamatory clauses) the past participle:

Hiergeblieben!	**Stillgestanden!**
Stay here!	Stand still!

5. an adverb or adverbial phrase:

Schneller!	**Lauter!**	**Kopf weg!**
Faster!	Louder!	Mind your head!

Auf die Plätze, fertig, los!
On your marks, get set, go!

6. a noun:

Achtung!	**Vorsicht!**	**Ruhe!**
Look out!	Be careful!	Silence!

242. The Passive Voice

The passive voice is the active voice inverted—that is, the direct object of the active becomes the subject of the passive, and the active subject becomes the agent; hence only transitive verbs can have a true passive.

243. The Passive with **werden**

Present Indicative	*Imperfect Indicative*
I am (being) praised, etc.	I was (being) praised, etc.

ich werde ⎫		ich wurde ⎫	
du wirst ⎪		du wurdest ⎪	
er ⎫ ⎪		er ⎫ ⎪	
sie ⎬ wird ⎬ gelobt		sie ⎬ wurde ⎬ gelobt	
es ⎭ ⎪		es ⎭ ⎪	
wir werden ⎪		wir wurden ⎪	
ihr werdet ⎪		ihr wurdet ⎪	
Sie werden ⎪		Sie wurden ⎪	
sie werden ⎭		sie wurden ⎭	

Present Infinitive: **gelobt (zu) werden,** to be praised.

1. This passive is formed by means of **werden** (= 'to become') + the past participle of the verb to be conjugated.

2. In accordance with the meaning of **werden,** this form of the passive indicates a passing into and continuing in a state or condition.

3. It is used whenever agency is specified or implied; the personal agent is denoted by **von**+dative; other agency by **durch** or **mit**:

Kleine Jungen werden oft von den größeren tyrannisiert.
Small boys are often bullied by the bigger ones.

Die Flüsse werden durch Abwässer verschmutzt.
The rivers are polluted by sewage.

Die Rechnung wurde mit einem Scheck bezahlt.
The bill was paid by cheque.

244. The Passive with sein

1. A passive is also formed by means of the various tenses of **sein**+the past participle of the verb to be conjugated.

2. This form of the passive indicates a state or condition regarded as complete and permanent, and as resulting from the action of the verb; it is never used when agency is expressed or implied, and must be carefully distinguished from the passive with **werden**:

Das Fenster ist geschlossen.
The window is closed (*state*).

Das Fenster wird jetzt geöffnet.
The window is now being opened.

Ein Kind wird geboren.
A child is born.

Ich bin am 24. Dezember 1928 geboren.
I was born on 24th December 1928.

But also: **Ich wurde am 24. Dezember 1928 geboren.**

Er war gelangweilt.
He was bored.

But occasionally a permanent condition is expressed by the passive with **werden**:

Amerika wird durch den Atlantischen Ozean von Europa getrennt.
America is separated from Europe by the Atlantic Ocean.

245. Limitations of the Passive

1. When the direct object of a transitive verb is a thing (not a person), the thing becomes the subject in the passive, the person remaining as indirect object:

Sie versprachen mir Hilfe (*active*).
They promised me help.

Mir wurde von ihnen Hilfe versprochen (*passive*).
I was promised help by them.

Ihm wurde der Photoapparat abgenommen.
The camera was taken away from him.

Der Kaffee wurde ihr gebracht.
The coffee was brought to her.

NOTE: Verbs having only an indirect personal object in German (often transitive in English) have no passive form: **Der Hund folgte ihm,** 'He was followed by the dog'.

2. Purely intransitive verbs can have a passive in the impersonal form only:

Es wurde gestern getanzt.⎫
Gestern wurde getanzt. ⎬ There was dancing yesterday.

Ich glaube, daß jetzt getanzt wird.
I think there is dancing going on now.

Es wurde viel gelacht.
There was a great deal of laughing.

In der Diskussion wurde viel durcheinandergeredet.
In the discussion there was a lot of confused speaking.

NOTE: 1. **Es** of this construction is omitted, unless it immediately precedes the verb; the impersonal construction is sparingly used, and is usually replaced by the **man** construction (§100).
2. The impersonal passive is sometimes used to express a command (especially to children): **Jetzt wird gegessen und nicht gealbert!** 'Get on with your meal and don't play about!'; **Jetzt wird gearbeitet, geschlafen,** etc., 'Now it is time to work, sleep', etc. See also §241, 2.

3. The passive is much less used in German than in English, being often replaced by a **man** construction (§100) and occasionally by a reflexive, especially with **lassen:**

Es wird sich schon finden.
It will doubtless be found.

Das läßt sich leicht machen.
That can easily be done.

With certain verbs the passive is replaced by the active +
past participle:

Er bekam es viele Male gesagt, nicht zu spät zu kommen.
He was told on many occasions not to arrive late.

Ich bekam heute ein Paket geschickt.
I received a parcel today.

Sie führten ihn gefesselt herein.
They brought him in in chains.

246. Alphabetical List of Strong and Irregular Verbs

1. The following list contains only verbs in common use.

2. Compound verbs are omitted, as a rule, and their conjugation is to be inferred from that of the corresponding simple verb—e.g., **verbinden,** see **binden; betrügen,** see **trügen;** but compounds which have no corresponding simple verbs will be found in the list.

3. The vowel of the 2nd and 3rd persons singular present indicative and of the 2nd person singular imperative is given only when it differs from that of the infinitive.

4. The vowel of the imperfect subjunctive is given only when it differs from that of the imperfect indicative.

5. Forms in parenthesis are less usual.

6. Verbs followed by (*sein*) are conjugated with **sein** only; those followed by (*sein, haben*) are sometimes conjugated with **haben** (§217, 2); all others with **haben** only.

Infinitive	Imperfect Indic.	Past Part.	Pres. Ind.	Imperative	Imperf. Subj.
backen, bake	backte or **buk**	gebacken	a or ä		

Infinitive	Imper-fect Indic.	Past Part.	Pres. Ind.	Impera-tive	Imperf. Subj.
befehlen, command	befahl	befohlen	ie	ie	ä or ö
beginnen, begin	begann	begonnen			ä or ö
beißen, bite	biß	gebissen			
bergen, hide	barg	geborgen	i	i	ä or ü
bersten (sein), burst	barst (borst)	geborsten	i	i	ä (ö)
bewegen[1], induce	bewog	bewogen			
biegen, bend	bog	gebogen			
bieten, offer	bot	geboten			
binden, bind	band	gebunden			
bitten, ask	bat	gebeten			
blasen, blow	blies	geblasen	ä		
bleiben (sein), remain	blieb	geblieben			
braten, roast	briet	gebraten	ä		
brechen, break	brach	gebrochen	i	i	
brennen, burn	brannte	gebrannt			brennte
bringen, bring	brachte	gebracht			
denken, think	dachte	gedacht			
dreschen, thresh	drosch	gedroschen	i	i	
dringen, press	drang	gedrungen			
dünken, seem	deuchte or dünkte	gedeucht or gedünkt	dünkt or deucht		
dürfen, may	durfte	gedurft	darf, darfst, darf		
empfehlen, recom-mend: see befehlen					
erbleichen (sein), turn pale	erblich	erblichen			
erlöschen[2] (sein), be extinguished	erlosch	erloschen	i	i	
erschallen,[3] resound	erscholl	erschollen			
erschrecken[4] (sein), be frightened	erschrak	erschrocken	i	i	
essen, eat	aß	gegessen	i	i	
fahren (sein, haben), go, drive	fuhr	gefahren	ä		
fallen (sein), fall	fiel	gefallen	ä		
fangen, catch	fing	gefangen	ä		
fechten, fight	focht	gefochten	i	i	
finden, find	fand	gefunden			
flechten, plait	flocht	geflochten	i	i	

Infinitive	Imperfect Indic.	Past Part.	Pres. Ind.	Imperative	Imperf. Subj.
fliegen[5] (sein), fly	flog	geflogen			
fliehen (sein), flee	floh	geflohen			
fließen (sein), flow	floß	geflossen			
fressen, eat	fraß	gefressen	i	i	
frieren (sein, haben), freeze	fror	gefroren			
gebären, bear	gebar	geboren	ä (ie)	ä (ie)	
geben, give	gab	gegeben	i	i	
gedeihen (sein), thrive	gedieh	gediehen			
gehen (sein), go, walk	ging	gegangen			
gelingen (sein), succeed	gelang	gelungen			
gelten, be worth	galt	gegolten	i	i	ä or ö
genesen (sein), recover	genas	genesen			
genießen, enjoy	genoß	genossen			
geraten (sein), get into: see raten					
geschehen (sein), happen	geschah	geschehen	ie		
gewinnen, win	gewann	gewonnen			ä or ö
gießen, pour	goß	gegossen			
gleichen, be like	glich	geglichen			
gleiten[6] (sein), glide	glitt	geglitten			
graben, dig	grub	gegraben	ä		
greifen, seize	griff	gegriffen			
haben, have	hatte	gehabt	hast, hat		
halten, hold	hielt	gehalten	ä		
hängen, hangen, hang	hing	gehangen	ä		
hauen, hew	hieb	gehauen			
heben, lift	hob	gehoben			
heißen, be called; command	hieß	geheißen; heißen			
helfen, help	half	geholfen; helfen	i	i	ä or ü
kennen, know	kannte	gekannt			kennte
klingen, sound	klang	geklungen			
kneifen, pinch	kniff	gekniffen			
kommen (sein), come	kam	gekommen			
können, can	konnte	gekonnt; können	kann, kannst, kann		

Infinitive	Imper-fect Indic.	Past Part.	Pres. Ind.	Impera-tive	Imperf. Subj.
kriechen[5] (sein), creep	kroch	gekrochen			
laden, load; invite	lud	geladen	ä		
lassen, let	ließ	gelassen	ä		
laufen (sein, haben), run	lief	gelaufen	äu		
leiden[7], suffer	litt	gelitten			
leihen, lend	lieh	geliehen			
lesen, read	las	gelesen	ie	ie	
liegen, lie, be	lag	gelegen			
lügen, tell a lie	log	gelogen			
meiden, shun	mied	gemieden			
melken[3], milk	molk	gemolken	i	i	
messen, measure	maß	gemessen	i	i	
mißlingen, fail: see gelingen					
mögen, may; like	mochte	gemocht; mögen	mag, magst, mag		
müssen, must	mußte	gemußt; müssen	muß, mußt, muß		
nehmen, take	nahm	genommen	nimmst, nimmt	nimm!	
nennen, name	nannte	genannt			nennte
pfeifen, whistle	pfiff	gepfiffen			
preisen, praise	pries	gepriesen			
quellen (sein), gush out	quoll	gequollen	i	i	
raten, advise	riet	geraten	ä		
reiben, rub	rieb	gerieben			
reißen (haben, sein), tear	riß	gerissen			
reiten[8] (sein, haben), ride	ritt	geritten			
rennen (sein, haben), run	rannte	gerannt			rennte
riechen, smell	roch	gerochen			
ringen[9], wring; wrestle	rang	gerungen			
rinnen (sein), flow	rann	geronnen			ä or ö
rufen, call	rief	gerufen			
saufen, drink	soff	gesoffen	äu		
saugen, suck	sog	gesogen			
schaffen[10], create	schuf	geschaffen			
schallen[3] (sein, haben), sound	scholl	geschallt			

Infinitive	Imper-fect Indic.	Past Part.	Pres. Ind.	Impera-tive	Imperf. Subj.
scheiden (*haben, sein*), part	schied	geschieden			
scheinen, shine	schien	geschienen			
schelten, scold	schalt	gescholten	i	i	ö
scheren[11], shear	schor	geschoren			
schieben, shove	schob	geschoben			
schießen, shoot	schoß	geschossen			
schlafen, sleep	schlief	geschlafen	ä		
schlagen[12], strike	schlug	geschlagen	ä		
schleichen (*sein*), creep	schlich	geschlichen			
schleifen[10], grind	schliff	geschliffen			
schließen, shut	schloß	geschlossen			
schlingen, tie; swallow	schlang	geschlungen			
schmeißen, fling	schmiß	geschmissen			
schmelzen[13] (*sein, haben*), melt	schmolz	geschmolzen	i	i	
schneiden, cut	schnitt	geschnitten			
schreiben, write	schrieb	geschrieben			
schreien, scream	schrie	geschrie(e)n			
schreiten (*sein*), stride	schritt	geschritten			
schweigen, be silent	schwieg	geschwiegen			
schwellen[14] (*sein*), swell	schwoll	geschwollen	i	i	
schwimmen (*sein, haben*), swim	schwamm	ge-schwommen			ä *or* ö
schwinden (*sein*), decline	schwand	geschwunden			
schwingen, swing	schwang	geschwungen			
schwören, swear	schwor *or* schwur	geschworen			ü
sehen, see	sah	gesehen; sehen	ie	ie	
sein (*sein*), be	war	gewesen	bin, bist, ist	sei!	
senden[3], send	sandte	gesandt			sendete
sieden[3], boil	sott	gesotten			
singen, sing	sang	gesungen			
sinken (*sein*), sink	sank	gesunken			
sinnen, think	sann	gesonnen			ä *or* ö
sitzen, sit	saß	gesessen			

Infinitive	Imperfect Indic.	Past Part.	Pres. Ind.	Imperative	Imperf. Subj.
sollen, ought, shall, am to	sollte	gesollt; sollen	soll, sollst, soll		o
speien, spit	spie	gespie(e)n			
spinnen, spin	spann	gesponnen			ä or ö
sprechen, speak	sprach	gesprochen	i	i	
sprießen (sein, haben), sprout	sproß	gesprossen			
springen (sein, haben), spring	sprang	gesprungen			
stechen, prick	stach	gestochen	i	i	
stecken[15], stick	stak	gesteckt			
stehen, stand	stand	gestanden			ä or ü
stehlen, steal	stahl	gestohlen	ie	ie	ä or ö
steigen (sein), climb	stieg	gestiegen			
sterben (sein), die	starb	gestorben	i	i	ü
stinken, stink	stank	gestunken			
stoßen (haben, sein), push	stieß	gestoßen	ö		
streichen, stroke	strich	gestrichen			
streiten, fight	stritt	gestritten			
tragen, carry; wear	trug	getragen	ä		
treffen, hit; meet	traf	getroffen	i	i	
treiben, drive	trieb	getrieben			
treten, step (sein); kick (haben)	trat	getreten	trittst, tritt	tritt!	
triefen[15] (sein, haben), drip	troff	getroffen			
trinken, drink	trank	getrunken			
trügen, deceive	trog	getrogen			
tun, do	tat	getan			
verbleichen, grow pale	verblich	verblichen			
verderben[16] (sein), spoil	verdarb	verdorben	i	i	ü
verdrießen, vex	verdroß	verdrossen			
vergessen, forget	vergaß	vergessen	i	i	
verlieren, lose	verlor	verloren			
verzeihen, pardon	verzieh	verziehen			
wachsen (sein), grow	wuchs	gewachsen	ä		
wägen, weigh	wog	gewogen			
waschen, wash	wusch	gewaschen	ä		
weben[3], weave	wob	gewoben			
weichen[17] (sein), yield	wich	gewichen			

Infinitive	Imperfect Indic.	Past Part.	Pres. Ind.	Imperative	Imperf. Subj.
weisen, show	wies	gewiesen			
wenden[3], turn	wandte	gewandt			wendete
werben, advertise; woo	warb	geworben	i	i	ü
werden (sein), become	wurde (Poet: ward)	geworden; worden	wirst, wird		würde
werfen, throw	warf	geworfen	i	i	ü
wiegen, weigh	wog	gewogen			
winden, wind	wand	gewunden			
wissen, know	wußte	gewußt	weiß, weißt, weiß		
wollen, will, wish	wollte	gewollt; wollen	will, willst, will		wollte
wringen, wring	wrang	gewrungen			
ziehen, draw (haben); move (sein)	zog	gezogen			
zwingen, compel	zwang	gezwungen			

[1] bewegen, 'move', is weak. [2] löschen, 'extinguish', is weak. [3] Also regular weak. [4] Weak when transitive (='frighten'). [5] Has also **eu** for **ie** in 3rd person singular present indicative in poetic diction. [6] begleiten, 'accompany', is weak. [7] verleiden, 'spoil', is weak. [8] bereiten, 'prepare', is weak. [9] umringen, 'surround', is weak. [10] In other senses weak. [11] bescheren, 'to give presents', is weak. [12] beratschlagen, 'deliberate', is weak. [13] schmelzen, 'smelt', is sometimes weak. [14] Weak when transitive. [15] Mostly weak nowadays. [16] Past participle may be weak in a moral context—e.g. verderbte Jugend, 'corrupt youth.' [17] weichen, 'soften', is weak.

VII. ADVERBS

247. General Remarks

Adverbs are indeclinable words which express *how*, *when*, or *where* an action is performed or a situation exists—*e.g.* 'he coughed *loudly*', 'he left *yesterday*', 'the museum is *nearby*'. These are known as adverbs of *manner*, *time* and *place* respectively. There are also adverbs of *degree*, which tell the degree or extent to which they apply—*e.g.* '*too* much', '*very* little', '*practically* nil'.

In English, adverbs are often formed by adding '-ly' to the corresponding adjective (*e.g.* 'pleasant—pleasantly'), but in German, adjectival and adverbial forms are commonly identical: for example, **gut** may mean either 'good' (adjective) or 'well' (adverb). Other German adverbs are formed by means of suffixes added to other parts of speech—*e.g.* **ein**mal ('once'), **sicher***lich* ('certainly'), **möglicher***weise* ('possibly'), **vier***fach* ('fourfold'), **rück***wärts* ('backwards'); see §249. In addition, there are a number of very common monosyllabic adverbs, such as **schon** ('already'), **fast** ('almost'), **bald** ('soon'), **gern** ('willingly'), **ganz** ('quite').

In German an adverb may modify (i) a verb: **sie singt gut**, 'she sings well'; (ii) another adverb: **sie singt sehr gut**, 'she sings very well'; (iii) an adjective: **dieser Anzug ist ziemlich teuer**, 'this suit is rather expensive'; (iv) a preposition: **ich muß gleich nach dem Mittagessen wegfahren**, 'I must leave immediately after lunch'. It may also be used alone, with imperative force—*e.g.* **Herein!**, 'Come in!', **Vorwärts!**, 'Forward!' Some adverbs may be used predicatively — *e.g.* **Alles Bemühen um Rettung war vergebens (or umsonst)**, 'Every attempt at rescue was in vain', **Die Schule ist aus**, 'School is over'.

248. Formation of Adverbs

There are three main classes of adverbs in German:

1. those which comprise the oldest, most basic and most often used group, many of which are monosyllabic. Examples:

234

jetzt, 'now', **nun,** 'now', **dann,** 'then', **noch,** 'still', **oft,** 'often', **kaum,** 'scarcely', **sonst,** 'formerly' or 'usually' or 'otherwise', **je,** 'ever', **wieder,** 'again'; cf. also the adverbs treated in §§256–273.

2. those which are formed by the addition of suffixes to other parts of speech—see §249, also §§282, 286.

3. those which are identical with uninflected adjectival and participial forms—see §250.

249. Adverbial Suffixes

The following are among the commonest adverbial suffixes in German:

1. **-lich:** Equivalent to the English suffix '-ly', both as adjective (*e.g.* **ein freundliches Lächeln,** 'a friendly smile') and adverb (*e.g.* **ich bin ihm kürzlich begegnet,** 'I recently met him'). Other adverbs ending in the suffix **-lich** are: **sicherlich,** 'certainly', **lediglich,** 'solely', 'simply', **schwerlich,** 'hardly', 'scarcely', **treulich,** 'faithfully', **freilich,** 'of course', **kürzlich,** 'not long ago', **ewiglich,** 'eternally', **bitterlich,** 'bitterly', **bekanntlich,** 'as is well known'.

2. **-s:** Adverbs ending in the suffix **-s** may be derived either from adjectives (*e.g.* **anders,** 'otherwise', **rechts,** 'on the right', **links,** 'on the left', **besonders,** 'particularly') or from nouns (*e.g.* **anfangs,** 'in the beginning', **nachmittags,** 'in the afternoon', **abends,** 'in the evening'), or from a combination of both (*e.g.* **jedenfalls,** 'in any case', **meistenteils,** 'for the most part', **allerdings,** 'certainly').

3. **-lings:** Derived from nouns (mostly now obsolete) with genitive singular **-s** endings. Examples: **blindlings,** 'blindly', 'headlong', **jählings,** 'suddenly', 'abruptly', **rücklings,** 'from behind', **rittlings,** 'astride', **meuchlings,** 'treacherously'.

4. **-weise:** Cf. the English suffix '-wise' (or '-ways'), as in 'crosswise', 'crossways', **kreuzweise.** It is therefore commonly found among adverbs of manner—*e.g.* **teilweise,** 'partly', **stückweise,** 'piecemeal', **glücklicherweise,** 'fortunately', **ausnahmsweise,** 'by way of exception', **vorzugsweise,** 'for preference'.

5. **-maßen:** This suffix is occasionally used to form adverbs of

manner, in the same way as **-weise** above—*e.g.* **(un)verdienter-maßen**, '(un)deservedly'—but is more frequent in adverbs of degree—*e.g.* **einigermaßen**, 'to some extent', **dermaßen (,daß ...)**, 'to such a degree (that ...)'.

6. **-halb, -halben**: (*a*) A number of adverbs ending in **-halb** or **-halben** convey the sense of 'on account of'—*e.g.* **deshalb**, 'on that account', 'for that reason', **seinethalben**, 'on his account', 'for his sake', **meinethalben**, 'on my account', 'for my sake.' (*b*) The suffix **-halb** is also used adverbially (as well as prepositionally) in such words as **außerhalb**, 'outside', **innerhalb**, 'inside', **oberhalb**, 'above', **unterhalb**, 'below'.

7. **-wärts**: Cf. English '-ward(s)', as in 'forward(s)', **vorwärts**, and 'backward(s)', **rückwärts**. Other examples: **seitwärts**, 'sideways', **abwärts**, 'downward(s)', **einwärts**, 'inward(s)', **auswärts**, 'outward(s)', **nordwärts**, 'northward(s)', **südwärts**, 'southward(s)'.

8. **-e**: Formerly common, this suffix is now usually omitted, being regarded as archaic or poetical (*e.g.* **balde** for **bald**, 'soon', **stille** for **still**, 'peacefully'); but it still survives in a few adverbs, such as **gerne** (or **gern**), 'willingly', **nahe** (or **nah**), 'near(by)', and **lange** (or **lang**), 'long', where the **-e** form is much preferred.

NOTE: For the adverbial suffixes **-mal** and **-ens**, see §§282 and 286 respectively. For adjectival suffixes, see §149.

250. Adjective as Adverb

1. Most adjectives may be used as adverbs in German without change. Thus **schön** = 'beautiful' or 'beautifully', **scharf** = 'sharp' or 'sharply'. Other examples:

Sie singt gut.	She sings well.
Er lernt schnell.	He learns quickly.
Ich arbeite langsam.	I am working slowly.

2. Participles used as adjectives can also be used as adverbs:

Das ist eine *fesselnd* geschriebene Geschichte.
This is a fascinatingly written story.

Ein Kind fragte *weinend* etwas, und eine Stimme antwortete *beruhigend*.
A child asked something tearfully, and a voice answered soothingly.

Ich habe ihn gestern ganz *unverhofft* getroffen.
I met him yesterday quite unexpectedly.

See also §214, 3.

251. Word Order

1. In a sentence containing two or more adverbs or adverbial phrases the normal word order is: time, manner, place:

Ich fahre morgen mit der Eisenbahn nach Frankfurt.
I am going by train to Frankfurt tomorrow.

2. Adverbial expressions of time precede noun objects and other adverbs, but not pronouns not governed by a preposition:

Ich habe heute kein Geld.
I have no money today.

Mein Vetter ist heute hier.
My cousin is here today.

Ich habe ihm gestern ein gutes Buch geschickt.
I sent him a good book yesterday.

3. When an adverb or adverbial phrase precedes the verb in a principal clause the subject comes after the verb, which is always the second idea (not necessarily the second word) in a principal assertive clause:

Heute ist das Wetter schön.
Today the weather is fine.

Eine Woche später wurden diese Stadtteile abgesperrt.
A week later these parts of the town were cordoned off.

4. The position of the adverb indicates its importance in the sentence:

Ich bin gestern ins Kino gegangen.
Gestern bin ich ins Kino gegangen.
Ins Kino bin ich gestern gegangen.

NOTE: The last example would only be used after the question **Wohin bist du gestern gegangen?** (with the stress on **wohin**), '*Where did you go yesterday?*'

5. The subject and finite verb of a main clause cannot be separated by an adverb in German, as they sometimes are in English:

Wir gehen manchmal ins Kino.
We sometimes go to the cinema.

Er kam gleich auf uns zu.
He immediately came towards us.

6. Adverbs follow pronouns:

Sie können das leicht verstehen.
They can easily understand that.

252. The Position of **nicht**

1. Generally, **nicht** is placed immediately before the word negated:

Das ist nicht wahr.
That is not true.

Ich konnte nicht eher kommen.
I could not come any sooner.

Nicht alle Leute sind so freigebig wie er.
Not everyone is as generous as he.

2. In a main clause **nicht** does not, however, immediately precede the finite verb it negates:

Gestern war ich nicht zu Hause.
Yesterday I was not at home.

Wir dürfen nicht kommen.
We are not allowed to come.

3. When the predicate as a whole is negated, **nicht** stands last except for an infinitive, past participle, or a predicative noun or adjective:

Er sieht den Wald vor lauter Bäumen nicht.
He can't see the wood for the trees.

Ich kann seine Haltung in dieser Sache nicht verstehen.
I can't understand his attitude in this matter.

Er war sich der Sensation, die er erregte, nicht bewußt.
He was not aware of the sensation he was causing.

253. Negative Adverbs

nein, no (*as opposed to* **ja,** 'yes')
nicht, not
noch nicht, not yet
gar nicht ⎫
ganz und gar nicht ⎬ not at all
überhaupt nicht ⎭
nicht mehr, no more, no longer
nie ⎫
niemals ⎭ never
nie und nimmer, never (*intensive*)
nie mehr ⎫
nie wieder ⎭ never again
noch nie, never (yet)
nirgends ⎫
nirgendwo ⎭ nowhere
keinesfalls, under no circumstances
keineswegs, not in the least
keinmal, not a single time

Er ist noch nicht angekommen.
He has not yet arrived.

Ich kann ihm überhaupt nicht mehr glauben.
I can't believe him at all any more.

Er kommt nie mehr nach Hause zurück.
He's never coming home again.

Nie und nimmer werde ich das vergessen.
I shall never, never forget that.

Nirgendwo war eine lebende Seele zu erblicken.
Nowhere was there a living soul to be seen.

Er will sich keinesfalls binden.
He does not want to tie himself down on any account.

Das stört mich keineswegs.
That doesn't bother me in the least.

Er hat mich keinmal besucht.
Not a single time did he visit me.

254. The Interrogative Adverbs **womit? wovon?** etc.

In the dative and accusative with prepositions, **was?** is replaced by **wo (wor** before vowels) prefixed to the preposition and written as one word with it:

Wodurch kann das erreicht werden?
By what means can that be achieved?

Womit soll ich anfangen?
What shall I start with?

Woran erkennt man ihn?
How (= by what) does one recognize him?

Worauf wartest du noch?
What are you waiting for?

Worin hast du meine Taschentücher gewaschen?
What did you wash my handkerchiefs in?

Worüber lachst du?
What are you laughing about?

Worum handelt es sich?
What is it (all) about?

Wovon spricht er?
What is he talking about?

Wozu soll das gut sein?
What is that supposed to be good for?

NOTE: In colloquial speech, the above interrogative forms are often replaced by the preposition with **was**—*e.g.*, **Um was** (for **Worum)** **handelt es sich?**

255. Some Other Interrogative Adverbs

1. **Weshalb?, weswegen?** 'on account of what?', 'why?'

Weshalb kommst du nicht mit?
Why don't you come too?

Weswegen müssen Sie schon so früh nach Hause?
Why must you go home so early?

NOTE: 1. **Wes** is an archaic form of **wessen**, surviving only in a few words and expressions—*e.g.*, **Wes Geistes Kind ist er?** 'What sort of a man is he?', **weshalb** and **weswegen.**
2. **Weshalb?** is in commoner use than **weswegen?**, but far commoner than either is **warum?** Note also **wieso**, identical in meaning but rather colloquial.

2. **Woher?, wohin?** 'where from?', 'where to?'

Woher stammt er? Where does he originate from?
Wohin gehen Sie? Where are you going (to)?

See also §205, 5 (*a*) and (*b*).

256. Idiomatic Uses of Adverbs

The following sections contain examples of the more difficult idiomatic uses of certain adverbs, namely:

auch	**gar**	**lauter**	**nur**
doch	**gern(e)**	**mal, einmal**	**schon**
eben	**irgend**	**nämlich**	**wohl**
erst	**ja**	**noch**	**zuerst**
	jetzt		

257. Auch

1. = 'also', 'too', 'in addition':

Er ist Schauspieler und auch Regisseur.
He is an actor and also a producer.

Ich bin müde.—Ich auch.
I am tired.—So am I.

2. = 'even':

Es war auch nicht das kleinste bißchen Staub auf den Möbeln.
There wasn't even the smallest speck of dust on the furniture.

Er ging fort, ohne auch nur auf Wiedersehen zu sagen.
He went away without even saying goodbye.

Auch das geringste Geräusch machte ihn nervös.
Even the slightest noise made him nervy.

NOTE: **Auch** does not cause inversion of verb and subject when, as in the last example above, it modifies a member of the sentence which precedes the verb.

3. (*concessive, corresponding to the English* '-ever'):

Wer auch immer es sein mag, er wird streng bestraft werden.
Whoever it may be, he will be severely punished.

Was auch geschieht, ich werde dir helfen.
Whatever happens I will help you.

Was er auch tut, er macht es ausgezeichnet.
Whatever he does, he does it excellently.

Wie dem auch sei, jetzt können wir nichts mehr daran ändern.
However that may be, there's nothing we can do about it now.

So nett er auch ist, er geht mir doch auf die Nerven.
However nice he is, he still gets on my nerves.

4. = 'really' (*often expressing a slight doubt*):

Kann ich mich aber auch darauf verlassen, daß du mich morgen um sechs Uhr weckst?

But can I really rely on your waking me at six o'clock tomorrow?

5. (*to confirm or explain a statement already made*):

Er hat uns nicht geschrieben, aber wir haben es auch nicht von ihm erwartet.

He has not written to us—but then, we didn't expect him to.

6. (*to express exasperation*):

Du bist auch nie zufrieden!

You're never satisfied, are you!

258. Doch

1. (*in answer to a negative question*) = 'yes' (cf. French '*si*'):

Hast du es nicht gehört?—Doch.

Didn't you hear it?—Yes, I did.

2. (*contradictory*) = 'but', 'nevertheless':

Ich fühle mich nicht wohl, doch krank bin ich nicht.

I don't feel well, but I'm not ill.

Ich habe es nicht getan.—Sie haben es ¹doch getan.

I didn't do it.—Yes, you did.

3. (*correcting statement, etc.*) = 'after all', 'all the same':

Er wird ¹doch kommen.

He will come after all.

4. (*urging, encouraging, etc.*) (*English verb stressed*):

Habe ich es doch gesagt!

I said so, didn't I!

Kommen Sie doch herein!

Do come in!

Ich stelle die Schüssel auf den Tisch.—Nicht doch! sie ist schmutzig!

I'll put the dish on the table.—Don't! it's dirty!

5. (*to express anxiety or uncertainty*):

Er wird doch kommen?

He will come, won't he?

6. (*for emphasis*) (*sometimes not translated*):

Denk doch nicht daran, es regt dich nur auf.
Don't think about it—it only upsets you.

7. (*optative*) = 'if only':

Hättest du es mir doch gesagt!
If only you had told me!

Wenn er doch einmal die Tür leise zumachen würde!
If only he would close the door quietly for once!

8. (*to express indignation*):

Das ist denn doch die Höhe!
Well, that's the limit!

9. **oder doch** = 'or at least', 'at all events':

Er ist krank oder doch nicht ganz gesund.
He is ill or at least not quite well.

259. Eben

1. (*stressed*) = 'just', 'exactly':

Eben das meine ich auch.
That's just what I think too.

2. (*stressed*) (*time*) = 'just', 'just now', 'a moment ago':

Das wollte ich eben sagen!
I was just going to say that!

Er ist eben (*more emphatic:* **soeben**) **angekommen.**
He has just (this moment) arrived.

Ich habe eben noch mit ihm gesprochen.
I was speaking to him just a moment ago.

3. (*unstressed*) (*underlining the obvious*) = 'simply', 'just':

**Die Kinder haben die ganze Wohnung auf den Kopf gestellt.
Man kann sie eben nicht allein lassen.**

The children have turned the whole house upside down. You simply can't leave them on their own.

4. (*stressed/unstressed*) = 'precisely', 'just (so)':

Und er wollte mitkommen?—Ja ¹eben! (*stressed*)
And he wanted to come too?—Precisely!

Das ¹ist es eben! (*unstressed*)
That's just it!

5. **nicht eben** (*unstressed*) = 'not exactly':

Sie ist nicht eben schön zu nennen.
You couldn't exactly call her beautiful.

260. Erst

1. = 'first', 'at first':

Erst denken, dann sprechen.
First think, then speak.

Erst wollte er nicht.
He didn't want to at first.

2. = 'only', 'only just':

Er ist gerade erst angekommen.
He has only just arrived.

Er ist erst vor drei Wochen angekommen.
He arrived only three weeks ago.

3. (*to emphasize a statement*) = 'really', 'just':

Wir haben immer viel zu tun, aber im Sommerschlußverkauf geht es erst richtig los.
We always have a lot to do, but in the summer sale it gets *really* busy.

4. = 'not until', 'not sooner than':

Er kommt erst am Freitag.
He isn't coming till Friday.

Er tat es erst, als er dazu aufgefordert wurde.
He did it only when he was called upon to.

    5. **wenn . . . erst (einmal)** = 'once . . .':

**Wenn er erst einmal seine Prüfung bestanden hat, werden wir
schon eine Stellung für ihn finden.**
Once he has passed his examination we shall find a job for him.

    6. **wenn . . . doch erst** = 'if only':

Wenn ich doch erst da wäre!
If only I were there!

261. Gar

    1. **gar nicht** = 'not at all', 'by no means':

Wir sind gar nicht zufrieden.
We are not at all satisfied.

Ich war gar nicht überrascht.
I was by no means surprised.

    2. **gar nichts** = 'nothing at all':

Ich weiß gar nichts von Landwirtschaft.
I know nothing at all about farming.

Ich habe gar nichts gegen ihn einzuwenden.
I have absolutely nothing against him.

    3. **ganz und gar** = 'completely', 'absolutely':

Er hat ganz und gar recht.
He is absolutely right.

Du bist wohl ganz und gar verrückt!
You must be stark, staring mad!

    4. = 'full', 'very' (*literary*):

Ich weiß es gar gut.
I know it full well.

Er hat gar wenig Takt.
He has precious little tact.

5. =**sogar**, 'even':

Es sind Seeschwalben oder (so)gar Sturmvögel.
They are terns or perhaps even petrels.

6. (*emotive particle*):

Gar manches Mal.
Many a time (and oft).

NOTE: 1. **Gar,** which is always intensive in character, is not normally stressed in verbal constructions but is always stressed in nonverbal constructions.
2. See also §138, 2, note 2.
3. **Gar** can also be an adjective, used predicatively only, meaning, of food, 'cooked', 'done', and also, of soil, processed substances, etc., 'ready for use'.

262. Gern(e)

1. ='gladly', 'willingly', 'readily':

Ich würde es gern tun.
I should gladly do it.

Das glaube ich gern.
I can readily believe that.

2. (*with verbs*) 'to like', 'to be fond of (someone, something, doing something)':

Sie hat ihn gern.
She is fond of him.

Ich esse gern Fisch.
I like fish.

Ich gehe gern ins Theater.
I like going to the theatre.

3. **gut und gern**='at least', 'easily':

Ich hätte gut und gern zweimal soviel essen können.
I could easily have eaten twice as much.

4. (*idioms*):

Das mag gern sein.
That may well be.

Man braucht schon einen halben Tag, um mit dem Auto von Paris nach Boulogne zu fahren.—Das glaube ich gern.
You really need half a day to drive from Paris to Boulogne.—
I can well believe that.

Haben Sie vielen Dank für Ihre Hilfe!—Gern geschehen!
Thank you very much for your help.—That's quite all right!
Don't mention it!

Kommen Sie doch auch morgen zu der Party!—Herzlich gern!
Do come to the party tomorrow.—Yes, I'd love to.

NOTE: The comparative and superlative forms of **gern** are irregular —**lieber, am liebsten: Er käme gern, er möchte** *lieber* **nicht kommen, er möchte** *am liebsten* **zu Hause bleiben,** 'He would like to come, he would *rather* not come, he would like *most of all* to stay at home'.

263. Irgend

1. = 'possibly' (*of frequent occurrence in conditional clauses*):

Ich werde kommen wenn irgend möglich.
I'll come if at all possible.

Ich werde kommen, wenn ich nur irgend Zeit finde.
I'll come if I can possibly find the time.

Kommen Sie so schnell wie Sie nur irgend können!
Come as quickly as you possibly can.

2. **Irgend** is also prefixed to a number of words with intensive indefinite force. The words may be

(*a*) Adverbs—*e.g.* **irgendeinmal,** 'sometime (or other)', **irgendwann,** 'some time', 'any time', **irgendwie,** 'somehow (or other)', **irgendwo,** 'somewhere (or other)', **irgendwoher,** 'from somewhere (or other)', **irgendwohin,** 'to some place (or other)'.

(b) Pronouns—*e.g.* **irgend etwas** *or* **irgendwas,** 'something', 'anything', **irgend jemand,** 'someone', 'anyone', **irgendeiner,** 'someone', 'anyone', **irgendwer,** 'someone'. Note that the pronominal element of each of the last three declines; thus their accusative forms are **irgend jemanden** (*or* **irgend jemand**—see §98), **irgendeinen, irgendeine, irgendeines,** and **irgendwen.**

(c) Adjectives—*e.g.* **irgendwelcher, irgendwelche, irgendwelches,** 'any', 'of any kind', as in the sentence **Bestehen irgendwelche Differenzen?** 'Are there any differences?', 'Are there differences of any kind?'

264. Ja

1. = 'yes':

Sind Sie hungrig?—Ja.
Are you hungry?—Yes.

2. (*to amplify a statement*) = 'indeed':

Das Ergebnis war überraschend, ja erstaunlich.
The result was surprising, indeed astonishing.

3. (*to emphasize the reason for what precedes*):

Du brauchst keinen Mantel mitzunehmen, es ist ja nicht kalt.
You don't need to take an overcoat, it's not cold.

4. (*to admonish*):

Tu ja, was ich dir sage.
Be sure to do what I tell you.

5. (*concessive*):

Ich möchte ihn ja nicht schlechtmachen, aber er ist einfach kein guter Schauspieler.
I should not like to run him down, but he simply is not a good actor.

6. (*confident assertion*):

Er soll sich ja nicht denken, daß er das Geld bekommt.
He mustn't think that he's going to get the money.

7. (*to reassure*):

Keine Angst, der Hund beißt ja nicht.
Don't worry, the dog doesn't bite.

265. Jetzt

1. = 'now', 'at the present time':

Sie muß jetzt eine alte Dame sein.
She must be an old lady now.

Jetzt haben wir alles, was wir brauchen.
Now we have everything we need.

2. (*immediate future*):

Was fange ich jetzt an?
What shall I do now?

Sie hören jetzt die dritte Sinfonie in Es-dur von Beethoven.
You will now hear Symphony No. 3 in E flat major by
    Beethoven.

3. (*in narrative*):

Er war jetzt schon auf dem Wege.
He was now already on his way.

Jetzt war alles bereit.
All was now ready.

4. (*present circumstances*):

Es wird jetzt nicht mehr lange dauern.
It won't take long now.

Jetzt, wo er schon einmal hier ist, kann er auch helfen.
Now that he's here he may just as well help.

5. **jetzt eben, jetzt gerade** = 'just now', 'just this minute'.

Sie ist jetzt eben (*or* jetzt gerade) angekommen.
She has just this minute arrived.

NOTE: Whereas **jetzt** relates generally to the present time or the
immediate future, **nun** implies some logical connection with what has

gone before. Both **von jetzt ab** and **von nun ab** mean 'from now on', but whereas the first means 'from this present time on', the second denotes rather 'from that time on', viewed from a past point in time. **Jetzt** is sometimes used in preference to **nun** as being more emphatic.

266. Lauter

= 'nothing but', 'only':

Es sind lauter Engländer hier.
There are only English people here.

Das Licht ließ das Wasser wie lauter Silber aussehen.
The light made the water look like pure silver.

Erzähle mir doch nicht lauter Lügen!
Don't tell me a pack of lies.

Er sieht den Wald vor lauter Bäumen nicht.
He can't see the wood for the trees.

267. Mal, Einmal

As an adverb and emotive particle, **mal** is often interchangeable with **einmal** but is somewhat more colloquial.

1. = 'once' (*as in* **wieder (ein)mal, noch (ein)mal**, 'once again', **schon (ein)mal**, 'once before', **erst (ein)mal**, 'once' (*future*)):

Er ist wieder (ein)mal (*or* noch (ein)mal) zu spät!
He's late again!

Ich muß ihn irgendwo schon (ein)mal gesehen haben.
I must have met him somewhere before.

Wenn wir erst (ein)mal dort sind, können wir uns ausruhen.
Once we are there we can have a rest.

2. (*always unstressed*) **nicht (ein)mal** = 'not even':

Er wollte sie nicht (ein)mal sehen.
He didn't even want to see her.

Nicht (ein)mal lesen kann er!
He can't even read!

3. = 'at one time', 'once' (*past*), 'some time' (*future*):

Dieser Hemdkragen war (ein)mal weiß.
This shirt-collar was once white.

Wenn du sie (ein)mal triffst, sag ihr bitte, daß ich sie nicht vergessen habe.
If you meet her some time, please tell her that I have not forgotten her.

4. (*always unstressed*) (*emotive particle, often not translated, sometimes almost meaningless*):

(*a*) (*summing up previous thoughts, feelings, remarks, etc.*):

Das ist nun (ein)mal so.
That's the way it is.

Das ist nun (ein)mal so im Leben.
Such is life.

(*b*) (*with imperative, intensifying*):

Hör (nur) (ein)mal! Schau (nur) (ein)mal!
(Just) listen! (Just) look!

Stell dir das nur (ein)mal vor!
Just fancy that!

268. Nämlich

1. = 'namely':

Die Woche hat sieben Tage, nämlich Sonntag, Montag usw.
The week has seven days, namely Sunday, Monday etc.

2. = 'because (you see . . .)':

Ich muß Überstunden machen, ich habe nämlich noch viel Arbeit zu erledigen.
I must work overtime because I still have a lot of work to get through.

Ich kann noch nicht wählen, ich bin nämlich noch nicht volljährig.
I can't vote yet because I'm not yet of age.

NOTE: **Nämlich** must not be confused with **namentlich**, which means
'especially': **Wein, namentlich Rotwein, trinke ich gern,** 'I like wine,
especially red wine.'

269. Noch

1. (*time*) = 'still', 'yet':

Ich weiß noch nicht, ob ich kommen kann.
I don't know yet whether I can come.

Ich war noch nie dort.
I have never been there.

Wir haben noch immer keine Nachricht von ihm.
We still have no news from him.

Noch heute werde ich ihm schreiben.
I shall write to him (not later than) today.

2. (*to specify something additional*):

Herr Ober! Noch einen Kaffee, bitte!
Waiter! Another coffee, please.

Was möchtest du dir noch ansehen?
What else would you like to see?

3. (*before a comparative*) = 'still more', 'even more':

Bei Mondlicht sieht der Dom noch imposanter aus.
By moonlight the cathedral looks even more imposing.

Ich habe noch weniger als Sie.
I have even less than you.

4. (*concessive*):

Und wenn er sich noch so sehr beeilt, *den* **Zug erreicht er nicht
mehr.**
However much he hurries, he won't catch *that* train now.

Note that **noch** precedes the negatives **nie, nicht,** etc.

270. Nur

1. 'only', 'just':

Sie hat nur ein Jahr hier gewohnt.
She only lived here a year.

Es war nur ein Traum.
It was just a dream.

2. (*to persuade, reassure*):

Kommen Sie nur herein!
Just come in, will you?

Lassen Sie nur, ich bezahle schon.
Don't bother, I'll pay.

Nur nicht ängstlich!
Don't be frightened.

3. (*to generalize a statement, often introducing an element of surprise*):

Was hat er nur, er ist so still?
What can be the matter with him, he's so quiet?

Wie kommt er nur auf ¹die Idee?
Where *did* he get that idea from?

Was hast du nur vor?
Whatever are you proposing to do?

4. (*idioms*):

Er fiel ins Wasser, daß es nur so spritzte.
He fell into the water and it splashed all over the place.

In dem Geschäft gibt es alles, was man sich nur wünschen kann.
In the shop there is everything you (*or* one) could possibly want.

271. Schon

1. = 'already', 'as early as', 'now', 'ever', etc.':

Sind Sie schon da?
Are you there already?

Das Schiff ist schon gestern angekommen.
The ship arrived (as early as) yesterday.

Ich bin schon acht Tage hier.
I've been here for a week now.

Ist sie schon in Rom gewesen?
Has she ever been to Rome?

Schon am folgenden Tag reisten sie wieder ab.
The very next day they set off again.

Jetzt ist er schon da.
He's there by now.

2. (*to reassure*):

Er wird schon noch kommen.
He will come, I'm sure.

Es wird schon gehen, auch wenn wir für uns allein kochen müssen.
It will be all right, even if we have to do our own cooking.

3. (*concessive*—'I admit . . . but'):

Es stimmt schon, daß das Wetter in der letzten Woche schön war, aber Sommer kann man das nicht nennen.
It's true (I grant you) that the weather was fine during this last week, but you can't call that summer.

4. (*for added emphasis*):

Ich komme schon!	**Schon gut!**
I'm coming!	All right! O.K.!

Sie interessierte sich nicht sehr für Sport und für Fußball schon gar nicht.
She was not very interested in sport and not at all in football.

5. = 'if for no other reason':

Schon weil er klein ist, konnte er es nicht sehen.
Because he is small, if for no other reason, he could not see it.

272. Wohl

1. = 'to be sure (. . . but)':

Er ist wohl krank, aber es ist nicht gefährlich.
He is ill, to be sure, but it isn't dangerous.

2. = 'no doubt', 'probably', 'I suppose':

Es ist wohl das beste, ihn jetzt in Ruhe zu lassen.
I suppose it's best to leave him in peace now.

Er wird wohl den Zug verpaßt haben, da er noch nicht hier ist.
He probably missed the train, seeing that he is not here yet.

Das wird wohl das letzte Mal gewesen sein, daß wir in diesem Jahr Tennis gespielt haben.
I suppose that was the last time we played tennis this year.

3. (*of mental or physical health or bodily comfort*) 'well':

Mir ist nicht wohl.
I'm not well.

Ich fühle mich in dieser netten Wohnung äußerst wohl.
I feel extremely comfortable in this nice flat.

Mir ist wohl zumute.
I feel at ease (*or* comfortable).

4. (*for added emphasis*):

Du bist wohl verrückt!
You must be mad!

Das ist wohl möglich.
That is quite possible.

Er hat wohl zehnmal dasselbe gesagt.
He must have said the same thing ten times over.

5. (*in exclamations*):

Leben Sie wohl!
Farewell! Goodbye!

Wohl bekomm's!
Your health!

273. Zuerst

1. = '(at) first', 'to begin with':

Ich gehe zuerst zur Bibliothek, danach gehe ich einkaufen.
I'm going first to the library, and afterwards I'm going shopping.

Wegen der vielen fremden Leute war sie zuerst sehr schüchtern.
Because of the many strange faces she was very shy to begin with.

Wer zuerst kommt, mahlt zuerst.
First come, first served.

2. (*precedence*):

Zuerst ist er Politiker, dann Rechtsanwalt.
He is first a politician, then a lawyer.

Zuerst kommt der Beruf, dann die Familie.
The job comes first, then the family.

3. = **als erster:**

Er kam zuerst an (= Er kam als erster an).
He was the first to arrive.

274. Comparison of Adverbs

Positive	*Comparative*	*Superlative*
leicht	**leichter**	**am leichtesten**
easily	more easily	most easily
streng	**strenger**	**am strengsten**
strictly	more strictly	most strictly
schnell	**schneller**	**am schnellsten**
quickly	more quickly	most quickly
richtig	**richtiger**	**am richtigsten**
correctly	more correctly	most correctly
schön	**schöner**	**am schönsten**
beautifully	more beautifully	most beautifully
pünktlich	**pünktlicher**	**am pünktlichsten**
punctually	more punctually	most punctually
kräftig	**kräftiger**	**am kräftigsten**
powerfully	more powerfully	most powerfully

Positive	*Comparative*	*Superlative*
heftig	**heftiger**	**am heftigsten**
violently	more violently	most violently

Ich fuhr *schnell*, aber mein Bruder fuhr *schneller*, und mein Freund *am schnellsten*.
I drove fast, but my brother drove faster, and my friend fastest.

Ich habe noch nie ein *schöner* möbliertes Haus gesehen.
I have never seen a more beautifully furnished house.

Das Hauptquartier wurde *schärfer* bewacht als je zuvor.
The headquarters were more strictly guarded than ever before.

Der Feind zog sich *schneller* zurück, als die Alliierten vorrücken konnten.
The enemy retreated more quickly than the Allies could advance.

Der Teilnehmer, der das Problem nach Ansicht des Chefredakteurs *am erfolgreichsten* löst, ist der Gewinner.
The competitor who in the editor's view solves the problem most successfully will be declared the winner.

1. The positive form of adverbs is identical with the uninflected form of adjectives.
2. The comparative of adverbs is identical with the uninflected form of the comparative of adjectives (§150).
3. The superlative of adverbs is formed by am + -en added to the uninflected form of the superlative of the adjective (§150).

275. The Comparative Absolute of Adverbs

The comparative absolute is used to denote a higher degree than is expressed by the simple adverb, although no direct comparison is made:

Heute verbringen die Leute *häufiger* ihre Ferien in Skandinavien.
Today people spend their holidays quite often in Scandinavia.

Er hat mich schon *länger* nicht mehr besucht.
He has not visited me for quite some time now.

For the comparative absolute of adjectives, see §152.

276. The Superlative Relative of Adverbs

The superlative relative is used to denote the highest degree attained by someone or something as compared with someone or something else:

Er liest *am besten*.
He reads best (i.e., better than anyone else).

Er lief *am schnellsten* von allen.
He ran the fastest of all.

For the superlative relative of adjectives, see §153.

277. The Superlative Absolute of Adverbs

1. English 'most', indicating a quality in a very high degree, but without comparative force, is expressed in German by an intensive adverb such as **sehr, höchst,** or **äußerst:**

Sie war äußerst freundlich.
She was most (= exceedingly) friendly.

Er hat sehr (*or* äußerst *or* höchst) klug gehandelt.
He has acted most (= very, extremely) wisely.

2. The superlative absolute of adverbs may also be expressed by **aufs** (= **auf das,** though in such constructions this is *not* an alternative form) prefixed to a superlative adjective:

Sie empfing mich aufs freundlichste.
She received me in the most friendly way.

3. Adverbs ending in **-ig, -lich, -sam,** and a few monosyllabic adverbs, such as **höchst** and **längst,** use the uninflected form in the superlative absolute:

Er läßt freundlichst grüßen.
He wishes to be most kindly remembered.

Es ist mir höchst unangenehm, daß ich Sie warten lassen mußte.
I feel most embarrassed at having had to keep you waiting.

Er sollte doch längst hier sein!
But he should have been here long ago!

4. A few superlative adverbs end in **-ens** with special meanings: **höchstens,** 'at most', **meistens,** 'for the most part', **wenigstens,** 'at least', **mindestens,** 'at least', **spätestens,** 'at the latest', **nächstens,** 'shortly', 'soon', **bestens,** 'very well':

Er ist höchstens 30 Jahre alt.
He is at most 30 years old.

Sie geht meistens zu Fuß zur Arbeit.
She walks to work mostly.

Ich habe wenigstens viermal geklingelt, bevor jemand öffnete.
I rang at least four times before anyone opened the door.

Er hätte sich mindestens davon überzeugen müssen.
He ought at least to have made sure.

Ich komme spätestens morgen.
I'm coming tomorrow at the ´latest.

Nächstens werden wir euch besuchen.
Soon we'll be paying you a visit.

Es geht ihr bestens.
She is very well (*or* She is in the best of health).

For ordinal adverbs ending in **-ens,** see §286.

278. Irregular Comparison of Adverbs

The following adverbs are irregular in the comparative and superlative:

	Comparative	*Superlative*
bald, soon	**eher,** sooner	**am ehesten,** soonest
gern(e), gladly	**lieber,** rather	**am liebsten,** most
oft, often	**öfter,** more often	**am öftesten,** most often
gut, well	**besser,** better	**am besten,** best
viel, much	**mehr,** more	**am meisten,** most

VIII. NUMERALS

279. Cardinal Numerals

1. eins	11. elf	21. einundzwanzig
2. zwei	12. zwölf	22. zweiundzwanzig
3. drei	13. dreizehn	30. dreißig
4. vier	14. vierzehn	40. vierzig
5. fünf	15. fünfzehn	50. fünfzig
6. sechs	16. sechzehn	60. sechzig
7. sieben	17. siebzehn	70. siebzig
8. acht	18. achtzehn	80. achtzig
9. neun	19. neunzehn	90. neunzig
10. zehn	20. zwanzig	100. hundert

101. hundert(und)eins	123. hundertdreiundzwanzig
200. zweihundert	1,001. tausend(und)eins
1,000. tausend	1,066. tausendsechsundsechzig
1,900. neunzehnhundert	1,000,000. eine Million
1,969. neunzehnhundert-neunundsechzig	

1. The form **eins** is used in counting (BUT 'one car' = **ein Auto**).

2. In compound numbers from 21 upwards, the units precede the tens, and are joined to them by **und**: 25 = **fünfundzwanzig** (cf. old English 'five and twenty'); 156 = **hundertsechsundfünfzig**.

3. The numerals ending in English in '-teen' (13–19) are rendered in German by the addition of **-zehn** to the relevant number preceding *with the exception of* 16 (**sechzehn**) and 17 (**siebzehn**).

4. The numerals ending in English in '-ty' (20, 30, etc. → 90) are rendered in German by the addition of **-zig** to the relevant number preceding *with the exception of* 30 (**dreißig**), 60 (**sechzig**), and 70 (**siebzig**).

5. **Hundert** and **tausend** generally omit **ein** before and may omit **und** after them.

280. Remarks on Numerals

1. **Ein** is used adjectivally after the definite article:

Der eine Bruder ... der andere Bruder.	The one brother ... the other brother.
Auf der einen Seite ... auf der anderen Seite.	On the one hand ... on the other hand.
Das eine Mal.	The one (single) occasion.

2. **Ein** is also used substantivally with the definite article, in both singular and plural:

Der eine oder der andere.	The one or the other.
Die einen sagten dies, die anderen das.	Some said this, (the) others that.

3. **Beide,** 'both', is used as a pronoun and as an adjective; as a pronoun it also has the neuter singular form **beides**:

Meine Eltern sind beide hier.	My parents are both here.
Die (meine) beiden Brüder.	The (my) two brothers, both the (my) brothers.
Beides ist richtig.	Both (facts, alternatives, etc.) are correct.

See also §§91, 129.

281. Multiplication

When two or more numbers are multiplied, the product—i.e., the number resulting from the multiplication—is in German always preceded by the verb in the *singular*, not plural as sometimes in English, and in such expressions the word **mal** is written separately:

Zwei mal drei ist (*or* macht *or* gibt) sechs.
Two threes are six, twice three is six.

Vier mal vier mal vier ist vierundsechzig.
Four times four times four is sixty-four.

Der Teppich ist drei mal zwei Meter.
The carpet is three metres by two.

Der erste Vorlauf wird über vier mal (ein)hundert Meter gelaufen.
The first heat will be run over four by one hundred metres.

282. Multiplicative Adverbs

Multiplicative adverbs, which indicate 'how many times', are formed by adding the suffix **-mal** (from **das Mal,** 'time, occasion') to the cardinal numerals:

Einmal, zweimal, zehnmal, hundertmal, hundert(und)einmal, tausendmal, tausendfünfhundertmal, millionenmal; vieltausendmal (= viele tausend Male).
Once, twice, ten times, a hundred times, a hundred and one times, a thousand times, one thousand five hundred times, a million times; many thousands of times.

Note also **anderthalbmal,** 'one and a half times' (**Dies ist anderthalbmal soviel wie das andere,** 'This is one and a half times as much as the other'). Cf. §291, 2, note 2.

283. The Suffix -fach

The suffix **-fach** (= English '-fold') is added to cardinal numerals, and also indefinite numerals, to form adjectives and adverbs—*e.g.* **einfach,** 'single', **zweifach,** 'twofold', **dreifach,** 'threefold', **zehnfach,** 'tenfold', **hundertfach,** 'hundredfold', **tausendfach,** 'thousandfold'; **mehrfach, vielfach, mannigfach,** 'manifold'. In addition, nouns and verbs can be formed from the adjectives, as in (*c*) and (*d*) below respectively.

(*a*) *Adjectives.* These decline in the normal way.

Examples:

Ein dreifacher Sieg; in dreifacher Ausfertigung.
A threefold victory; in triplicate.

Ein dreifaches Hoch auf jemanden ausbringen.
To give three cheers for someone.

Die vierfache Menge; in hundertfacher Vergrößerung.
Four times the amount; magnified a hundred times.

Ein vielfacher Millionär.
A millionaire many times over.

NOTE: 1. **Einfach,** besides meaning 'single' (*e.g.* **eine einfache Fahrkarte,** 'a single (i.e. one-way) ticket', **der einfache Fahrpreis,** 'the single fare'), also has the meaning 'simple' in the sense of 'uncomplicated'—*e.g.* **eine einfache Aufgabe,** 'a simple task'.
2. **Zweifach,** 'twofold', is occasionally found in the rather literary form **zwiefach.**
3. The same distinction exists in German between **zweifach** and **doppelt** as in English between 'twofold' and 'double'.
4. The suffix **-fältig** (or **-faltig**) is still occasionally used as an alternative form of **-fach,** but is practically obsolete. Thus, for example, **achtfältig** ('eightfold', 'octuple') is nowadays largely replaced by **achtfach.** But, in the case of **einfältig,** although the meaning 'single' is now virtually obsolete, the meaning 'simple', both in the sense of 'naive' and in the sense of 'stupid', survives, together with the nouns **die Einfalt** and **die Einfältigkeit.** Note also **vielfältig,** 'manifold', 'multiple'.

(*b*) *Adverbs.*
Achtfach geteilt; zehnfach vergrößert,
Divided into eight; magnified ten times.

Das hat sich hundertfach bewährt.
That has proved its worth a hundred times.

(*c*) *Nouns.* Neuter nouns may be formed from the adjectival forms, as follows:

Das Dreifache nehmen.
To take three times the amount, to take three times as much.

Achtzehn ist das Neunfache von zwei.
Eighteen is nine times two.

Etwas um das Tausendfache vermehren.
To increase something a thousandfold.

(*d*) *Verbs.* These may be formed by prefixing **ver-** and adding the infinitive ending **-en,** as follows:

verdreifachen, to treble
vervierfachen, to quadruple

verfünffachen, to increase fivefold, to quintuple

—and so on to **verzehnfachen,** to increase tenfold.

NOTE: 1. **Vereinfachen** = 'to simplify', as in **ein Herstellungs-verfahren vereinfachen,** 'to simplify a manufacturing process'.
2. 'To double' is **verdoppeln.**

284. Distributive Article

The English indefinite article is replaced by the definite article in German when used distributively (= 'each').

Dreimal die Woche; viermal das Jahr.	Three times a week; four times a year.
Drei Mark das Meter.	Three Marks a metre.

NOTE: In expressions of time and of price, as above, the noun is in the accusative (see also §24).

285. Expressions of Quantity

1. **Hundert Pfennig ergeben eine Mark.** — A hundred Pfennigs make one Mark.

   Hundert Zentimeter sind ein Meter. — A hundred centimetres make one metre.

   Vier Pfund; tausend Mann. — Four pounds; a thousand men.

   Eine Mark; fünf Mark; zwanzig Pfennig. — One Mark; five Marks; twenty Pfennigs.

2. **Zwei Flaschen.** — Two bottles.

   Drei Tassen Tee. — Three cups of tea.

   Sechs Dutzend Flaschen Wein. — Six dozen bottles of wine.

3. **Ein Glas Bier; fünf Glas Bier.** — One glass of beer; five glasses of beer.

   Mit zwei Paar Schuhen. — With two pairs of shoes.

   Sechs Meter von diesem Stoff. — Six metres of this material.

   Noch ein Glas von diesem Bier. — Another glass of this beer.

   Noch ein Glas helles Bier, bitte. — Another glass of pale ale, please.

4. **Der Stock ist einen Fuß lang.** — The stick is a foot long.

1. Nouns expressing measure, weight, or number (except feminines ending in -e) retain the uninflected form of the singular, even when the sense is plural.

2. Feminines ending in -e add -n in the plural.

3. The noun the quantity of which is expressed is usually in apposition to the noun expressing the quantity, unless preceded by a determinative (§116, 1, note).

4. The measure of distance, weight, etc., is in the accusative.

5. Meter ('metre') and its compounds (**Zentimeter, Kilometer,** etc.) are optionally masculine or neuter,

286. Ordinals

Der zweite, vierte, fünfte Tag.	The second, fourth, fifth day.
Das erste, dritte, achte Mal.	The first, third, eighth time.
Der hundertfünfte (or **hundertundfünfte) Bewerber.**	The hundred and fifth applicant.
Der neunundzwanzigste Band.	The twenty-ninth volume.
Die zweiundvierzigste Lektion.	The forty-second lesson.
Erstens, zweitens, drittens.	In the first place, secondly, thirdly.

1. The stem of ordinal adjectives is formed from the cardinals by adding -t, up to 19 (except **erst-,** 'first', **dritt-,** 'third', **acht-,** 'eighth'), and -st from 20 upwards.

2. Compound ordinals add the suffix to the last component only.

3. Ordinal adverbs are formed by adding -ens to the ordinal stem.

NOTE: 1. The numeral before **Band,** 'volume', **Kapitel,** 'chapter', **Seite,** 'page', etc., is read as an ordinal (and is written **1., 2.,** etc.) when it precedes, and as an undeclined cardinal when it follows; **Nummer,** 'number', is followed by the cardinal: **Das dritte Kapitel,** 'The third chapter'; **Kapitel drei,** 'Chapter three'; **Nummer fünf,** 'Number five'.

2. In common use are the adverbial forms **zu zweit** and **zu dritt,** meaning 'two of us (or you or them)' and 'three of us (or you or them)' respectively—cf. the colloquial English expressions 'as a twosome', 'as a threesome'. Examples: **Sie kamen zu dritt,** 'Three of them came', **Sie gingen zu zweit ins Kino,** 'They went as a twosome to the cinema', **Wir waren zu dritt, meine Mutter, meine kleine Schwester und ich,** 'There were three of us, my mother, my little sister and I'.

287. Ordinals with Personal Names

The ordinals after proper names of sovereigns, etc., are written with a capital letter, and must be declined throughout, as well as the article:

Nom.: **Karl der Erste.**	Charles the First.
Acc.: **Karl den Ersten.**	Charles the First.
Gen.: **Karls des Ersten.**	Of Charles the First.
Dat.: **Karl dem Ersten.**	(To, for) Charles the First.

NOTE: The Roman numerals I, II, etc., after such names must be read as above: **Karl V. = Karl der Fünfte; Karls I. = Karls des Ersten,** etc.

288. The Time of Day

Wieviel Uhr ist es?⎫ **Wie spät ist es?** ⎭	What time is it?
Es ist ein Uhr.⎫ **Es ist eins.** ⎭	It is one o'clock.
Um zwölf Uhr mittags.	At (twelve) noon.
Um zwölf Uhr nachts.	At (twelve) midnight.
Es ist Viertel nach eins.⎫ **Es ist Viertel zwei.** ⎭	It is a quarter past one.
Es ist halb zwei.	It is half past one.
Es ist Viertel vor zwei.⎫ **Es ist dreiviertel zwei.** ⎭	It is a quarter to two.
Um halb eins.	At half past twelve.
Um 23 Minuten nach eins.	At 23 minutes past one.
Es ist 21 Minuten vor zwei.	It is 21 minutes to two.
Acht Uhr morgens (vormittags).	Eight o'clock in the morning, 8 A.M.
Drei Uhr nachmittags.	Three o'clock in the afternoon, 3 P.M.
Sechs Uhr abends.	Six o'clock in the evening, 6 P.M.
Gegen acht Uhr hoffe ich dort zu sein.	About eight o'clock I hope to be there.

1. The verb **sein** in these expressions is singular.
2. **Uhr** remains uninflected, and may be omitted.

3. 'At' = **um** (*except* in the expressions **um Mittag, um Mitternacht** (or, equally, **gegen Mittag, gegen Mitternacht**), which mean '*about* midday, *about* midnight').

4. **Ein** remains uninflected, but **eins** is used when **Uhr** is omitted.

5. The 'quarter past' may be expressed either by **Viertel nach** + the number of the hour past or by **Viertel** + the number of the hour following. The former is the usual method, the latter being mainly South German.

6. The 'half past' is expressed by **halb** + the number of the hour following.

7. The 'quarter to' may be expressed either by **Viertel vor** + the number of the hour following or by **dreiviertel** + the number of the hour following. Again, the former is more usual, the latter being mainly South German.

8. The 'minutes past' are expressed by **nach**; the 'minutes to' by **vor.**

9. The abbreviation 'A.M.' = **morgens** or **vormittags;** 'P.M.' = **nachmittags, abends,** or **nachts,** according to the lateness of the hour.

NOTE: 1. The time may also, as always in railway timetables, be expressed thus: **Ein Uhr fünfzehn** = 1.15; **ein Uhr dreißig** = 1.30; **ein Uhr fünfundfünfzig** = 1.55.

2. The use of the 24-hour clock is becoming increasingly common in Germany.

289. Dates

Der wievielte ist heute? **Den wievielten haben wir heute?** }	What day of the month is it?
Was für ein Datum haben wir heute?	What is the date today?
Es ist der zehnte. **Wir haben den zehnten.** }	It is the tenth.
Am 1. (= ersten) Januar.	On the first of January.
London, den 3. April 1969 (= **London, den dritten April, neunzehnhundertneunundsechzig).**	London, 3rd April 1969.
Goethe starb 1832 (*or* **im Jahre 1832).**	Goethe died in (the year) 1832.

1. In dates, the ordinals are used adjectivally before the names of the months, the figures (1, 2, 3, etc., followed by a full stop) being read as ordinals with the definite article and the proper adjective ending.

2. The year number is either written and read without a preposition or preceded by **im Jahre.**

290. House Numbers and Addresses

1. In street-names, the preposition and article are omitted in giving an address and in addressing letters, and the street-name is written as one word, unless: (*a*) the name consists of several words, in which case they should be hyphenated—*e.g.* **Albert-Schweitzer-Straße;** (*b*) the adjective of a street-name can be inflected, in which case the adjective and street-name are written separately—*e.g.* **Kleine Budengasse** (= literally 'Little Market-stall Lane'); similarly if the adjective ends in **-er** or **-isch** and is derived from the name of a place or country—*e.g.* **Hallisches Tor, Nürnberger Straße.**

2. In addressing letters, the name of the town precedes that of the street and number:

Herrn Karl Schneider,
69 Heidelberg,
Schloßstraße 15/IV.

The number before the name of the town is the postal number (**Postleitzahl,** *f.*). The roman numeral after the house number indicates the storey (**Etage,** *f.*, or **Stock,** *m.*).

291. Fractions

1. They are regularly formed by adding **-tel** to the ordinal stem minus its final **-t,** and are neuter nouns: **ein Drittel** = one third; **drei Viertel** = three-quarters; **fünf Einundzwanzigstel** = five twenty-firsts.

NOTE: The termination **-tel** is a weakened form of **Teil,** 'part', which was once neuter but is now generally masculine, except in some compounds—*e.g.*, **das Gegenteil,** 'the opposite', **das Abteil,** 'compartment', **das Urteil,** 'verdict'.

2. 'The half' = die Hälfte; 'half' as adjective or adverb = halb; as adjective, halb is inflected and follows the determinative (§116, 1, note):

Die Hälfte meines Vermögens. } Half my property.
Mein halbes Vermögen.

Die halbe Schweiz.   Half of Switzerland.

Ich habe das Buch nur zur Hälfte gelesen.
I have only read half the book.

Der Umschlag muß alle halbe Stunde gewechselt werden.
The poultice must be changed every half an hour.

Ich habe das Radio zum halben Preis bekommen.
I obtained the radio at half-price (for half the price).

Wir mußten auf halbem Wege umkehren, da es heftig zu regnen begann.
We had to return half-way because it began to pour with rain.

NOTE: 1. With place-names not requiring the article, the uninflected **halb** may be used: **halb Frankreich**, 'half of France'.
2. **Anderthalb** is an invariable adjective meaning 'one and a half' —e.g., **anderthalb Jahre**, 'a year and a half'. 'Two and a half' is **zweieinhalb** (or **zweiundeinhalb**), 'three and a half' is **drei(und)einhalb**, and so on, these being either invariable adjectives with noun in the plural or variable adjectives with noun in the singular: **Er lief fünfzehneinhalb Kilometer** or **Er lief fünfzehn und einen halben Kilometer**, 'He ran fifteen and a half kilometres'.
3. Other mixed numbers are read as follows: $15\frac{7}{8}$ = **fünfzehn sieben Achtel.**

3. The fraction **Viertel** is prefixed to its noun:

Eine Viertelstunde.   A quarter of an hour.
Eine Dreiviertelstunde.   Three-quarters of an hour.

Ich habe eine Dreiviertelstunde auf ihn gewartet.
I waited for him for three-quarters of an hour.

IX. PREPOSITIONS

292. General Remarks

A preposition is a word which expresses a relation between a noun or a pronoun which it governs and some other word—a verb or adjective, or another noun or pronoun. For example, in the sentence 'He works in a factory', the preposition 'in' expresses a relation between the noun 'factory' and the verb 'works'. The word 'preposition' is so called because it is normally placed before the noun or pronoun which it governs (Latin *præ*, 'before', *positum*, 'placed'), though in English the preposition in fact often follows—*e.g.* 'What are you looking *for*?'

Prepositions are closely related to adverbs, but whereas prepositions take an object, adverbs do not—'He went *up the stairs*' (prepositional phrase consisting of preposition + object), 'He went *up*' (adverb); the prepositional phrase 'up the stairs' is, at the same time, an adverbial phrase, since it describes *where* he went.

Because prepositions take their meanings from the phrases in which they stand, they are capable of having a wide variety of meanings; thus when they are being rendered into another language it is essential to take into account the whole phrase in which they stand, especially where verbs are concerned; for example, the German preposition **an** is used to translate a number of different English prepositions in certain specific contexts, such as **erkennen an,** 'to recognize *by*', **sich rächen an,** 'to avenge oneself *on*', **sterben an,** 'to die *of*', **sich gewöhnen an,** 'to get accustomed *to*', **glauben an,** 'to believe *in*', etc.

A further difficulty is that whereas in English *all* prepositions govern the accusative case, in German some govern the accusative, others the dative, or the genitive, or either dative or accusative according to context.

293. Prepositions with Dative

The following eight prepositions govern the dative only:

aus	gegenüber	nach	von
bei	mit	seit	zu

294. Aus

1. = 'out of' (*motion, or direction from inside to outside*):

Heute gehe ich nicht aus dem Haus.
Today I am not going out of the house.

Sie schaute aus dem Fenster.
She looked out of the window.

Er trinkt die Milch gleich aus der Flasche.
He is drinking the milk straight out of the bottle.

2. = '(made) of' (*material*):

Die Vase ist aus Glas.
The vase is (made) of glass.

Das Kleid ist aus Baumwolle.
The dress is of cotton.

Die Uhr ist aus Gold.
The watch is (made) of gold.

3. = 'from' (*origin*):

Er ist aus Hamburg.
He is from Hamburg.

Die Gläser sind aus dem achtzehnten Jahrhundert.
The glasses are from the eighteenth century.

Sie lesen eine Szene aus dem ,,Faust".
They are reading a scene from "Faust".

4. = 'from', 'out of' (*motive*):

Sie tat es aus Furcht (Rache, Ehrgeiz, Eifersucht).
She did it out of fear (revenge, ambition, jealousy).

Er wurde aus Mangel an Beweisen freigesprochen.
He was acquitted for lack of evidence.

Aus welchem Grund mag er es getan haben?
For what reason might he have done it?

5. (*figurative and idiomatic uses*):

Was ist aus ihm geworden?
What happened to him? (What became of him?)

Aus ihrem Plan wurde nichts.
Nothing came of her plan.

Aus den Augen, aus dem Sinn.
Out of sight, out of mind.

295. Bei

1. = 'by', 'near', 'next to' (*proximity in space*):

Croydon liegt bei London.
Croydon is situated near London.

Ich saß bei ihm.
I sat next to him.

Er stand bei der Tür.
He stood by the door.

2. = 'with', 'at (the house of)' (cf. French *chez*):

Er wohnt bei seinen Eltern.
He lives with his parents.

Bei uns in Deutschland fahren die Autos auf der rechten Straßenseite.
Here in Germany cars drive on the right-hand side of the road.

Haben Sie ein Konto bei der Bank?
Have you an account at (with) the bank?

3. = 'on', 'with':

Ich habe kein Geld bei mir.
I have no money on (with) me.

Bei ihm wurden gefährliche Rauschgifte gefunden.
Dangerous drugs were found on him.

4. ='by', 'in', 'during' (*time*):

Stör mich nicht bei der Arbeit.
Don't disturb me while I am working.

Bei schlechtem Wetter bleiben wir zu Hause.
In bad weather we stay at home.

Vorsicht beim Überschreiten der Fahrbahn!
Take care when crossing the road.

NOTE: With the neuter verbal noun, **beim** (see the last example above) can never be resolved into **bei dem**. See §323.

5. (*state, mood, etc.*):

Ich bin jetzt nicht bei Laune.
I am not in the mood now.

Er ist wohl nicht bei Trost!
He must be out of his senses!

296. Gegenüber

1. ='opposite', 'facing':

Wir wohnen dem Polizeirevier gegenüber (*or* gegenüber dem Polizeirevier).
We live opposite the police station.

Mir gegenüber saßen zwei ältere Damen.
Opposite me sat two elderly ladies.

NOTE: This preposition may precede or follow the noun, but it always follows a personal pronoun.

2. ='towards', 'with regard to':

Seinem Vater gegenüber wagt er nicht, so frech zu sein.
He doesn't dare be so impertinent with his father.

3. ='by comparison with':

Dir gegenüber war er doch immer sehr nett.
By comparison with you he was always very nice.

297. Mit

1. = 'with' (*instrument*):

Sie schreibt mit einem Kugelschreiber.
She writes with a ball-point pen.

Sie fahren mit dem Bus zur Schule.
They go to school by bus.

Schicken Sie mir das Buch mit der Post.
Send me the book by post.

2. = '(along) with', 'in company with':

Sie gingen mit ihrem Lehrer ins Museum.
They went with their teacher to the museum.

Ich werde mit ihr sprechen.
I'll have a word with her.

Er besitzt das Haus mit seinem Vater zusammen.
He owns the house jointly with his father.

298. Nach

1. = 'after' (*time, order*):

Was machst du nach der Schule?
What are you doing after school?

Nach einer Weile fanden sie das Spiel langweilig.
After a while they found the game boring.

Nach dem Präsidenten ist er der mächtigste Mann im Staat.
After the President he is the most powerful man in the state.

2. = 'to' (*with proper names of places*):

Sie fuhren nach München, nach Frankreich.
They travelled to Munich, to France.

3. (*direction*):

Sie sahen nach oben, nach unten.
They looked up(wards), down.

Fahren Sie nach rechts, nach links!
Drive to the right, to the left!

Wir gingen nach Hause.
We went home.

Sie griff nach dem Buch.
She reached for the book.

4. = 'according to' (*may follow its noun in this sense*):

**Er wählte den Anzug nicht nach dem Preis, sondern nach der
Qualität.**
He chose the suit not according to the price but according to the
quality.

**Nach meiner Meinung (*or* Meiner Meinung nach) war das Stück
ausgezeichnet.**
In my opinion the play was excellent.

Aller Voraussicht nach wird es einen kalten Winter geben.
In all probability there will be a cold winter.

299. Seit

= 'since':

Seit dem zweiten Weltkrieg ...
Since the Second World War ...

Er ist seit acht Tagen hier.
He has been here for a week now.

Wie lange wohnen Sie schon in London?—Seit zwei Jahren.
How long have you been living in London?—For two years.

Observe the use of the present tense in the second and third
examples.

300. Von

1. = 'from' (*direction*):

Der Zug kommt von Moskau.
The train is coming from Moscow.

Sie stammt nicht von hier.
She is not from these parts.

Von vorn sieht das Haus sehr schön aus.
From the front the house looks very beautiful.

Von wo kommt das Geräusch?
Where is the noise coming from?

Der Zirkus zog von Stadt zu Stadt.
The circus went from town to town.

2. = 'from' (*time*):

Ich werde von jetzt an (von heute an) früher aufstehen.
From now on (as from today) I shall get up earlier.

**Ich habe von vornherein (von Anfang an) nicht an das Gelingen des
Planes geglaubt.**
From the outset (from the very beginning) I have had no faith
in the success of the plan.

3. = 'of' (*measure*):

Ein Buch von 600 Seiten.
A book of 600 pages.

Eine Leiter von 4 Meter Länge.
A ladder 4 metres in length.

Eine Frau von 30 Jahren.
A woman of 30.

4. = 'of' (*quality*):

Sie ist eine Frau von außerordentlicher Schönheit.
She is a woman of extraordinary beauty.

Er ist von blasser Hautfarbe.
He is of a pale complexion.

Er ist ein Mann von Charakter.
He is a man of (strong) character.

5. 'of', 'from' (*partitive*):

Sie aßen von dem Kuchen.
They ate a bit (*or* some) of the cake.

Er riß ein Blatt vom Block.
He tore a sheet from the pad.

Jeder von ihnen war beschwipst.
Every one of them was tipsy.

6. (*indicating cause, authorship, connection, agent, etc.*):

Er ist sehr müde; das kommt vom späten Fernsehen.
He is very tired; that is the result of watching television late.

Die Sinfonie ist von Brahms.
The symphony is by Brahms.

Wissen Sie von dem Unfall?
Do you know about the accident?

Das Dach ist vom Wind abgerissen worden.
The roof has been ripped off by the wind.

Ich bekam eine Uhr von meinem Vater.
I got a watch from my father.

NOTE: 1. The English preposition 'of' with a noun must generally be rendered in German by a genitive without a preposition, whenever it can be turned into the English possessive, otherwise by **von: der Kopf eines Hundes**, 'the head of a dog' ('a dog's head'); **die Mutter dieser Kinder**, 'the mother of these children'; **wir reden von dem Mädchen**, 'we are talking of the girl'.

2. **Von** replaces the genitive with unqualified plural nouns—*e.g.*, **Besitzer von zwei Warenhäusern**, 'owner of two department stores'; also to avoid repetition of genitives, and usually after partitives: **Das Haus vom Bruder meines Vaters**, 'the house of my father's brother'; **einer von meinen Freunden**, 'one of my friends'.

301. Zu

1. = 'to' (*people, places*):

Wir gehen zur Schule, zur Kirche, zu Bett, zum Frisör, zum Fleischer usw.
We are going to school, to church, to bed, to the hairdresser's, to the butcher's, etc.

Sie geht zu ihrer Mutter.
She goes to her mother.

Kommen Sie schnell zu mir!
Come quickly to me!

Welcher Weg führt zum Rathaus?
Which is the way to the Town Hall?

2. = 'at' (*places, positions*):

Der Dom zu Köln.
The cathedral at Cologne.

Wir bleiben zu Hause.
We stay at home.

Zu seiner Rechten saß der Bürgermeister, zu seiner Linken der Pfarrer.
On his right sat the mayor, on his left the vicar.

3. (*time*):

Wir kamen gerade noch zur rechten Zeit.
We came just in time.

Wir werden zu Ostern verreisen.
We shall be going away for Easter.

Zu jener Zeit gab es noch keine Autos.
At that time there were still no motor-cars.

Zu Anfang des Jahres trat er seine neue Stellung an.
At the beginning of the year he started his new job.

4. (*means of transport—usually* **mit**):

Er geht zu Fuß zur Schule.
He goes to school on foot.

Sie kamen zu Pferd.
They came on horseback.

5. (*ratio, proportion*):

Wir machen den Ausflug zu dritt.
There are three of us going on the excursion.

Er könnte zum mindesten grüßen.
He could at least say hello.

Im Verhältnis zum Einkommen sind die Lebenskosten zu hoch.
In relation to income, the cost of living is too high.

Sein Deutsch ist viel besser geworden im Vergleich zu früher.
His German has improved a lot compared with how it used to
be.

6. (*result of an action*):

Er wurde zum Vorsitzenden gewählt.
He was elected chairman.

Die deutsche Grammatik ist wirklich zum Verrücktwerden!
German grammar really is enough to drive one mad!

7. = 'for' (*of purpose*):

Sie lernt Spanisch zum Vergnügen.
She is learning Spanish for pleasure.

Sie kauft sich Stoff zu einem Kleid.
She buys material for a dress.

Er hat es nur zum Spaß gesagt.
He only said it for a joke.

8. (*providing something additional*):

Nehmen Sie Gebäck zum Tee?
Will you have some biscuits with your tea?

Er legte den Brief zu den anderen.
He put the letter with the others.

9. = 'at', 'of' (*price*):

Stoff zu 3 Mark das Meter.
Material at 3 Marks a metre.

Das Stück zu 25 Pfennig.
25 Pfennigs each.

Das Pfund zu 2 Mark.
2 Marks a pound.

302. Less Common Prepositions with the Dative

The following prepositions all take the dative, but are less common than those already mentioned:

(*a*) **entgegen**, 'contrary to'; 'towards':

Dem Rat seines Vaters entgegen (*or* Entgegen dem Rat seines Vaters) verkaufte er das Haus.
Contrary to his father's advice he sold the house.

Dem Süden entgegen.
Towards the south.

NOTE: As with **entlang** (§322,4), the preposition **entgegen** may be combined with a verb—*e.g.* **entgegenkommen**, 'to approach': **Seine Schwester ist ihm entgegengekommen, Seine Schwester kam ihm entgegen**, 'His sister came up to him'.

(*b*) **gemäß**, 'in accordance with':

Er handelte meinem Wunsche gemäß (*or* gemäß meinem Wunsche).
He acted in accordance with my wish.

(*c*) **gleich**, 'like':

Das Kamel lagerte gleich einem Felsblock (*or* einem Felsblock gleich) im Sand.
The camel lay like a lump of rock in the sand.

(*d*) **nächst, zunächst**, 'next to':

Nächst (*or* Zunächst) dem Hause (*or* Dem Hause zunächst) stand ein Tulpenbaum.
Next to the house stood a tulip-tree.

(*e*) **nebst, samt**, 'together with':

Das Landhaus ist zu verkaufen nebst (*or* samt) den anstoßenden Grundstücken.
The country house is up for sale together with the abutting plots of land.

(*f*) **zuwider**, 'contrary to':

Dem Friedensvertrag zuwider führten sie Waffen in das Land ein.
Contrary to the peace treaty they imported arms into the country.

NOTE: **Zunächst** usually follows the dative; **entgegen, gleich, gemäß** may precede or follow; **nächst, nebst, samt** always precede, **zuwider** always follows.

303. Prepositions with Accusative

The following prepositions govern the accusative only:

bis   durch   für   gegen   ohne   um   wider

304. Bis

1. (*a*) = 'till, until':

Können Sie bis nächsten Montag warten?
Can you wait until next Monday?

(*b*) = (*of time*) 'by':

Ich muß die Arbeit bis nächsten Montag fertig haben.
I must have the work ready by next Monday.

(*c*) = 'as far as':

Ich fahre bis Berlin.
I am going as far as Berlin.

(*d*) = (*with numerals*) 'or', 'to':

Vier bis fünf.	**Sechs bis acht Mark.**
Four or five.	Six to eight Marks.

2. **Bis** is very commonly used as an adverb followed by a preposition; the case of the following noun is then governed by the preposition. Examples:

(*a*) (*time*):

Der Zug hat manchmal bis zu einer halben Stunde (*dat.*) Verspätung.
The train is sometimes up to half an hour late.

Er arbeitete bis in die späte Nacht (*acc.*) hinein.
He worked late into the night.

Es regnete bis gegen Abend (*acc.*).
It was raining till early evening.

(*b*) (*space*).

Ich bringe Sie bis zur Bushaltestelle (*dat.*).
I'll take you as far as the bus stop.

Der Garten reicht bis an den Fluß (*acc.*).
The garden extends to the river.

Er ging mit ihr die Treppe hinunter bis vor die Tür (*acc.*).
He went down the stairs with her as far as the door.

See also §313, 2, note.

305. Durch

1. = 'through':

Wir gehen durch die Stadt.
We walk through the town.

Sie sehen durch das Schlüsselloch.
They look through the keyhole.

2. = (*agency*) 'through', 'by means of', 'by the agency of':

Sie schickte das Geld durch die Post.
She sent the money through the post.

Durch die ungewöhnliche Kälte fror die Wasserleitung ein.
On account of the exceptional cold the water-pipes froze.

Er starb durch Gift.
He died of poison.

306. Für

1. = 'for':

Ich habe einen Brief für deinen Vater.
I have a letter for your father.

2. = 'for, on behalf of':

Die Sammlung war für das Rote Kreuz.
The collection was for (on behalf of) the Red Cross

307. Gegen

1. = 'towards':

Sie war sehr unfreundlich gegen ihn.
She was very unfriendly towards him.

Sie kamen gegen acht Uhr an.
They arrived about eight o'clock.

   2. = 'against':

Er boxt gegen den Weltmeister.
He boxes against the world champion.

Die Leiter lehnt gegen die Mauer.
The ladder is leaning against the wall.

Er schwimmt gegen den Strom.
He is swimming against the current.

   3. = 'about, approximately':

Es waren gegen fünftausend Menschen da.
There were about five thousand people present.

   4. = 'in exchange for':

Er tauschte ein Fernglas gegen eine Kamera ein.
He exchanged a pair of binoculars for a camera.

Ich wette hundert gegen eins.
I'll bet you a hundred to one.

308. Ohne

= 'without':

Er kam, aber ohne seine Frau.
He came, but without his wife.

Er kehrte ohne einen einzigen Pfennig zurück.
He returned without so much as a penny.

Er ist ja nur ein Strohmann ohne allen Einfluß.
He is only a figurehead without any (devoid of) influence.

Ohne dich bin ich nichts.
Without (but for) you I am nothing.

309. Um

1. = (*place*) 'round, around':

Um den Garten ist ein Zaun.
Around the garden is a fence.

Das Geschäft ist gleich um die Ecke.
The shop is just around the corner.

Sie fahren um die Stadt herum.
They drive round (the circumference of) the town.

NOTE: The adverb **herum** is always added after the object in this sense. The sense 'They drive about in the town' would be rendered **Sie fahren in der Stadt herum** (*or* **umher**). Similarly: **Sie liefen dreimal um das Gebäude herum,** 'They ran three times round (the outside of) the building', but **Sie liefen im Gebäude herum** (*or* **umher**), 'They ran around in(side) the building'. **Umher** implies less definite direction ('this way and that', 'hither and thither') than **herum,** but this distinction is not always observed nowadays, and **herum** is tending to displace **umher** in most contexts.

Die Erde dreht sich um die Sonne.
The earth goes round the sun.

2. = (*time*) 'at':

Um diese Zeit; um zwei Uhr.
At this time; at two o'clock.

310. Wider

= 'against, contrary to':

Wider Erwarten hatte er Erfolg bei den Wahlen.
Contrary to expectation he was successful at the polls.

Es geschah wider seinen Willen.
It happened against his will.

Sie mußte wider Willen lachen.
She could not help laughing.

311. Prepositions with Dative or Accusative

The following nine prepositions govern the dative when they indicate locality merely, and answer the question 'where?' or 'in what place?', the accusative when they imply motion, direction, or tendency towards the object of the preposition, and answer the question 'whither?' or 'to what place or person?'

an	hinter	neben	unter	zwischen
auf	in	über	vor	

312. An, 'on, upon, to, at, in'

1. Of place (*surface non-horizontal*):

(*a*) With dative = 'on, upon (adjacent to), at, (leaning, lying) against':

Das Bild hängt an der Wand.
The picture hangs on the wall.

Ich sitze am Tisch.
I am sitting at the table.

Die Leiter steht an der Mauer.
The ladder is standing against the wall.

(*b*) With accusative = 'on, to (towards)':

Er hängt das Bild an die Wand.
He hangs the picture on the wall.

Er geht ans Fenster.
He goes to the window.

Ich schreibe an meinen Vater.
I am writing to my father.

2. Of time and date, with dative only = 'on, in, at':

Am Vormittag, am Abend, etc.
In the morning, in the evening, etc.

Am zweiten Juli, am Montag, am Wochenende.
On the second of July, on Monday, at the weekend.

An dem Tag, an dem er ankan, war der große Streik.
On the day on which he arrived there was the great strike.

313. Auf, 'on, upon, to, for'

1. Place (*surface horizontal*):

(*a*) With dative = 'on, upon, on top of':

Das Buch ist auf dem Tisch.
The book is on the table.

Auf dem Kirchturm ist ein Wetterhahn.
On (top of) the church tower there is a weathercock.

(*b*) With accusative = 'on, to, up':

Legen Sie das Buch auf den Tisch!
Put the book on the table.

Er geht auf den Markt.
He is going to the market.

Sie gehen auf den Berg.
They are going up the mountain.

2. Of future time, with accusative only = 'for':

Er kommt auf zwei Tage.
He is coming for two days.

Sie fuhren auf ein paar Tage in die Schweiz.
They went for a few days to Switzerland.

Er wurde zu Gefängnis auf Lebenszeit verurteilt.
He was sentenced to life imprisonment.

NOTE: **Bis auf**+accusative may mean either (i) 'up to but not including' or (ii) 'up to and including'. The context should make the meaning clear—for example, **Er aß alle Äpfel bis auf einen** = 'He ate all the apples but one'; **Sie fielen bis auf den letzten Mann** = 'They fell (were killed) to a man'. See also §303, 2.

3. Of mode, with accusative only:

Er fuhr per Anhalter nach Hamburg; auf diese Weise sparte er das Fahrgeld.
He hitch-hiked to Hamburg; in this way he saved the fare.

Er leerte das Glas auf einen Zug.
He emptied the glass at a single draught.

Das sollst du auf keinen Fall machen.
You mustn't do that on any account.

314. Hinter, 'behind'

Der Hund liegt hinter dem Ofen.
The dog lies behind the stove.

Er kriecht hinter den Ofen.
It creeps behind the stove.

315. In, 'in, into'

1. Of place, with dative = 'in'; with accusative = 'into':

Er arbeitet im Garten.
He is working in the garden.

Er geht ins Zimmer.
He goes into the room.

2. Of time, with dative only = 'in':

Er tat es in einer Stunde.
He did it in an hour.

316. Neben, 'beside, by, near, next to, besides, in addition to'

Er steht neben dem Tisch.
He is standing beside the table.

Stelle es neben die Tür!
Put it by (near) the door.

Das junge Mädchen sitzt neben ihm.
The young girl is sitting next to him.

Neben seiner Rente bekommt er regelmäßig Geld von seinen Kindern.
In addition to his pension he regularly receives money from his children.

317. Über, 'over, across, of, about, concerning'

1. Of place, with dative = 'over (above)'; with accusative = 'over (across)':

Die Wolke hängt über dem Berg.
The cloud hangs over the mountain.

Sie gingen über die Straße.
They went across the road.

2. Of excess, with accusative only = 'over':

Das kostet über zehn Mark.
That costs over ten Marks.

3. With accusative only = 'of, about, concerning':

Er redete über seine Reise.
He talked about his journey.

318. Unter, 'under, among, less than'

1. Of place, with dative or accusative = 'under (beneath, below)':

Die schwarze Katze war unter dem Tisch.
The black cat was under the table.

Sie kroch unter den Tisch.
It crept under the table.

2. Of number, with dative or accusative = 'among':

Er fühlte sich nicht wohl unter all den fremden Leuten.
He did not feel at ease among all the strange people.

Sie mischte sich unter die Menge der Schaulustigen.
She mingled with the crowd of onlookers.

3. With dative = 'less than':

Sie verkauften die Bücher unter dem Verkaufspreis.
They sold the books at less than the list price.

Der Film ist für Jugendliche unter 18 Jahren nicht zugelassen.
The film must not be shown to (*literally*, is not permitted for)
young people under 18 years of age.

NOTE: This use of **unter** is not to be confused with the adverbial
use in such sentences as **Unter drei Gläser Wein trinkt er nicht,** where
unter is an adverb of degree (= **weniger als**).

319. Vor, 'before, in front of, ago'

1. Of place, with dative or accusative = 'before, in front of':

Der Stuhl steht vor der Tür.
The chair is in front of the door.

Stelle ihn vor die Tür!
Put it in front of the door.

2. Of order, with dative only = 'before, ahead of':

Sie sind vor mir an der Reihe.
It's your turn before mine.

3. Of time, with dative only = 'before, ago':

Vor nächster Woche wird er nicht hier sein.
He won't be here before next week.

Er kam vor zwei Tagen an.
He arrived two days ago.

NOTE: 1. In expressions of feeling **vor** + dative = 'with' or 'for'
—*e.g.*, **vor Freude tanzen,** 'to dance for joy', **vor Kälte zittern,** 'to
shiver with cold'.
2. In certain other expressions **vor** + dative = 'from'—*e.g.*, **die
Ernte vor dem Verderb bewahren,** 'to keep the crops from being
ruined', **jemanden vor seinen Gläubigern retten,** 'to save someone
from his creditors', **sich vor dem Wind schützen,** 'to protect oneself
from the wind'.

320. Zwischen, 'between'

Der Stuhl steht zwischen der Tür und dem Fenster.
The chair stands between the door and the window.

Stellen Sie ihn zwischen die Tür und das Fenster!
Put it between the door and the window.

321. Prepositions with the Genitive

The prepositions governing the genitive are easily recognizable because, in many cases, the corresponding English includes the word 'of'. The following are those of common or fairly common occurrence:

> **angesichts,** in view of, considering
> **anstatt,** instead of
> **außerhalb,** outside
> **diesseits,** (on) this side of
> **halber,** for the sake of
> **infolge,** as a result of
> **inmitten,** in the midst of
> **innerhalb,** inside, within
> **jenseits,** (on) the other side of
> **kraft,** by virtue of
> **mangels,** for lack of
> **mittels,** by means of
> **oberhalb,** above
> **statt,** instead of
> **um . . . willen,** for the sake of
> **unterhalb,** below
> **unweit, unfern,** not far from
> **vermittels,** by means of
> **vermöge,** by virtue of
> **während,** during
> **wegen,** on account of

NOTE: 1. **Halber** always follows the genitive.
2. With **um . . . willen** the genitive stands between **um** and **willen**—
e.g., **um Himmels willen!** 'for heaven's sake!'
3. **Wegen** may precede or follow the genitive.

4. Before **wegen,** . . . **willen,** the genitives of the personal pronouns
have the forms **meinet-, deinet-, seinet-, unsert-, euret-, ihret-, Ihret-:
unsertwegen, um Ihretwillen.** Similarly with the adverbial suffix
-halben: deinethalben, 'for your sake', 'on your account'.

5. To the above list may be added the following, especially common in officialese: **abseits,** 'away from'; **anhand** (or **an Hand**+geni-
tive or **anhand von**+dative), 'with the aid of, by means of'; **anstelle**
(or **an Stelle** + genitive or **anstelle von** + dative), 'in place of';
aufgrund (or **auf Grund**+genitive or **aufgrund von**+dative), 'because
of'; **ausschließlich,** 'exclusive of, excluding'; **einschließlich,** 'inclusive
of, including'; **gelegentlich** or **anläßlich** (better: **aus Anlaß**+genitive),
'on the occasion of'; **hinsichtlich** or **bezüglich** (better: **mit Hinsicht
auf**+accusative, **in Bezug auf**+accusative), 'with regard to'; **unbe-
schadet,** 'despite' *or* 'without detriment to'; **ungeachtet,** 'notwith-
standing'; **vorbehaltlich,** 'subject to'; **zwecks,** 'with a view to'.

322. Prepositions with Varying Case

1. **außer**
(*a*) with dative:

(i) 'out of':

Wir können niemanden außer der Reihe bedienen.
We can serve nobody out of turn.

Sie besprachen sich über die Sache außer Hörweite der andern.
They discussed the matter out of earshot of the others.

(ii) 'except, apart from':

Er traf niemanden außer seinem Freund.
He met nobody apart from his friend.

Außer einem Brötchen hatte er nichts gegessen.
Apart from a roll he had eaten nothing.

(iii) 'besides, in addition to':

**Außer uns zweien waren mindestens zehn seiner ehemaligen
Freunde zugegen.**
In addition to the two of us, at least ten of his former friends
were present.

(*b*) with accusative (with verbs of motion):

Durch die Zeugen wurde seine Unschuld außer allen Zweifel gesetzt.
Through the witnesses his innocence was established beyond all doubt.

Die Banknote wurde außer Kurs gesetzt.
The banknote was withdrawn from circulation.

(*c*) with genitive (in a very few set phrases):

Er beabsichtigt, außer Landes zu gehen.
He intends to leave the country (go abroad).

2. **binnen,** 'within' (of time), genitive or (more commonly) dative: **binnen eines Monats** *or* **binnen einem Monat,** 'within a month'.

3. **dank,** 'thanks to', genitive more often than dative nowadays: **dank seiner** *or* **seinen Bemühungen,** 'thanks to his efforts'.

4. **entlang,** 'along', takes a preceding accusative or **an+** dative: **den Fluß entlang** *or* **am Fluß entlang,** 'along the river'. Observe in the following examples the combining of preposition and verb: **eine Straße entlanggehen,** 'to walk along a street'; **die Mauer** (*or* **an der Mauer**) **entlangkriechen,** 'to crawl along the wall'.

5. **längs,** 'along', genitive or dative: **längs des Ufers** *or* **längs dem Ufer,** 'along the bank'. Much less common are the forms **am Ufer längs** and **das Ufer längs;** modern German prefers the use of **entlang** (see 4, above) with these constructions.

6. **laut,** 'according to, in accordance with', may be followed (*a*) by genitive or dative, when the noun is preceded by an article or adjective: **laut dieses Berichtes** *or* **laut diesem Bericht,** 'according to this report'; (*b*) by an uninflected singular noun: **laut Bericht;** (*c*) by a noun in the dative plural: **laut Berichten.**

7. **trotz,** 'in spite of', dative or (more commonly) genitive: **trotz dem Regen** *or* **trotz des Regens,** 'in spite of the rain'. The dative is more usual if the following noun is plural and belongs to the strong declension—*e.g.,* **trotz Verweisen,** 'in spite of reprimands'.

8. **zufolge,** 'according to', may precede or follow the noun;

if it precedes, the genitive is used: **zufolge des Gesetzes,** 'according to the law'; if it follows (as is preferable), the dative is used: **dem Gesetz zufolge.**

9. **zugunsten,** 'for, in favour of', and **zuungunsten,** 'against', may precede or follow the noun; if they precede, the genitive is used: **Der Fall wurde zugunsten (zuungunsten) des Angeklagten entschieden,** 'The case was decided in favour of (against) the accused'; if it follows (which it rarely does in modern German), the dative is used: **dem Angeklagten zu(un)gunsten.**

323. Contraction of Prepositions with the Definite Article

1. The prepositions **an** and **in** are generally (in expressions of time always) contracted with the unemphasized definite article (see §10) as follows:

an dem → am	in dem → im
an das → ans	in das → ins

2. The prepositions **bei, von,** and **zu** have the following contractions:

bei dem → beim	von dem → vom	zu dem → zum
		zu der → zur

3. The preposition **auf** is contracted with **das** only:

auf das → aufs

4. The prepositions **durch, für,** and **um** are sometimes contracted with the neuter of the unemphasized definite article:

durch das → durchs   für das → fürs   um das → ums

Both forms can be used in writing (in certain set expressions the contraction is obligatory), but the contracted forms are commoner in speech.

5. The following contractions are less common, but are used in colloquial speech and in certain set expressions:

hinters (hinter das)	hinterm (hinter dem)
übers (über das)	überm (über dem)
unters (unter das)	unterm (unter dem)
vors (vor das)	vorm (vor dem)

324. Use of Prepositions with Verbs

One of the major problems for English-speaking students of German concerns the correct choice of preposition—and the correct case to use with that preposition—after verbs. The following paragraphs contain most of the commoner verbs with the preposition(s) they can take, listed in alphabetical order of the prepositions:

NOTE: For prepositions with reflexive verbs, see §222, 6.

1. AN:

abnehmen an (+ *dat.*), to decrease in (size)
arbeiten an (+ *dat.*), to work at, on
befestigen an (+ *dat. or acc.*) (*also* + **auf**), to fasten to
binden an (+ *acc.*), to bind to
erinnern an (+ *acc.*), to remind of
erkennen an (+ *dat.*), to recognize by
erkranken an (+ *dat.*), to fall ill with
fassen an (+ *acc.*), to snatch at
fehlen an (+ *dat.*), (*impersonal*), to lack
fesseln an (+ *acc.*), to fetter to; to confine to (bed)
gewinnen an (+ *dat.*), to gain (in)
gewöhnen an (+ *acc.*), to accustom to
glauben an (+ *acc.*), to believe in
haben:
> **Anteil haben an** (+ *dat.*), to have a share in
> **Mangel haben an** (+ *dat.*), to stand in need of
> **Überfluß haben an** (+ *dat.*), to abound in

hängen an (+ *acc.*), to hang on
hindern an (+ *dat.*), to prevent from
ketten an (+ *acc.*), to chain to
kleben an (+ *acc. or dat.*), to stick to
kommen an (+ *acc.*), to come by, to lay hands on
leiden an (+ *dat.*), to suffer from
leimen an (+ *acc.*), to glue to
nageln an (+ *acc.*), to nail to
nehmen:
> **Anstoß nehmen an** (+ *dat.*), to take offence at

Anteil nehmen an (+*dat.*), to take an interest in
Interesse nehmen an (+*dat.*), to take an interest in
richten an (+*acc.*), to address (letter, petition, etc.) to
schließen an (+*acc.*), to fasten to
schreiben an (+*acc.*), to write to (a person)
sterben an (+*dat.*), to die of
stoßen an (+*acc.*), to knock against
teilnehmen (*sep.*) **an** (+*dat.*), to take part in
verweisen an (+*acc.*), to refer (someone) to
verzweifeln an (+*dat.*), to despair of
ziehen an (+*dat.*), to pull at
zweifeln an (+*dat.*), to doubt

2. AUF:

abzielen (*sep.*) **auf** (+*acc.*), to aim (remarks, etc.) at
achten auf (+*acc.*), to pay attention to
achtgeben (*sep.*) **auf** (+*acc.*), to take care of; to beware of
anspielen (*sep.*) **auf** (+*acc.*), to allude to, to refer to
antworten auf (+*acc.*), to answer (a question)
bauen auf (+*acc.*), to rely upon (someone)
beharren auf (+*dat.*), to persist in
beruhen auf (+*dat.*), to be based on
beschränken auf (+*acc.*), to restrict to
bestehen auf (+*dat.*), to insist on
beziehen auf (+*acc.*), to relate (something) to
blicken auf (+*acc.*), to look at
eingehen (*sep.*) **auf** (+*acc.*), to go into (details, etc.)
feuern auf (+*acc.*), to fire at
gründen auf (+*acc.*), to base on
herabsehen (*sep.*) **auf** (+*acc.*), to look down on (someone)
herabsetzen (*sep.*) **auf** (+*acc.*), to reduce to (a lower price)
hinarbeiten (*sep.*) **auf** (+*acc.*), to strive towards (a goal)
hindeuten (*sep.*) **auf** (+*acc.*), to point to (*literally and figuratively*)
hinweisen (*sep.*) **auf** (+*acc.*), to point out, to draw attention to
hoffen auf (+*acc.*), to hope for
hören auf (+*acc.*), to listen to
klettern auf (+*acc.*), to climb (up)
lauschen auf (+*acc.*), to listen to, for
losgehen (*sep.*) **auf** (+*acc.*), to let fly at

rechnen auf (+*acc.*), to count on
reduzieren auf (+*acc.*), to reduce to
richten auf (+*acc.*), to direct (one's attention, etc.) to
schießen auf (+*acc.*), to shoot at
schimpfen auf (+*acc.*), to inveigh against
schwören auf (+*acc.*), to swear on (Bible, etc.)
sehen auf (+*acc.*), to look at (the clock)
sinnen auf (+*acc.*), to be thinking about, to meditate
trinken auf (+*acc.*), to drink to (someone's health)
verzichten auf (+*acc.*), to renounce
warten auf (+*acc.*), to wait for
weisen auf (+*acc.*), to point to, at
wenden auf (+*acc.*), to direct (one's attention, etc.) to
wirken auf (+*acc.*), to influence
zeigen auf (+*acc.*), to point to
zielen auf (+*acc.*), to aim at
zugehen (*sep.*) **auf** (+*acc.*), to go up to
zukommen (*sep.*) **auf** (+*acc.*), to come up to
zurückkommen (*sep.*) **auf** (+*acc.*), to return to, to revert to

3. AUS (+*dat.*):

auftauchen (*sep.*) **aus**, to emerge from
bestehen aus, to consist of
entspringen aus, to arise from, to spring from
entstehen aus, to arise from
ersehen aus, to gather from, to understand from
hervorgehen (*sep.*) **aus**, to be descended from, to stem from; to emerge from
lernen aus, to learn from (a book)
machen aus, to make from (leather, etc.)
schließen aus, to infer from
stammen aus, to originate from (a place); to date back to (a time)
werden aus, to become of

4. BEI (+*dat.*):

anhalten (*sep.*) **bei**, to stop (off) at
arbeiten bei, to work with (a firm), for (a person)
bleiben bei, to stay (at someone's house) with

dienen bei, to serve with (the Forces, etc.)
nehmen bei, to take by (the hand)
packen bei, to seize by (the hair, etc.)
schwören bei, to swear by
verweilen bei, to dwell upon (a theme, etc.)
vorsprechen (*sep.*) **bei,** to call on, to visit

5. FÜR (+*acc.*):

aussagen (*sep.*) **für,** to testify in favour of (someone)
gelten für, to count as, to be reckoned as, to be considered
halten für, to regard as
schwärmen für, to be enthusiastic about, to rave about

6. GEGEN (+*acc.*):

abstechen (*sep.*) **gegen,** to contrast strongly with
tauschen gegen, to exchange for

7. IN:

ankommen (*sep.*) **in** (+*dat.*), to arrive at (a place)
anlangen (*sep.*) **in** (+*dat.*), to reach, arrive at
einwilligen (*sep.*) **in** (+*acc.*), to consent to

8. MIT (+*dat.*):

aufhören (*sep.*) **mit,** to stop (work, etc.)
handeln mit, to trade with; to deal in
prahlen mit, to boast about

9. NACH (+*dat.*):

aussehen (*sep.*) **nach,** to be on the look-out for
duften nach, to smell (sweetly) of
dürsten nach (*impersonal*), to thirst for (*figurative*)
fahnden nach, to search for (deserter, smuggled goods, etc.)
fischen nach, to fish for
forschen nach, to search for
fragen nach, to enquire about
graben nach, to dig for
greifen nach, to reach out for, to grab at
haschen nach, to grab at; to fish for (compliments)
hungern nach (*impersonal*), to hunger for (*figurative*)
riechen nach, to smell of

schicken nach, to send for
schielen nach, to leer at
schmecken nach, to taste of
suchen nach, to search for
urteilen nach, to judge by

10. ÜBER:

(In all these figurative expressions the preposition governs the accusative.)

grübeln über, to ponder on
herfallen (*sep.*) **über,** to attack, to fall upon
hinausgehen (*sep.*) **über,** to exceed, to go beyond
klagen über, to complain of, about
knurren über, to grumble about
kommen über, to come across
lachen über, to laugh at, about
murren über, to grumble about
nachdenken (*sep.*) **über,** to reflect on
scherzen über, to joke about
spotten über, to mock at
sprechen über, to speak about
verfügen über, to have at one's disposal
weinen über, to cry about

11. UM (+*acc.*):

beneiden um, to envy (someone) for
betrügen um, to swindle (someone) out of
bitten um, to ask for, to beg for
bringen um, to do (someone) out of
feilschen um, to haggle over
flehen um, to beg for, to plead for
kämpfen um, to fight for
kommen um, to lose, to be deprived of
ringen um, to wrestle for, to struggle for
spielen um, to play for (money, etc.)

zurückschrecken (*sep.*) **vor,** to shrink from

14. **ZU** (+*dat.*):

beglückwünschen zu, to congratulate on
dienen zu, to serve, to be useful for
gelangen zu, to reach, to attain
gratulieren zu, to congratulate
taugen zu, to be fit for, good for
werden zu, to become

325. Use of Prepositions with Adjectives and Participles

Not only do verb+preposition constructions provide special difficulty for English-speaking students of German, but also adjective or participle+preposition constructions. The following paragraphs contain a selection of the commoner adjective or participle+preposition constructions, listed in alphabetical order of the prepositions:

1. **AN:**

anstoßend an (+*acc.*), bordering on, contiguous to
arm an (+*dat.*), poor in
gesund an (+*dat.*), sound in
gleich an (+*dat.*), equal in (size, etc.)
krank an (+*dat.*), ill with, sick with
reich an (+*dat.*), rich in
überlegen an (+*dat.*), superior in

2. **AUF:**

achtsam auf (+*acc.*), mindful of
angewiesen auf (+*acc.*), dependent on
anwendbar auf (+*acc.*), applicable to
ärgerlich auf (+*acc.*), cross with (someone)
aufmerksam auf (+*acc.*), conscious of; attentive to
bedacht auf (+*acc.*), mindful of, concerned about
begierig auf (+*acc.*), eager for

blind auf (+*dat*.), blind in (one eye)
böse auf (+*acc*.), annoyed with
eifersüchtig auf (+*acc*.), jealous of
eitel auf (+*acc*.), vain of, about
erpicht auf (+*acc*.), keen on, (dead) set on (something)
geeicht auf (+*acc*.), versed in
gefaßt auf (+*acc*.), prepared for
gierig auf (+*acc*.), greedy for (power, etc.)
lahm auf (+*dat*.), lame in (one leg); paralysed on (one side)
neidisch auf (+*acc*.), envious of
neugierig auf (+*acc*.), curious about
stolz auf (+*acc*.), proud of
taub auf (+*dat*.), deaf in (one ear)
übertragbar auf (+*acc*.), transferable to
versessen auf (+*acc*.), mad about (money, etc.)
wachsam auf (+*acc*.), watchful of
zornig auf (+*acc*.), angry at, with

3. AUS (+*dat*.):

ersichtlich aus, evident from
gebürtig aus, born in, a native of

4. BEI (+*dat*.):

beliebt bei, popular with
verlegt bei, published by

5. FÜR (+*acc*.):

blind für, blind to (someone's faults, etc.)
eingenommen für, well-disposed towards
empfänglich für, susceptible to
nachteilig für, injurious to
schädlich für, detrimental to
unempfänglich für, unreceptive to

6. MIT (+*dat*.):

verlobt mit, engaged to
verwandt mit, related to

7. NACH (+*dat.*):

begierig nach, eager for
gierig nach, greedy for (power, etc.)

8. ÜBER:

(In all these figurative expressions the preposition governs
the accusative.)

ärgerlich über, cross with, annoyed at
aufgebracht über, angry at, infuriated by
bekümmert über, concerned about, worried about
bestürzt über, dismayed at
beunruhigt über, worried by, about
entrüstet über, indignant at
erstaunt über, surprised at, amazed at

9. UM (+*acc.*):

bange um, uneasy about
besorgt um, anxious about
verlegen um, at a loss for

10. VON (+*dat.*):

abhängig von, dependent on, subject to
berauscht von, drunk with (power, etc.), wild with (joy, etc.)
eingenommen von, intrigued by; biased in favour of
entbrannt von, burning with (passion, etc.)
entzückt von, delighted with
erstickt von, choked with (tears, etc.)
unabhängig von, irrespective of
verzehrt von, eaten up with (ambition, etc.)

11. VOR:

(In all these figurative expressions the preposition governs
the dative.)

blaß vor, pale with (fear, etc.)
bleich vor, pale with (fear, etc.)

krank vor, sick with (anger, etc.)
rasend vor, mad with (rage, etc.)
steif vor, stiff with (the cold, etc.)

12. **ZU** (+*dat.*):

aufgelegt zu, in the mood for
bereit zu, ready for
geeignet zu, suitable for
tauglich zu, fit for, good for

326. Equivalents of English Prepositions

English and German differ widely in the idiomatic use of prepositions. For convenient reference, the most commonly occurring English prepositions are given below in alphabetical order with examples showing their German equivalents.

About

Was weißt du von ihm (über ihn)?	What do you know about him?
Sie stritten sich ums Geld.	They quarrelled about the money.
Ungefähr (*or* etwa) 10 DM.	About 10 Marks.
Und deine Schwester, kommt sie auch?	What about your sister, is she coming too?
Was soll das alles heißen?	What's it all about?

At

In der Schule (Kirche).	At school (church).
Im Theater (Konzert).	At the theatre (concert).
Am Tisch; bei Tisch.	At the table; at table.
An der Tür.	At the door.
Auf dem Markt.	At (the) market.
Auf der Post.	At the post office.
Er studiert (lehrt) an der Universität Frankfurt.	He is studying (teaching) at the University of Frankfurt.
Auf jeden Fall.	At all events.
In diesem Augenblick.	At this (*or* that) moment.
Um halb vier.	At half-past three.

Bei Tagesanbruch.	At daybreak.
Zur rechten Zeit (Stunde).	At the right time (hour).
Zu Weihnachten (Ostern).	At Christmas (Easter).
Kaffee zu 9 DM das Pfund.	Coffee at 9 Marks a pound.
Zum halben Preis.	At half price.

By

Er wurde von seiner Mutter abgeholt.	He was met (fetched) by his mother.
Durch die Post.	By post.
Durch Krankheit verhindert.	Prevented by illness.
Mit der Eisenbahn reisen.	To travel by rail.
Bei (or an) der Hand ergreifen.	To seize by the hand.
Bei Tageslicht.	By daylight.
Zu Land.	By land.

For

Ich tat es für ihn.	I did it for him.
Schönes Wetter zum Spazierengehen.	Fine weather for walking.
Er reist zum Vergnügen.	He travels for pleasure.
Zum Beispiel.	For example.
Er ist seit zwei Tagen hier.	He has been here for two days.
Ich verreise für (or auf) eine Woche.	I am going away for a week.
Er war einen Monat hier.	He was here for a month.
Fürs erste.	For the time being.
Zum zweiten Mal.	For the second time.

In

Im Hause; in einer Woche.	In the house; in a week.
Im Himmel; am Himmel.	In heaven; in the sky.
Des Abends, abends.	In the evening.
Auf der Straße; auf dem Land(e).	In the street; in the country.
Auf diese Weise.	In this manner.
Auf die Dauer.	In the long run.
Unter Karl V.	In the reign of Charles V.
Bei kaltem Wetter.	In cold weather.

| Meiner Meinung nach. | In my opinion. |
| Zum Gedächtnis (zu Ehren)+ gen. | In commemoration (honour) of. |

Of

Ich spreche von ihm.	I am speaking of him.
Der König von Dänemark.	The king of Denmark.
Einer von meinen Freunden.	One of my friends.
Zur Tür hinaus.	Out of the door.
Die Schlacht von Waterloo.	The battle of Waterloo.
Was soll aus mir werden?	What will become of me?

On

Haben Sie Geld bei sich?	Have you any money on you?
Auf dem Tisch; auf der Bank.	On the table; on the bench.
Auf der Erde.	On the ground.
Auf der Reise nach Prag.	On the journey to Prague.
Am zweiten März.	On the second of March.
Die Schiffe auf dem Fluß.	The ships on the river.
New York liegt am Hudson und am Meer.	New York is on the Hudson and on the sea.
Zu Pferd; zu Fuß	On horseback; on foot.
Im Begriff, etwas zu tun.	On the point of doing something.
Bei dieser Gelegenheit.	On this occasion.
Bei seiner Ankunft.	On his arrival.
Unter dieser Bedingung.	On this condition.

To

Nach Europa; nach London.	To Europe; to London.
Ich fahre in die Stadt.	I am going to town.
Er fährt aufs Land.	He is going to the country.
Gehst du zur Schule?	Are you going to school?
Er ging ins Theater.	He went to the theatre.
Gehe ans (or zum) Fenster!	Go to the window.
Auf den (or zum) Markt gehen.	To go to (the) market.
Auf die Universität gehen.	To go to the University (as a student).
Zur Universität gehen.	To go to the University (buildings).
Bis auf den letzten Tropfen.	To the last drop.

With

Mit einem Stock schlagen.	To beat with a stick.
Von ganzem Herzen.	With all my heart.
In dieser Absicht.	With this intention.

327. Prepositions with Verbs, Adjectives, and Nouns

The object of many verbs, as well as the complement of nouns and adjectives corresponding to them in signification, is indicated by prepositions. The proper use of prepositions in such cases must be learnt from practice and from a good dictionary; but below is given, for convenient reference, the grammatical government of particular classes of verbs, etc., which differ most widely from their English equivalents.

1. 'At', 'of':

Of joy, wonder, etc. = **über** + accusative:

Er klagt über die Hitze.
He complains of the heat.

Er lacht über uns.
He is laughing at us.

Ihr Erstaunen über die Nachricht.
Her surprise at the news.

2. 'For':

(*a*) Of expectation, etc. = **auf** + accusative:

Sie war nicht darauf gefaßt.
She was not prepared for that.

Wir hoffen auf gutes Wetter.
We are hoping for good weather.

Er wartete auf Sie.
He was waiting for you.

(b) Of longing, inquiry, etc. = nach:

Streben nach Ruhm.
Striving for fame.

Sie sehnt sich nach Ruhe.
She longs for rest.

Suche nach der Wahrheit.
Search for the truth.

(c) Of entreaty, etc. = um:

Ich bat ihn um Geld.
I asked him for money.

Meine Sorge um ihn.
My concern for him.

3. 'From':

Of protection, etc. = vor + dative:

Retten Sie mich vor meinen Verfolgern!
Save me from my persecutors.

4. 'In':

(a) Of plenty, want, etc. = an + dative:

Arm an Bodenschätzen.   **Reich an Ideen.**
Poor in mineral resources.   Rich in ideas.

(b) Of confidence, etc. = auf + accusative:

Vertrauen Sie auf mich!
Trust in me.

5. 'Of':

(a) Of plenty, want, doubt, etc. = an + dative:

Es fehlt überall an Lehrkräften.
There is a general lack of teachers.

Mangel an Geld.
Lack of money.

Er verzweifelte fast an der Genesung seines Sohnes.
He almost despaired of his son's recovery.

    (*b*) Of remembrance, etc. = **an** + accusative:

Ich denke an Sie.
I am thinking of you.

Erinnere ihn daran!
Remind him of it.

    (*c*) Of envy, pride, etc. = **auf** + accusative:

Er ist neidisch auf mich.
He is envious of me.

Sie ist stolz auf ihren Sohn.
She is proud of her son.

    (*d*) Of fear, etc. = **vor** + dative:

Furcht vor dem Blitz.
Fear of lightning.

Mir graut vor der Seereise.
I dread the thought of the sea-voyage.

    6. 'To':

    (*a*) Of address, etc. = **an** + accusative:

Ich schreibe an einen Freund.
I am writing to a friend.

Ein an mich weitergeleiteter Brief.
A letter sent on to me.

Wenden Sie sich an ihn!
Apply to him.

    (*b*) After many nouns and adjectives signifying an affection of the mind = **gegen**:

Er benahm sich schlecht gegen seine Frau.
He behaved badly to his wife.

Er zeigt sich immer freundlich gegen alte Leute.
He is always friendly to old people.

Seine Hilfsbereitschaft gegen andere machte ihn überall beliebt.
His helpfulness to others made him popular with everyone.

328. Da(r) with Prepositions

With the following prepositions **da(r)** replaces pronouns used for inanimate objects and abstractions (compare §329):

(*a*) **an: Ich glaube nicht daran** (*e.g.*, **an seine Geschichte**).
I don't believe it (his story).

(*b*) **auf: Ich bin gespannt darauf** (*e.g.*, **auf das Prüfungsergebnis**). I am waiting eagerly for it (the examination result).

(*c*) **aus: Daraus werde ich nicht schlau** (*e.g.*, **aus diesem Brief**).
I can't make head or tail of it (this letter).

(*d*) **bei: Es gibt einen Garten dabei** (*e.g.*, **bei dem Haus**). It has a garden attached to it (the house).

(*e*) **durch: Das Nadelöhr ist zu schmal: der Faden kommt nicht dadurch.** The eye of the needle is too small: the thread won't go through.

(*f*) **für: Er hat viel Geld dafür bezahlt** (*e.g.*, **für das Auto**). He paid a lot of money for it (the car).

(*g*) **gegen: Ich bin ganz einverstanden; dagegen ist wirklich nichts zu sagen.** I absolutely agree; there is really nothing to be said against it.

(*h*) **hinter: Er öffnete die Tür und verbarg sich dahinter.** He opened the door and hid behind it.

(*i*) **in: Er öffnete das Kästchen und fand darin einen Manschettenknopf.** He opened the box and found in it a cuff-link.

(*j*) **mit: Die Katze fraß die Maus nicht, sondern spielte nur damit.** The cat did not eat the mouse, but just played with it.

(*k*) **nach: Wir haben Erbsensuppe und danach kalten Aufschnitt gegessen.** We ate pea soup and after that slices of cold meat.

(*l*) **neben: Die Post ist gleich daneben** (*e.g.*, **neben dem Rathaus**). The post office is right next to it (the town hall).

(*m*) **über: Machen Sie sich keine Sorgen darüber!** (*e.g.*, **über die Beförderung Ihres Gepäckes**). Don't worry about it (the forwarding of your luggage).

(*n*) **um: Das Haus hat einen Garten mit einem Zaun darum.** The house has a garden with a fence round it.

(*o*) **unter: Er hob den Stein auf und fand einen Käfer darunter.** He lifted the stone and found a beetle beneath it.

(*p*) **von: Ich kenne den Ort, den Sie meinen, denn ich wohne nicht weit davon.** I know the place you mean as I live not far away from it.

(*q*) **vor: „Vor der Kaserne, vor dem großen Tor, stand eine Laterne und steht sie noch davor"** (*Lili Marleen*). In front of the barracks, in front of the tall gate, used to stand a (street) lamp and still it stands there in front of it.

(*r*) **zu: Dazu habe ich keine Zeit** (*e.g.*, **zum Spazierengehen**). I have no time for that (for walking).

(*s*) **zwischen: Dazwischen war eine Pause** (*e.g.*, **zwischen den beiden Akten des Stückes**). Between them there was an interval (between the two acts of the play).

NOTE: 1. **Da(r)** cannot be combined with the prepositions **außer, bis, entlang, gegenüber, ohne, seit, wider.**

2. **Da(r)** may also refer back to a whole sentence or look forward to a clause or an infinitive phrase—*e.g.*, **Ich glaube, daß er mein Feuerzeug gestohlen hat. Dafür habe ich aber keinen Beweis,** 'I think that he has stolen my lighter. But I have no proof of it'; **Ich bin dagegen, daß die Kinder allein bleiben,** 'I am against the children being left alone'; **Er sprach davon, sein Auto zu verkaufen,** 'He talked of selling his car'.

3. The substitution of **da** for **das** is not made before a relative: **Ich dachte an das, was Sie sagten,** 'I was thinking of what you were saying'.

4. The following abbreviated forms are not uncommon, especially in colloquial speech: **dran** (= **daran**), **drauf** (= **darauf**), **draus** (= **daraus**), **drin** (= **darin**), **drüber** (= **darüber**), **drum** (= **darum**), **drunter** (= **darunter**).

5. When not emphatic, these words are stressed on the second syllable (*e.g.*, **da'rüber**). When used emphatically, however, they are stressed on the first syllable (*e.g.*, **'darüber**). Compare the sentences **Man wird keine Brücke da'rüber bauen können,** 'They won't be able to

build a bridge over it' and **'Darüber wird man keine Brücke bauen können,** 'They won't be able to build a bridge over *that*'.

329. Hier with Prepositions

Just as **das** and **jenes** are replaced by **da(r)** (see §328), so **dies** is replaced by **hier**, prefixed to a preposition and written as one word with it:

(*a*) **an: Halt dich hieran fest!** Hold on (tight) to this!

(*b*) **auf: Mit Tinte kann man hierauf nicht schreiben.** You can't write on this with ink.

(*c*) **für: Hierfür biete ich Ihnen zwanzig Mark.** I'll give you twenty Marks for this.

(*d*) **mit: Hiermit will ich schließen.** With this I will close.

(*e*) **von: Hiervon bin ich überzeugt.** I am convinced of this.

(*f*) **zu: Stellen Sie die neuen Bücher hierzu!** Put the new books with these.

There are many other such combinations, for example, **hieraus,** 'from it (*or* them)'; **hierbei,** 'near it'; **hierneben,** 'next to it (*or* them)'; **hierüber,** 'over it (*or* them)'.

NOTE: 1. The translation of such words depends on the translation of the preposition in connection with the verb, etc., in question. The above examples illustrate the most literal meanings; there are, besides, numerous extended uses.

2. When not emphatic, these words have equal stress (*e.g.*, **'hier'für**). When used emphatically, however, they are stressed on the first syllable (*e.g.*, **'hierfür**). Compare the sentences **Ich biete Ihnen zwanzig Mark 'hier'für,** 'I'll give you twenty Marks for this' and **'Hierfür biete ich Ihnen zwanzig Mark,** 'I'll give you twenty Marks for *this* one'.

330. Infinitive with Prepositions

1. Only the prepositions **um, (an)statt,** and **ohne** can govern an infinitive (with **zu**) directly, and then only with identical subject:

Er kaufte die Blumen, um seiner Frau damit eine Freude zu machen.
He bought the flowers in order to please his wife.

Er fuhr ins Ausland, um seine Sprachkenntnisse aufzufrischen.
He went abroad to brush up his knowledge of foreign languages.

Anstatt ruhig über die Angelegenheit zu sprechen, machte sie eine schreckliche Szene.
Instead of speaking calmly about the matter she made a dreadful scene.

Anstatt ins Kino zu gehen, blieben sie zu Hause.
Instead of going to the cinema they stayed at home.

Ohne ein Wort zu sagen, ging er aus dem Zimmer.
Without saying a word he went out of the room.

Er kritisierte das Buch, ohne es je gelesen zu haben.
He criticized the book without ever having read it.

2. Observe from the above that the English gerund, or verbal noun ending in '-ing', answers to this German construction, except after **um**.

3. The English gerund is a noun, and may stand as subject or object; it must be carefully distinguished from the English present participle, which is an adjective and must refer to some noun, expressed or understood—*e.g.*, Fishing (*gerund subject*) is exciting (*participial adjective*); I like fishing (*gerund object*); I am tired of fishing (*gerund object of preposition*).

4. The preposition governing an English gerund is not always required in German, and the gerund is then rendered by an infinitive:

Die Gabe, gut zu sprechen.
The gift of speaking well.

Er hat alle Ursache, sich über das Geschenk zu freuen.
He has every reason for being delighted with the present.

5. If the verb in the governing clause requires a preposition, the preposition is usually preceded by **da(r)** and

(*a*) in the case of identical subject, there follows the infinitive with **zu**:

Ich bin damit beschäftigt, ein Buch zu schreiben.
I am engaged in writing a book.

Ich denke nicht daran, ein neues Auto zu kaufen.
I am not thinking of buying a new car.

(b) in the case of different subjects, there follows a subordinate clause introduced by **daß**:

Ich habe nichts dagegen, daß Ihr Bruder bleibt.
I have no objection to your brother staying.

Wir verlassen uns darauf, daß Sie kommen.
We rely on your coming.

6. When the English gerund governed by a preposition expresses an adverbial relation, it must be expanded in German into a subordinate clause:

Als er uns sah, lief er fort.
On seeing us, he ran away.

Indem wir andere überreden, überreden wir uns selbst.
In persuading others we persuade ourselves.

X. CONJUNCTIONS

331. General Remarks

Conjunctions are uninflected words which connect words, phrases, or clauses—*e.g.* 'and', 'whether', 'although'. In German, all conjunctions cause the verb to be placed at the end of its clause, except **aber, allein, denn, oder, sondern,** and **und,** and correlative conjunctions (§340), which do not affect the normal word order. There are three kinds of conjunctions, namely:

Co-ordinating conjunctions: These are conjunctions that join clauses of the same rank or order—*e.g.* 'He waved goodbye *and* boarded the aircraft', 'They threw tomatoes at him *but* he went on singing'.

Subordinating conjunctions: These connect a subordinate statement with a principal statement or with another subordinate statement, and in German the verb must come at the end of the clause—*e.g.* **Frage ihn, *ob* er kommen will,** 'Ask him *whether* he wants to come', **Ich glaube, *daß* er kommt,** 'I think that he'll come'.

Correlative conjunctions: These consist of pairs of words habitually used together, the second part being necessary to complete the first—*e.g.* **nicht nur . . . sondern auch,** 'not only . . . but also'.

332. Co-ordinating Conjunctions

1. The following co-ordinating conjunctions do not affect the word order:

aber, but	**oder,** or
allein, but, (and) yet	**sondern,** but (on the contrary)
denn, for, as	**und,** and

Examples:

Ich habe das Buch gelesen, aber es gefiel mir nicht.
I have read the book but I did not like it.

streiten um, to quarrel about
trauern um, to mourn for

12. VON (+ *dat.*):

abhängen (*sep.*) **von,** to depend on
benachrichtigen von, to inform of, to notify about
erschallen von, to resound with
freisprechen (*sep.*) **von,** to acquit of
handeln von, to deal with, to be about
heilen von, to cure of
leben von, to live on
sprechen von, to speak of
träumen von, to dream of
triefen von, to drip with; to overflow with (wisdom, etc.)
überzeugen von, to convince of
widerhallen von, to resound with
wimmeln von, to seethe with, to swarm with

13. VOR:

(In all these figurative expressions the preposition governs the dative.)

beben vor, to tremble with (anger, etc.)
brennen vor, to burn with (impatience, etc.)
erröten vor, to blush for (shame, etc.)
fliehen vor, to flee from
glühen vor, to be aflame with (longing), to glow with (enthusiasm)
hüpfen vor, to jump for (joy)
kochen vor, to boil with (rage, etc.)
retten vor, to rescue from
schäumen vor, to foam with (rage, etc.)
schützen vor, to protect from
strahlen vor, to be radiant with (happiness, etc.)
umkommen (*sep.*) **vor,** to die of (boredom, etc.)
warnen vor, to warn of
weinen vor, to weep with (joy, etc.)
zittern vor, to tremble with (fear, etc.)

Er hat viel Geld, allein er weiß nichts damit anzufangen.
He has a lot of money but he doesn't know what to do with it.

NOTE: In speech **aber** is more frequently used than **allein**.

**Er hatte großes Glück, die Stellung zu bekommen, denn es gab
viele Bewerber.**
He was very lucky to get the job as there were many applicants.

Geht ihr ins Kino, oder seht ihr euch die Ausstellung an?
Are you going to the cinema or are you going to see the exhibition?

Er zögerte nicht lange, sondern (er) nahm das Angebot an.
He did not hesitate for long, but accepted the offer.

NOTE: **Sondern** corrects or contradicts a preceding negative
statement in a sentence in which the subject of both statements is
identical. If, however, there is no correction or contradiction expressed
or implied, **aber,** not **sondern,** is used; compare the following
two sentences: **Er ist nicht reich, sondern (er ist) arm,** 'He is not rich
but (on the contrary) poor'; **Er ist nicht reich, aber er ist ehrlich,**
'He is not rich, but he *is* honest'.

Er setzte sich auf den Stuhl, und der Stuhl zerbrach.
He sat down on the chair, and the chair broke.

2. When two principal clauses connected by **und** have a common
subject, the verb of the latter clause usually follows the
conjunction immediately and there is no comma before **und**:

Mein Freund ist krank und muß das Haus hüten.
My friend is ill and has to stay indoors.

333. Combinations of Co-ordinating Conjunctions

Some common co-ordinating conjunctions—*e.g.*, **und, aber,
denn**—are used together with other co-ordinating conjunctions.
The clause introduced by the two conjunctions is inverted and
separated from the first clause by a comma. (NOTE: There is no
inversion in the second clause, however, if the two conjunctions
are separated by subject and verb; compare the two examples
under **und deshalb** below). Its subject is a personal pronoun if it is
the same as in the first clause.

Examples:

(*a*) **und auch: Es gab keinen Strom, und auch das Gas war abgestellt.** There was no electricity, and even the gas was cut off.

und dann: Sie tranken noch ein Glas Bier, und dann gingen sie nach Hause. They drank another glass of beer and then they went home.

und deshalb: Drei Busse fielen wegen eines Unfalls aus, und deshalb kam er zwei Stunden zu spät ins Büro. Three buses were cancelled because of an accident, and therefore he arrived at the office two hours late.

Es fing an zu regnen, und wir gingen deshalb nach Hause. It started to rain and we therefore went home.

und dennoch: Er ist ein seltsamer Mensch, und dennoch habe ich ihn gern. He is a strange person, but I still like him.

und doch: Alle Wünsche wurden ihm erfüllt, und doch war er unzufrieden. Every wish was granted him and yet he was not satisfied.

und zwar: Sie planten eine längere Reise, und zwar wollten sie in die Türkei fahren. They were planning a fairly long trip, and in fact they intended going to Turkey.

und somit: Das Projekt wurde genehmigt, und somit konnte mit seiner Verwirklichung begonnen werden. The project was approved, and so work could be started to bring it to realization.

(*b*) **aber auch: Er suchte den Füllhalter in der Schublade, aber auch dort fand er ihn nicht.** He looked for the fountain pen in the drawer, but even there he did not find it.

aber freilich: Er bestand die Prüfung mit „sehr gut", er hatte aber freilich auch Nachhilfestunden bekommen. He passed the examination with 'very good', but then of course he had had extra coaching.

aber dennoch, aber trotzdem: Alle bisherigen Versuche waren fehlgeschlagen, aber trotzdem experimentierte er weiter. All previous attempts had failed, but even so he went on experimenting.

aber wenn: Er wird nicht sehr leicht wütend, aber wenn es doch geschieht (wenn es aber doch geschieht), zerschlägt er gleich das

Geschirr. He does not very easily lose his temper, but when it does happen he immediately smashes the crockery.

(c) **denn auch: Er hörte auf zu arbeiten, denn auch die anderen arbeiteten nicht mehr.** He stopped working as the others were no longer working either.

denn doch: Sie warf die alten Kleider weg, denn es wollte sie doch niemand haben. She threw the old clothes away, as nobody wanted them anyway.

(d) **oder aber: Da die Eisenbahnen streiken, müssen wir uns ein Auto mieten oder aber per Anhalter fahren.** As the railways are on strike we must hire a car or else hitch-hike.

334. Adverbial Conjunctions

Adverbs and adverbial phrases often have the function of a connective conjunction, and introduce a clause co-ordinate with the preceding clause; the subject is then placed after the verb:

Ein Lehrer muß Geduld haben; insofern wär(e)st du nicht für diesen Beruf geeignet.
A teacher must have patience; in this respect you would not be suited to this profession.

Das Leben ist teuer, also müssen wir sparen.
Life is expensive, therefore we must economize.

NOTE: Adverbial conjunctions may also follow the verb as ordinary adverbs: **Das Leben ist teuer, wir müssen also sparen,** 'Life is expensive; we must therefore economize'.

335. Adverbial Conjunctions—Special Cases

1. **Es sei denn (, daß)** = 'unless' never begins a sentence:

Er wird schon noch kommen, es sei denn, er hat unsere Verabredung vergessen.
He'll be coming, unless he has forgotten our appointment.

Ich komme gern, es sei denn, daß ich selbst Besuch bekomme.
I'll be glad to come unless I have visitors myself.

NOTE: Both constructions are equally correct, but the one without **daß** is considered more elegant.

2. Likewise, **geschweige denn (, daß) = 'let alone, never mind'** never begins a sentence:

Er hat ihr zum Geburtstag nicht einmal eine Karte geschickt, geschweige denn ein Geschenk.
He didn't even send her a birthday card, let alone a present.

Ich glaube nicht einmal, daß er anruft, geschweige denn, daß er vorbeikommt.
I don't think he'll even ring, let alone call round.

3. Certain adverbial conjunctions—*e.g.*, **also, freilich, nun**—followed by a pause (indicated by a comma) cause no inversion:

Also, du glaubst nicht an seine Unschuld?
So you don't believe in his innocence?

Freilich, sie hätte wirklich etwas freundlicher sein können.
Of course, she could really have been a bit friendlier.

Nun, wir wollen nicht ungerecht sein, er hat sich alle Mühe gegeben.
Now, we don't want to be unjust, he did take a lot of trouble.

4. **Desgleichen** is an adverbial co-ordinating conjunction which connects two propositions of equal value:

Er nahm das Geld, desgleichen den Schmuck, und machte sich durch das Fenster davon.
He took the money, and with it the jewellery, and made off through the window.

Sie schickte den Brief per Eilpost, desgleichen das Paket.
She sent the letter by express delivery, and likewise the parcel.

336. Subordinating Conjunctions

1. Those most commonly occurring are:

als, as; when; than
als ob, als wenn, as if
bevor, before
bis, until
da, as, since; when
damit, in order that
daß, that
ehe, before
falls, in case
indem, as, while (*see* §338, 1)
insofern⎱ insofar as
insoweit⎰
nachdem, after
ob, whether, if
ob auch, (al)though
obgleich⎫
obschon⎬ although
obwohl⎭
ohne daß, without (+*gerund*)
seit(dem), since (*time*)

sobald, as soon as
so daß, so that
sofern, as far as
solange, as long as
sooft, as often as
soweit, as far as
sowie, as soon as; as well as
statt daß, instead of (+*gerund*)
trotzdem, in spite of the fact
    that (**obgleich** *is preferred*)
während, as, while
weil, because
wenn, if; when; whenever
wenn auch⎱ although,
wenngleich⎰   even if
wie, as, like
wofern, insofar as
wogegen   ⎱ whereas
wohingegen⎰
zumal, especially as

The following are also found, though rarely nowadays except in literary contexts:

auf daß, (in order) that
derweil(en), while
dieweil, as long as, while
indes(sen) ⎱ while
unterdessen⎰

obzwar, although
ungeachtet (daß), although
wennschon⎱ although
wiewohl ⎰

2. These conjunctions connect a subordinate statement with a principal statement or with another subordinate statement, and in German the verb must come at the end of the clause:

Ich glaube, daß er kommt.
I think that he'll come.

Ich weiß nicht, ob es wahr ist, daß er verreist.
I don't know whether it is true that he is going away.

337. Use of **wenn, als, wann**

Wenn ich eine Arbeit beende (beendet habe), bin ich froh.
When (*or* Whenever) I finish (have finished) a piece of work, I
am glad.

Ich habe immer meine Freunde besucht, wenn ich in der Stadt war.
I always visited my friends when(ever) I was in town.

Ich bin gestern ausgegangen, als es zehn Uhr war.
I went out yesterday when it was ten o'clock.

Als ich in Paris war, bin ich oft ins Museum gegangen.
When I was in Paris I often went to the museum.

Wenn immer ich in Paris bin, gehe ich ins Museum.
Whenever I am in Paris I go to the museum.

Wenn immer ich in Paris war, bin ich ins Museum gegangen.
Whenever I was in Paris I went to the museum.

Wann war sein Vater hier?
When was his father here?

Ich weiß nicht, wann sein Vater hier war.
I do not know when his father was here.

1. 'When' = **wenn** always with present or perfect.
2. 'When' = **wenn** with imperfect and pluperfect of a habitual
or repeated occurrence, state, or condition (= 'whenever').
3. 'When' = **als** with imperfect and pluperfect only, of a single,
definite occurrence, or of a state or condition once occurring.
4. 'Whenever', with present, future, or imperfect, is rendered
by **wenn immer** when an emphatic statement is being made.
5. 'When?' interrogative, both in direct and indirect propositions, = **wann?**

NOTE: Remember that **wenn** also = 'if'.

338. Subordinating Conjunctions— Special Cases

1. 'As' in the sense of 'while' = **während** (occasionally **indem**):

**Während (*or* indem) er dies niederschrieb, kam ihm ein neuer
Gedanke.**
As he was writing this down a fresh thought occurred to him.

NOTE: **Indem** usually=ʼby -ingʼ—*e.g.*, **Er entkam, indem er über die Mauer sprang,** 'He escaped by jumping over the wall'.

2. 'As' or 'since' indicating cause = **da**:

Er kann heute nicht kommen, da es regnet.
He can't come today as it is raining.

3. 'Since' as preposition = **seit**; as subordinating conjunction of time = **seitdem** (or **seit**):

Er ist schon seit voriger Woche hier.
He has been here since last week.

Ich habe nichts von ihm gehört, seit(dem) er verreist ist.
I have not heard from him since he went away.

4. 'Since' as adverb or co-ordinative adverbial conjunction = **seitdem**:

Den letzten Brief erhielt ich vor einem Monat. Seitdem habe ich nichts mehr von ihm gehört.
I received the last letter a month ago. Since then I have heard nothing more from him.

5. **Als** = 'but' after negatives; **alles andere als** = 'anything but':

Nichts als Unglück.
Nothing but bad luck.

Er ist alles andere als ein Held.
He is anything but a hero.

6. **Ob** = 'whether' in indirect questions:

Frage ihn, ob er mitkommen möchte.
Ask him whether he would like to come.

NOTE: 1. In **obgleich, wenngleich, obschon,** etc., 'although', the latter part used commonly to be separated and placed after the subject; this construction is often found in the Bible, but hardly ever in modern usage: **Ob er gleich reich ist, ...** (= **Obgleich er reich ist, ...**), 'Although he is rich, ...'
2. The **ob** or **wenn** is often omitted in **als ob, als wenn;** note the resulting change in word order: **Mir ist, als ob ich jemanden klingeln**

gehört hätte *or* Mir ist, als hätte ich jemanden klingeln hören, 'I thought I heard someone ring'.

7. **Bevor** expresses time only; **ehe** also expresses preference: (*a*) = 'before':

Ich möchte noch nach Hause kommen, ehe (*or* bevor) es dunkel wird.
I should like to reach home before it gets dark.

(*b*) = 'until':

Es hat keinen Sinn, dir das Schwimmen beizubringen, ehe (*or* bevor) du nicht deine Angst vor dem Wasser überwunden hast.
There is no point in teaching you how to swim until you have conquered your fear of water.

NOTE: Observe the expletive **nicht** in this use of **ehe** and **bevor**. (An expletive is a word not strictly necessary to the sense of a given construction).

(*c*) **ehe** also = 'rather than':

Ehe er sein Geheimnis preisgäbe, würde er lieber sterben.
Rather than yield his secret he would prefer to die.

8. Distinguish carefully between 'after' and 'before' as prepositions and as conjunctions:

(*a*) Prepositions:

Nach der Hochzeit fuhren sie nach Italien.
After the wedding they went to Italy.

Vor dem Abendessen machen wir einen Spaziergang.
Before the evening meal we go for a walk.

(*b*) Conjunctions:

Nachdem er fort war, entdeckte sie den Diebstahl.
After he had gone she discovered the theft.

Ich wußte nicht, wie nett sie ist, bevor (*or* ehe) ich sie richtig kennenlernte.
I did not know how nice she is until I really got to know her.

339. Subordinating Conjunctions used to render Participles of Time and Cause

1. The English present participle often has the force of an

adverbial clause of time or cause, and when so used is rendered in German by a sentence introduced by a subordinating conjunction.

2. The conjunctions thus used to express time are **als**, 'when', and **während** (occasionally **indem**), 'while':

Als ich ihn kommen sah, ging ich ihm entgegen.
Seeing him coming, I went to meet him.

Während er auf sein Manuskript blickte, fuhr er in seiner Rede fort.
Looking at his manuscript, he continued his speech.

Ich traf ihn, als (während, indem) ich in Europa umherreiste.
I met him when (while) travelling in Europe.

3. For time, expressed by the English perfect participle, **nachdem**, 'after', or **als**, 'when', is always used, followed by the pluperfect:

Nachdem (Als) ich den Brief gelesen hatte, warf ich ihn weg.
Having read the letter, I threw it away.

4. To express cause, **da**, 'as', 'since', or **weil**, 'because', is used:

Da ich ihn nicht angetroffen hatte, besuchte ich ihn am nächsten Tag noch einmal.
Not finding him at home, I called on him again the next day.

Weil er ehrlich ist, kann man ihm trauen.
Being honest, he is to be trusted.

340. Correlative Conjunctions

1. These conjunctions consist of two parts, the second being necessary to complete the first; the following are the most important:

(*a*) **entweder ... oder,** 'either ... or': **Entweder du gehst jetzt los, oder du kommst zu spät.** Either you set off now or you'll be late.

(*b*) **weder ... noch,** 'neither ... nor': **Er interessiert sich weder für Musik noch für Kunst.** He is interested neither in music nor in art.

(*c*) **nicht nur ... sondern auch,** 'not only ... but also': **Nicht**

nur die Geschäfte waren geschlossen, sondern auch die Banken.
Not only the shops but also the banks were closed.

(*d*) sowohl . . . als (*or* wie) (auch), 'both . . . and': Sie konnte
sowohl Klavier als (*or* wie) auch Geige spielen. She could play
both the piano and the violin. (See 2, below.)

(*e*) bald . . . bald, 'at one time . . . at another'; 'now . . . now
(then)': Bald regnete es, bald schneite es, das Wetter war scheußlich. Now it rained, now it snowed, the weather was dreadful.

(*f*) (eben)so . . . wie, '(just) as . . . as': So komisch, wie er in
seinen Filmen war, war er auch im Leben. He was just as comical
in real life as he was in his films.

(*g*) desto (*or* je) . . . desto (*or* je *or* um so), 'the . . . the': Je
höher die Löhne, desto mehr steigen die Preise. The higher the
wages, the more prices rise. (See 3, below.)

(*h*) so . . . so, 'as . . . as': So häßlich sie ist, so dumm ist sie
auch. She is as ugly as she is stupid. (See 4, below.)

(*i*) zwar . . . aber, 'it is true that . . . but': Zwar war sein
Wissen nicht groß, aber er wußte es geschickt anzuwenden. It is
true that his knowledge was not great, but he knew how to make
clever use of it.

(*j*) mal . . . mal, 'sometimes . . . sometimes': Mal gehe ich
ins Kino, mal ins Theater, je nach Laune. Sometimes I go to the
cinema, sometimes to the theatre, according to how I feel.

2. In sentences introduced by sowohl . . . als (*or* wie) (auch)
the verb sometimes agrees with the last subject:

Sowohl mein Bruder als (auch) mein Vetter ist angekommen.
Both my brother and my cousin have arrived.

More usual nowadays, however, is the plural:

Sowohl mein Bruder als (auch) mein Vetter sind angekommen.

3. Desto and je are used interchangeably in either member
of a proportional clause; the former member is subordinate,
the latter principal, but with inversion of subject and verb:

Je (*or* **desto**) **eher er kommt, desto** (*or* **je** *or* **um so**) **eher kann er gehen.**
The sooner he comes, the sooner he can go.

4. **So . . . so** introduce correlative clauses containing adjectives compared together in the positive degree, the former being subordinate:

So dumm er ist, so feige ist er auch.
He is as cowardly as he is stupid.

XI. GLOSSARY OF GRAMMATICAL TERMS

Note: More detailed information about many of the head-words will be found by consulting the Index.

ABSTRACT NOUN. See §33.

ACCUSATIVE CASE. The accusative is the case of the direct object of a verb—*e.g.* 'He posted *the letter*', 'I hope to see *my sister*'—thus answering the question 'what?' **(was?)** or 'whom?' **(wen?).** It has the same form as the nominative case, except in the masculine singular (see §22). Whereas in English *all* prepositions take the accusative case, in German only some do (see §§303-320). See also DIRECT OBJECT.

ACTIVE VOICE. The voice used when the subject of the verb performs the action—*e.g.* 'He sang a song', 'I am reading a book'—or is in the state described by the verb — *e.g.* 'We stood in the rain'. See VOICE and PASSIVE VOICE.

ADJECTIVAL NOUN. An adjective used as a noun—*e.g.* 'the rich and the poor', 'the high and the mighty', where the word 'people' is understood but not expressed. In German, such adjectives—and participles—are declined according to the rules for adjective declension—i.e., they are declined exactly as if a noun followed. For example, from the adjective **fremd** ('strange') is formed the adjectival noun **der Fremde** ('the stranger'), the full declension of which is given in §148. See also §147.

ADJECTIVE. For general remarks about adjectives, see §113. For declension of adjectives after the definite article and after **dieser, jener, jeder, welcher, mancher,** and **solcher,** see §§115, 116; after the indefinite article and after **kein** and the possessive adjectives **mein, dein, sein, unser, euer, ihr,** and **Ihr,** §§114-116; and for when the noun is preceded by an adjective alone, see

§116, 1. See also under ATTRIBUTIVE ADJECTIVE, PRE-DICATIVE ADJECTIVE.

ADVERB. See §247.

ADVERBIAL CONJUNCTION. A conjunction which serves as an adverb or adverbial phrase, having the function of a connective conjunction (see under CONNECTIVE) to intro-duce a clause co-ordinate with the preceding clause; the subject is then placed after the verb. For examples, see §§334, 335.

AFFIRMATIVE. A word or phrase which affirms or declares as a fact, answering 'yes' to a question; opposed to NEGATÌVE.

AGENT. The doer of an action as represented by a noun or pronoun—e.g., in the sentence 'He scored a goal', 'he' is the agent; in the sentence 'The goal was scored by him', 'him' is the agent. From the latter example it will be seen that agency is often associated with the passive voice and in English with the word 'by' in passive constructions. In German the passive with **werden** is used whenever agency is specified or implied; the personal agent is denoted by **von**+dative, other agency by **durch** or **mit** (see §243).

AGREEMENT. See §8, 2.

ANTECEDENT. An antecedent (literally, 'that which goes before') is a noun or noun-equivalent (either a phrase or clause) related to a personal or relative pronoun and preceding it. Thus, in the examples 'people who care', 'things which matter', 'people' is the antecedent of 'who' and 'things' the ante-cedent of 'which'; an example where the antecedent is a whole clause is: **Nach nur einer Woche machte er ihr einen Heiratsan-trag, was sie sehr überraschte,** 'After only a week he proposed to her, which surprised her very much'; here **was** is a relative pronoun and all that precedes it constitutes the antecedent.

In German, the pronoun must agree with its antecedent in gender, number, and (in the case of personal pronouns) person, though its case depends on its use in its own clause (see §§57, 59, 2).

APPOSITION/APPOSITIVE. A word, or word-group, is said to be in apposition with another when it refers to the same person(s) or thing(s) and provides additional information—*e.g.* 'Robin Hood, a legendary outlaw, . . .', 'The crew of the lifeboat, a courageous handful of men, . . .' In German, words and word-groups in apposition must agree in gender, number, person, and case (see §§45, 49). The adjective derived from 'apposition' is 'appositive'.

ARTICLES. See §8, 3.

ATTRIBUTIVE ADJECTIVE. If an adjective comes immediately before a noun (as in 'a *good* breakfast', 'a *magic* potion') it is said to be attributive. In German, as in English, adjectives are commonly used attributively, and when they are they must be declined (§§115, 116). See also §113 and PREDICATIVE ADJECTIVE.

AUXILIARY VERBS. Auxiliary (='helping') verbs are verbs which help to form the tenses, voices, or moods of other verbs.

(1) *Auxiliary verbs of tense:* In order to form a finite verb in the perfect or pluperfect, an auxiliary verb is used together with the past participle; in English the auxiliary is always 'to have'— *e.g.* 'I *have* spoken', 'I *had* spoken' (though cf. the archaic usage 'He *is* come into the world to save sinners')—but in German the auxiliary may be either **haben** or **sein** (*e.g.* **ich habe gesprochen, ich hatte gesprochen**, but **ich bin gekommen, ich war gekommen**—see §§217, 246). Note that both in English and in German, 'to be' and 'to have', **sein** and **haben**, besides their use as auxiliary verbs, can be used as normal independent verbs: thus 'I have a lighter', **ich habe ein Feuerzeug**: 'She is a cook', **sie ist Köchin.**

(2) **werden** *as an auxiliary of voice:* The passive voice is formed in German by using **werden** together with the past participle—*e.g.* **Der Gefangene wurde entlassen**, 'The prisoner was released'.

(3) *Auxiliary verbs of mood:* See §§224–230.

CARDINALS. Cardinals are numbers which express *how many*—*e.g.* 'one', 'six', 'ninety'. In German, except for **ein,** they are not nowadays normally inflected; cf. §279. See also ORDINALS.

CASE. See §8, 4.

CASE-ENDING. The one or more letters added to the stem of an inflected noun, pronoun, or adjective to denote the case— i.e., to show the part they play in a sentence. For example, the case-ending **-(e)s** is added to the stem of masculine and neuter nouns to indicate the genitive singular: **Brief-(e)s, Dorf-(e)s.** See also STEM, DECLENSION, and §8, 4.

CLAUSE. A group of words which contains a finite verb (thus distinguishing it from a phrase, which does not) and forms part of a sentence. A principal (or main) clause makes sense on its own, whereas a dependent (or subordinate) clause does not —*e.g.*, in the sentence 'He came when I called him', 'He came' is the principal clause and 'when I called him' is the dependent clause. A sentence may contain any number of clauses. In German, the verb comes last in a dependent clause.

COLLECTIVE (NOUN). See §33.

COLLOQUIAL. Conversational or informal, as opposed to literary or formal. Colloquial words and expressions (known as colloquialisms) are characteristic of everyday conversation and informal writings, but not of dignified speech or formal written discourse. Thus 'pot-holer' is colloquial for 'speleologist', 'up the creek' is colloquial for 'in trouble'. Cf. FAMILIAR (1).

COMMON NOUN. See §33.

COMPARATIVE. The comparative (or comparative degree) is the degree of comparison of an adjective (see §§150–157) or an adverb (§§274–278) expressing a higher degree or amount of the attribute denoted by the positive form—*e.g.* **kleiner, schöner** ('smaller', 'more beautiful') are the comparative forms of the simple adjectival forms **klein, schön** ('small', 'beautiful'). The comparative may be either relative, when it denotes a higher degree than any other considered (*e.g.* 'Make me a *better* offer'), or absolute, when it merely denotes a somewhat high degree (*e.g.* 'a fairly long stretch', rendered in German by **eine längere Strecke)**. See also COMPARISON, DEGREE, POSITIVE, SUPERLATIVE.

COMPARISON. For adjectives and adverbs there are three degrees of comparison—the positive (*e.g.* 'big', 'soon'), the comparative ('bigger', 'sooner'), and the superlative ('biggest', 'soonest'). See also COMPARATIVE, DEGREE, POSITIVE, SUPERLATIVE.

COMPLEMENT. The complement is that part of a sentence which completes its sense, by the addition of a word or words to certain verbs, such as 'to be' and 'to become'. Thus in the sentence 'She is a nurse', 'She' is the subject, 'is' is a part of the verb 'to be', and 'a nurse' is the complement. Note that in such sentences the subject and compliment are the same person, thing, etc., and therefore take the same case, always the nominative with the verbs 'to be' and 'to become'. See also PREDICATE.

COMPOUND NOUN. See §33.

COMPOUND TENSE. A tense which is composed of more than one verb element—namely, (1) one or more auxiliary verbs + a past participle (*e.g.* **ich habe gegeben,** 'I have given'— perfect), (2) an auxiliary verb + an infinitive (*e.g.* **ich werde geben,** 'I shall give'—future), (3) an auxiliary verb + a past participle + an infinitive (*e.g.* **ich werde gegeben haben,** 'I shall have given'—future perfect). Other compound tenses are the pluperfect (**ich hatte gegeben,** 'I had given'), the simple conditional (**ich würde geben,** 'I would give'), and the compound conditional (**ich würde gegeben haben,** 'I would have given'). The compound conditional is also sometimes called the past conditional or perfect conditional. Compound passive forms of verbs also occur—*e.g.* **er wurde verletzt,** 'he was injured', **er ist verletzt worden,** 'he has been injured'. See also SIMPLE TENSE.

COMPOUND VERB. See §200.

CONCRETE NOUN. See §33.

CONDITIONAL (TENSES). There are two conditional tenses—the simple (or present) conditional and the compound (or past or perfect) conditional. See §§180–182.

A conditional sentence is formed of two parts—the condition and the result, known technically as the *protasis* (= 'fore-saying') and the *apodosis* (= 'aftersaying'). The condition is usually introduced by the conjunction **wenn** ('if') and is a subordinate clause with the verb at the end, while the conclusion is the main (or principal) clause, in which the word order is inverted and often introduced by **so**—*e.g.* **Wenn ich Geld habe, so gebe ich es aus,** 'If I have money I spend it'; **Wenn ich Geld hätte, so würde ich es ausgeben,** 'If I had money I would spend it'; **Wenn ich Geld gehabt hätte, so hätte ich es ausgegeben,** 'If I had had money I would have spent it'. Thus in a conditional sentence the indicative expresses what actually happens under certain circumstances (I spend money *if*. . .), while the subjunctive or conditional expresses what would happen (or would have happened) under certain circumstances, but in fact does not (or did not) happen.

CONJUGATE. To conjugate a verb is to give, usually in a set sequence (as in the example in the next sentence), its various forms according to voice, mood, tense, number, and person. Thus the verb 'to go' is conjugated as follows in the active voice, indicative mood, present tense, in the singular and plural (number) in all persons: I go, [thou goest], he/she/it goes; we go, you go (*singular and plural*), they go. In German as in English, the compound past tenses are conjugated with the help of an auxiliary verb (+ past participle); in English the auxiliary is nowadays invariably 'to have' (*e.g.* 'I have come'—but cf. the archaic use of the verb 'to be', as in 'He *is* come to save us'), whereas in

German the auxiliary may be either **haben** (*e.g.* ich *habe* **gegeben,** 'I have given') or **sein** (*e.g.* ich *bin* **gegangen,** 'I have gone'). Note that only verbs are conjugated; nouns and adjectives are declined.

CONJUGATION. The conjugation of a verb is the variation of its forms according to voice, mood, tense, number, and person (see CONJUGATE). The word 'conjugation' has a second meaning, namely a group or class of verbs with the same kind of forms—i.e., conjugated in the same manner according to a set pattern. In German there are three kinds of conjugations: weak, strong, and mixed—see §160. The corresponding term applied to nouns and adjectives is 'declension'.

CONJUNCTION. See §331.

CONSTRUCTION. The way in which words are arranged in a sentence to convey a particular meaning. Construction involves *syntax*, which is that branch of grammar which deals with the rules and conventions which govern such arrangements and relationships; these are different for every language, and care should be taken to render a given construction in one language by the equivalent construction in another, which may be totally different. It is because of the variation in construction from one language to another that sentences can rarely be translated literally. Thus the German construction **Ein Mann wie ein Baum** (literally = 'A man like a tree') is rendered in English by a different construction, 'A mountain of a man'; **bei einbrechender Nacht** = 'when night closes in' or 'at nightfall'. Similarly, 'to love to do something' and 'to love doing something' are two different verbal constructions.

CONTEXT. The material which immediately precedes or follows a given text or passage or word which, so placed in its general setting, throws light upon its meaning. It is only when the context of a word is known that it can be correctly rendered in another language.

CONTRACTION. A shortened form of a word or words—
e.g. 'shan't' for 'shall not', 'p.' for 'page' (**S.** for **Seite).**
Many German prepositions have contracted forms in certain
set phrases, where the definite article loses its demonstrative
force and assumes an abstract and general force—*e.g.* **am
besten,** 'best (of all)', where **am** is a contraction of **an dem;
fürs erste,** 'for the time being', where **fürs** is a contraction of
für das. See §323.

CO-ORDINATING CONJUNCTIONS. See §331.

CORRELATIVE CONJUNCTIONS. See §331.

DATIVE CASE. The dative is the case of the indirect object
of a verb—*e.g.* 'He gave it *to the man*', 'I gave *him* it'—thus
answering the question 'to whom?' **(wem?).** It denotes the
person for whose advantage or disadvantage a thing is or is
done, corresponding not only to the English 'to' or 'for' but
also to 'from' (see §25). In German, many verbs and prepositions govern the dative case. The form of the dative singular of
nouns is often (in the case of feminine nouns, always) the same
as the nominative, but masculine and neuter monosyllables
sometimes add **-e** in the dative singular (*e.g.* **dem Manne, dem
Kinde);** though once usual, this **-e** is tending more and more to
disappear.

DECLENSION. The declension of a noun or adjective is
the variation, either by the addition of an ending or by a change
within the word, or both, of its forms according to its case,
gender, and number (see DECLINE). The word 'declension'
can also denote a group or class of nouns or adjectives with the
same kinds of forms—i.e., declined in the same manner according to a set pattern. For example, if in German an adjective is
preceded by **der, dieser, jeder,** etc., it conforms to the *weak* declension (*e.g.* **der gute Wein),** if standing on its own to the *strong*
declension **(guter Wein),** and if preceded by **ein, mein, dein,** etc.,
to the *mixed* declension (see §115). Nouns are classified into

those belonging to the *strong* declension (§34), the *weak* declension (§35), and the *mixed* declension (§36). The corresponding term applied to verbs is 'conjugation'. See WEAK, STRONG, MIXED.

DECLINE. To decline a noun or adjective is to give, usually in a set sequence, its various forms according to its case, gender, and number. The set sequence used in this Grammar and most others is: Nominative, Accusative, Genitive, Dative; thus the masculine noun **der Hund,** which belongs to the strong declension, is declined as follows in the singular: **der Hund, den Hund, des Hund(e)s, dem Hund(e);** and in the plural **die Hunde, die Hunde, der Hunde, den Hunden.** See §34. Attributive adjectives followed by a noun are declined variously according to what, if anything, precedes them (see under DECLENSION and also §§115, 116). Note that only nouns and adjectives are declined; verbs are conjugated.

DEFINITE ARTICLE. See §8, 3.

DEGREE. When applied to adjectives or adverbs, one of the three stages or grades of comparison—positive, comparative, superlative (which see).

DEMONSTRATIVE ADJECTIVE. A demonstrative adjective is one which distinctly points out that to which it refers— *e.g.* '*this* country', '*that* picture', '*those* considerations'.

DEMONSTRATIVE PRONOUN. See §50.

DEPENDENT. (1) Of clauses: see under CLAUSE. (2) Of other grammatical contexts the word is used to denote that one part of speech depends on or is related to another—*e.g.* in the sentence **Hier ist ein Brief, den ich eben erhalten habe** ('Here is a letter which I have just received') **den** (here a relative pronoun) is *dependent* on **Brief** (its antecedent) for number and person, though not for case.

DETERMINATIVES. Another name for 'limiting adjectives', §113.

DIMINUTIVE. A word formed from another by means of a suffix to denote a small one of the kind—for example, 'pig*let*' (a young pig), 'animal*cule*' (a microscopic animal)—or used as a term of endearment. In German, all diminutives ending in the suffixes **-chen** and **-lein** are neuter, regardless of sex—*e.g.* **das Fräulein,** 'young lady', **das Männlein** or **Männchen,** 'little man' (cf. English 'manikin', '-kin' here being a diminutive).

DIPHTHONG. A single speech sound made up of two separate vowel sounds, as *ou* in 'house' and *au* in **Haus**—though in German the first element is more deliberately uttered. See §7.

DIRECT OBJECT. A noun or pronoun governed by the action of a transitive verb. Thus in the sentence 'She sent a present', 'a present' is the direct object. In the sentence 'She sent a present to her mother', 'a present' is still the direct object, 'to her mother' being the *indirect* object. In a sentence containing both a direct and an indirect object, it is the direct object which is primarily affected by the action of the verb, the indirect object being only secondarily affected. The direct object is expressed in the accusative case, answering the question 'what?' or 'who?', and the indirect object is expressed in the dative case, answering the question 'to what?', 'to whom?' or 'for what?', 'for whom?' See ACCUSATIVE CASE, DATIVE CASE, OBJECT.

DISTRIBUTIVE. An adjective or pronoun which refers to each individual of a class separately—*e.g.* 'each', 'every', 'either', 'neither'. The English indefinite article is replaced by the definite article in German when used distributively—*e.g.* **dreimal** *die* **Woche,** 'three times *a* (=each) week', **drei Mark**

das **Meter,** 'three Marks *a* metre'; in such expressions of time and price the noun is in the accusative case.

ELLIPTICAL. A term used in grammar to denote that part of a construction has been omitted. For the use of the elliptical infinitive, which omits the finite part of the verb, see §§191, 241, 3.

EMOTIVE PARTICLE. A particle which provides added 'emotion' or feeling to a sentence, as, for example, the word **doch** in the sentence **Ich habe es ¹doch gesehen,** 'But I *did* see it', or **Was ist sie doch** (*unstressed*) **für ein hübsches Mädchen!,** 'What a pretty girl she is!' See, for further examples, §261, 6 and §267, 4; see also PARTICLE.

EMPHATIC PRONOUN. See §108.

ENDING. One or more letters or syllables added to a word or stem to indicate number, gender, case, person, mood, tense, or degree. Thus, for example, the *endings* '-er', '-est' are added to adjectives both in English and in German to form the comparative and superlative degrees—*e.g.* 'broader', 'broadest', **breiter, breitest;** the *ending* of the possessive adjective depends on the gender, number, and case of the noun it qualifies; the stem of a verb is what is left when the *ending* **-en** or **-n** is dropped from the infinitive. See STEM, INFLEXION.

ESSENTIAL PARTS. See §39.

ETHIC DATIVE. The 'ethic dative', otherwise known as the 'dative of advantage', is a colloquial use of the dative of a pronoun and is used to denote the person who has some interest in an action or thing—*e.g.* 'But hear *me* this' (Shakespeare). It is freely used in German colloquially to give a livelier tone to a sentence—for examples, see §112.

FAMILIAR. (1) = colloquial (which see). Familiar words and expressions are often designated *F*: in dictionaries. (2) Familiar address is distinguished in German by the use of the **du** form (cf. English 'thou' and French 'tu') as opposed to the formal or polite form **Sie** (cf. French 'vous'). **Du** and its corresponding possessive adjectives and verb forms are used when addressing close relatives, friends, children, or animals, etc.—see §52, 1, and FORMAL (2).

FEMININE. The gender of nouns and pronouns to which names of females normally belong, as opposed to the MASCU-LINE and NEUTER genders. In German, feminine nouns have the same form in all cases of the singular. See §8, 1, also §42.

FIGURATIVE, FIGURE OF SPEECH. Figurative language, as opposed to bare facts and literally true statements, adds force and variety to an idea to give a more emphatic or graphic effect. This is achieved by means of figures of speech, which are forms of expression differing from plain and normal usage and aimed at producing a striking effect. The word 'figurative' is often used simply as the opposite of 'literal'.

FINITE. The finite part of a verb is that which is used in the predicate and inflected in number and person; it is so called because it is distinctly limited to the subject (Latin 'finitus' = 'limited')—'he sings', 'she went', 'they disappear'. In the sentence **Ich habe meinen Hut verloren** ('I have lost my hat') the finite part of the verb is **habe** (have), not **verloren** (lost), which is a past participle.

FORM. The 'shape' or aspect which a word assumes when inflected, or when changed in spelling. Thus 'going', 'gone', and 'went' are *forms* of the verb 'to go'; 'seke' is an obsolete *form* of 'seek'.

FORMAL. (1) See under COLLOQUIAL. (2) Formal or polite address is distinguished in German by the use of the **Sie** form (cf. French 'vous') as opposed to the familiar **du** form (cf. French 'tu'). **Sie** and its corresponding possessive adjectives and verb forms are used when addressing strangers, mere acquaintances, and as a mark of respect to older people. See §52, 2, and FAMILIAR.

FUTURE PASSIVE PARTICIPLE. See under PAR-
TICIPLE.

FUTURE PERFECT TENSE. In German as in English, the
future perfect tense denotes a future act or event or state as past
in relation to a given future time; in German it also expresses
probability, etc.—for examples, see §179. It is formed in German
by inserting the past participle of the verb before the infinitive
of the future of the auxiliary—*e.g.* **ich werde gemacht haben** ('I
shall have made'), where **gemacht** is the past participle of the
verb **(machen)** and **werde . . . haben** the infinitive of the future
of the auxiliary.

FUTURE TENSE. In German as in English, the future tense
denotes an act or event or state which will happen or be at some
future time; in German it is also used to denote probability or
conjecture—for examples, see §177. It is formed in English with
'will' and 'shall', in German by adding the infinitive to the
present indicative of **werden,** as auxiliary—*e.g.* **ich werde gehen,**
'I shall go'. See also IMMEDIATE FUTURE.

GENDER. See §8, 1.

GENITIVE CASE. The use of the genitive case in German
is much the same as that of the English possessive, and answers
the question 'whose?', 'of whom?', or 'of what?' **(wessen?,
wovon?).** The genitive singular of feminine nouns is identical in
form with the nominative singular, but masculine and neuter
nouns usually have the genitive singular ending in **-s** or **-es.**
For prepositions which take the genitive case see §321. For adjectives which govern a genitive see §31, 1.

GERUND. The English gerund is a verbal noun (i.e., a
part of a verb which has lost all its function as a verb and is
used purely as a noun) ending in '-ing'; it may stand as subject
or object, and must be carefully distinguished from the English
present participle, which is an adjective and must refer to
some noun, expressed or understood—*e.g.* 'Fishing (*gerund
subject*) is exciting' (*participial adjective*); 'I like fishing'

(*gerund object*); 'I am tired of fishing' (*gerund object of preposition*). For the way in which these English constructions are rendered into German, see §330.

GLOTTAL STOP. The utterance of every German initial vowel, unless wholly unstressed, begins with the 'glottal stop', which consists in suddenly closing the glottis (the space between the vocal cords) and forcing it open by an explosion of breath, as in slight coughing.

GROUP-TERM. See 'Collective nouns', §33.

IDIOM(ATIC). An idiom is a mode of expression, often figurative, peculiar to a language. For instance, one may speak of buying a pig in a poke; in German the equivalent idiom is **die Katze im Sack kaufen.** This example serves to show that idioms, since they often convey a meaning different from that contained in the individual words, can rarely be rendered literally into another language. An *idiomatic* use of language is one which reflects these particular linguistic characteristics.

IMMEDIATE FUTURE. A form of the future tense exemplified by the sentence 'Tomorrow I am going home', in which a future meaning is conveyed by means of the present continuous tense ('am going'—a form of the present tense which does not exist in German). In Old English the present and future tenses had the same form, and this fact is reflected in the use, in modern German, of the *present* tense to render the English present continuous tense—**Morgen gehe ich nach Hause.**

IMPERATIVE (MOOD). The imperative expresses command or entreaty, and is therefore usually accompanied by an exclamation mark. The only true imperative forms in German are the second person singular and the second person plural (*e.g.* **mach!** or **mache!** (singular), **macht!** (plural)); for the remaining forms, which are present subjunctives with imperative force, see §238. For other ways of expressing the imperative in German, see §§239–241.

IMPERFECT TENSE. This is the past tense of historical narrative; it also denotes customary, repeated, or simultaneous action, answering to the English forms 'was doing', 'used to do', etc. For examples, see §171. The distinction made in English between the Imperfect (*e.g.* 'I was going') and the Past Definite (*e.g.* 'I went') does not exist in German because German has no continuous tenses, and therefore the Imperfect **(ich ging)** is used for both English forms.

IMPERSONAL VERB. An impersonal verb is one which is used only in (all tenses of) the third person singular (in English usually with 'it', in German with **es,** as subject)—*e.g.* **es regnete,** 'it was raining'. There are also the infinitive and past participial forms—**regnen** ('to rain') and **es hat geregnet** ('it has been raining'). Impersonal verbs may express natural phenomena (*e.g.* **es dunkelt,** 'it is getting dark', **es dämmert,** 'it is growing light'), or bodily or mental affection (*e.g.* **es ärgert mich,** 'I am annoyed', **es freut mich,** 'I am glad'), with the accusative, or various other sensations, etc. (*e.g.* **es tut mir leid,** 'I am sorry', **es ist mir kalt,** 'I am cold'), with the dative; for further examples, etc., see §218. See also §217. 4, for the only impersonal verbs conjugated with **sein.**

INDECLINABLE. This word is identical in meaning with INVARIABLE, but is applied only to nouns and adjectives. See also DECLINE.

INDEFINITE ADJECTIVE. An adjective, such as 'some', 'any', 'other', 'several', which does not define or determine the person, number, or quantity of the noun to which it refers.

INDEFINITE ARTICLE. See §8, 3.

INDEFINITE PRONOUN. See §50.

INDICATIVE (MOOD). The indicative is the mood of reality and direct statement or question—i.e., it states fact(s) or asks questions of fact: 'Venus is a planet', 'Is Venus a planet?' The indicative mood thus differs from the subjunctive mood, which represents something not as fact, from the imperative mood, which expresses command or entreaty, and from the infinitive mood, which expresses the idea or action or state of a verb without reference to person or number.

INDIRECT OBJECT. See under DIRECT OBJECT and DATIVE CASE.

INDIRECT QUESTION. A dependent clause which begins with an interrogative word such as 'who', 'what', 'whether', 'how', and expresses what was originally a direct question— *e.g.* 'He asked *who was there*', originally 'Who is there?' In German, the verb in the dependent clause is usually in the subjunctive if the verb in the governing clause is in a past tense—*e.g.* **Er fragte, wer da sei.** See §236.

INDIRECT STATEMENT. A statement which reports in a different tense a previous direct statement—*e.g.* 'He said that he was tired', where the previous direct statement was 'He said, "I am tired"'. Indirect statements are often introduced in English by 'that', in German by **daß**, though in both languages the conjunction can be omitted—*e.g.* **Er sagte, daß er müde sei** or **Er sagte, er sei müde** (note different position of verb), 'He said that he was tired' or 'He said he was tired'. Indirect statement is also known as 'reported speech'. See §236.

INFINITIVE (MOOD). See §184.

INFLEXION. The inflexion of a word is the variations or changes of form which it undergoes, usually by the addition of an ending, sometimes by an internal change, according to its voices, moods, tenses, numbers, and persons (in the case of a verb); its case, gender, and number (in the case of a noun or adjective); its degree, etc. German is a *highly inflected* language, in that such variations are numerous. See also CONJUGATION, DECLENSION, ENDING, STEM.

INSEPARABLE PREFIX. Certain prefixes (see §202) used in German with verbs are 'inseparable'—i.e., they cannot be detached from the rest of the verb. Such prefixes are always unstressed. Whereas separable prefixes usually retain their literal meaning (*e.g.* **ein,** 'in', **aus,** 'out'), inseparable prefixes have for the most part lost their original concrete meaning and in some instances developed a figurative meaning. Verbs with these prefixes omit the **ge-** of the past participle—*e.g.* the past participle of the inseparable verb **be¦grüßen,** 'to greet', is **be¦grüßt** (compare the simple verb **grüßen,** past participle **ge¦grüßt).** See also SEPARABLE PREFIX and COMPOUND VERB.

INTERROGATIVE ADJECTIVE. An adjective which is used to introduce a question; it may be indefinite ('*What* books do you like reading?') or definite ('*Which* boy won the prize?'). Interrogative adjectives are also used in indirect questions, such as 'I asked her *which* opera she preferred'. In German, when 'what' = 'what kind of', **was für ein** is used, otherwise **welcher** (see §§124, 125).

INTERROGATIVE PRONOUN. See §50.

INTONATION. The rise and fall in pitch (i.e., the range of intonation) of the voice in speech. Intonation, both in English and German, is noticeable chiefly in sense-groups, though single words such as 'What?' and 'Well' can be spoken with a variety of intonations, according to the meaning intended to be conveyed.

INTRANSITIVE VERBS. See §160; see also REFLEXIVE VERBS.

INVARIABLE. A term used in grammar to denote a word which does not change its form, regardless of mood, tense, or case, gender, number, or person, or degree. The word 'invariable' can be used of any part of speech to which it applies—for example, both in English and in German, all adverbs and conjunctions are invariable; **anderthalb** is an invariable adjective,

meaning 'one and a half'. See also INDECLINABLE, PAR-
TICLE, UNINFLECTED.

INVERSION. The reversal of normal word order in a sentence—*e.g.* '"I pray", *said she*, "that he will return"'. In
German, the rules of grammar require that inversion (or
'inverted word order') take place when a word other than the
subject stands first in the sentence: the verb then comes second,
followed, in relative order, by the subject (and its modifiers),
pronoun object, time, noun object, place, and other adverbial
expressions. See §§163, 251.

IRREGULAR. Not conforming to the normal pattern of
inflexion; for example, both in English and in German the
verb 'to be' is an irregular verb, in that its principal parts ('to
be, was, been'—**sein, war, gewesen)** differ from the normal
pattern of inflexion by which regular verbs are recognized. Cf.
REGULAR; see also STRONG, the list of irregular German
verbs in §246, and §160.

English *nouns* may also be said to be irregular if they form
their plurals by the addition of any ending other than '-s' or
'-es'—*e.g.* 'ox—oxen; child—children'.

LIMITING ADJECTIVES. Another name for 'determinatives', §113.

MAIN CLAUSE. =PRINCIPAL CLAUSE (see under
CLAUSE).

MASCULINE. The gender of nouns and pronouns to which
names of males normally belong, as opposed to the FEMININE
and NEUTER genders. See §8, 1, also §41.

MIXED. A term applied in grammar to (*a*) verbs, (*b*) nouns,
and (*c*) adjectives.

(*a*) For *mixed verbs,* see §160.

(*b*) A *mixed noun* is a noun which is declined strong in the
singular but weak in the plural. All mixed nouns are either
masculine or neuter. For models, see §36; for Reference Lists

of Nouns so declined see §38, 7, 8 and 9, and see also the Summary of Noun Declension, §37, *C*. Cf. also STRONG (*b*) and WEAK (*b*).

(*c*) The *adjective* takes the mixed form when it is preceded by a determinative of the **mein** model (see §115, III)—that is to say, it takes the endings **-er, -e, -es** in the nominative singular, and **-en, -e, -es** in the accusative singular; otherwise **-en** throughout. For the full declension see §§115, III, and 116, 3. Cf. also STRONG (*c*) and WEAK (*c*).

MODAL AUXILIARY. See §224. For conjugation and the uses of modal auxiliaries see §§225–230. See also AUXILIARY VERBS.

MODIFY. A word applied to adverbs; in the sentence 'He coughed loudly' the adverb 'loudly' modifies the verb 'coughed' —i.e., it limits or qualifies the sense of the verb. See ADVERB, and compare the word QUALIFY, used in connection with adjectives. For the use of the word 'modify' in another sense, see under UMLAUT.

MOOD. This word is used to express the idea or action or state of a verb in a given context. There are four moods, namely the Indicative, Subjunctive, Imperative, and Infinitive. All these terms are treated separately in this Glossary. For 'auxiliaries of mood' see MODAL AUXILIARY.

MULTIPLICATIVE ADVERB. Multiplicative adverbs indicate 'how many times' and are formed in German by adding the suffix **-mal** to the cardinal numerals—*e.g.* **dreimal,** 'three times'. See §282.

NEGATIVE. A word or phrase which expresses negation or denial, answering 'no' to a question; opposed to AFFIRMATIVE.

NEUTER. The gender of nouns and pronouns that are neither MASCULINE nor FEMININE. See §8, 1, also §43.

NOMINATIVE CASE. In German as in English, the

nominative case is mainly used as the subject of a verb (*e.g.*
'*The cow* jumped over the moon') or as the predicate of the
verb 'to be' (*e.g.* 'He is *a dustman*'). The subject of a sentence is
always in the nominative case, which answers the question
'who?' **(wer?)** or 'what?' **(was?)** placed before the main verb.

NOUN. See §33.

NUMBER. A form of a verb, noun, pronoun, etc., which
denotes 'one' (the singular number) or 'more than one' (the
plural number). See SINGULAR, PLURAL, also §8, 2.

NUMERALS. See CARDINALS, ORDINALS.

OBJECT. A noun or pronoun affected by the action of a
transitive verb. Transitive constructions of a verb may result in a
direct object, which answers the question 'whom?' or 'what?'
and is expressed in the accusative case, or an *indirect* object,
which answers the question 'to (or 'for') whom?' or 'to (or
'for') what?' and is expressed in the dative case. In English it is
the position in the sentence of the object (direct or indirect)
which determines the sense (compare 'The boy chased the
girl' with 'The girl chased the boy'). In the case of certain
pronouns the forms differ for subject and object ('he—him,
she—her, they—them, we—us'); in German, on the other hand,
the object is indicated by case endings of accompanying articles,
adjectives, etc., and the pronouns—sometimes also the nouns—
have distinctive forms or endings. See DIRECT OBJECT,
ACCUSATIVE CASE, DATIVE CASE, also §160.

ORDINALS. Ordinals are numbers which express order of
sequence or position in a series—*e.g.* 'first', 'second', 'third'—
as opposed to CARDINAL numbers ('one', 'two', 'three').
Ordinals usually have an adjectival function—*e.g.* 'the *first*
Noël', 'the *second* time'. In German they are formed, with a
few exceptions (see §286), by adding **-t** to the cardinal number
up to 19 and **-st** from 20 upwards, with suitable adjectival endings. They may be adverbial in function too—*e.g.* **zweitens,**
'secondly'—in which case they are formed by adding **-ens**

to the ordinal stem. With personal names, ordinal numerals
are written in German with a capital letter and are declined—
e.g. **Karl der Erste** (nominative), 'Charles the First', **Karls des
Ersten** (genitive), 'of Charles the First' (see §287). In dates,
the ordinals are used adjectivally before the names of the
months—*e.g.* **Am ersten (1.) Januar,** 'On the first (1st) of
January' (see §289). Fractions are regularly formed by adding
-tel to the ordinal stem minus its final **t**—*e.g.* **ein Drittel,** 'one
third' (stem: **dritt)** (see §291).

PARTICIPLE. A part of a verb that often has characteristics
of both a verb and an adjective. In English there are two kinds
of participles—the *present* participle, ending in '-ing' (*e.g.*
'going', 'performing', 'sleeping'), and the *past* participle, usually
ending in '-ed', '-d', '-t', '-n', or '-en' *e.g.* 'played', 'saved',
'spent', 'known', 'written'). In German there are three participles—the *present* participle, ending in **-end** (*e.g.* **schlafend,**
'sleeping', **denkend,** 'thinking'); the *past* participle, usually
formed, in the case of weak verbs, by prefixing **ge-** to the stem
and adding **-t** or **-et** (*e.g.* **ge-spiel-t,** from **spielen,** 'to play';
ge-bad-et, from **baden,** 'to bathe'), and in the case of strong
verbs by prefixing **ge-** to the stem and adding **-en,** usually also
with change of stem-vowel (*e.g.* **ge-sung-en,** from **singen,** 'to
sing'); and the *future passive* participle, which has the form of
the present participle preceded by **zu,** is formed from transitive
verbs only, and is always used attributively (*e.g.* **eine ernstzunehmende Angelegenheit,** 'a matter to be taken seriously'). All
three types of participle are used in German as attributive
adjectives—*e.g.* **ein singender Vogel,** 'a singing bird', **singende
Vögel,** 'singing birds', **die geflüsterten Worte,** 'the whispered
words', **geflüsterte Worte,** 'whispered words' (see §214). The
past participle is a regular part of the compound tenses of the
verb (*e.g.* **ich habe gelacht,** 'I have laughed') and of the passive
voice (*e.g.* **ich wurde gelobt,** 'I was praised').

PARTICLE. A minor part of speech, usually short, which
is indeclinable or invariable, such as an adverb or conjunction.
See also EMOTIVE PARTICLE.

PARTS OF SPEECH. The names by which words are grammatically identified with reference to the part they play in a phrase, clause, or sentence. Nouns, pronouns, adjectives, prepositions, conjunctions, verbs, adverbs, and interjections are all parts of speech.

PASSIVE VOICE. The *passive* voice is used when the subject of the verb *suffers* the action, as opposed to the *active* voice, in which the subject of the verb *performs* the action. The agent (i.e., the doer of the action) may or may not be specified in a passive construction—*e.g.* 'He was jeered' (no agent), 'He was jeered by the crowd' (agent specified—'the crowd'). Otherwise expressed, the passive voice is the active voice inverted—that is, the direct object of the active becomes the subject of the passive, and the active subject becomes the agent; hence only transitive verbs can have a true passive. Purely intransitive verbs can have a passive in the impersonal form only—for examples, see §245, 2. The passive is formed in German by means of **werden** (='to become') + the past participle of the verb to be conjugated; the prefix **ge-** of the past participle **geworden** (from **werden**) is dropped throughout in the perfect tense of the passive—*e.g.* **sie ist gelobt worden,** 'she has been praised'. The passive is used wherever agency is specified or implied (§243, 3), or where a state or condition regarded as complete and permanent, and as resulting from the action of the verb, is indicated (§244, 2). The passive is much less used in German than in English, being often replaced by a **man** construction (§100, 7) and by other means. See VOICE, ACTIVE VOICE, AGENT.

PAST PARTICIPLE. See PARTICIPLE.

PERFECT TENSE. This tense indicates an event in past time, continuing up to, but not including, the present. It is particularly used in speech. It often answers to the English simple past tense, especially when referring to an action or state that is complete and that has happened or been in the recent past, or to an event as a separate and independent fact. For examples, see §173. In German the perfect tense is formed either with **haben** or with **sein** as auxiliary, the present of the auxiliary being added to the past participle—*e.g.* **ich** *habe* **gespielt,** 'I have played', **ich** *bin* **gegangen,** 'I have gone'.

PERSON. Personal pronouns have three persons—the *first* person, which represents the speaker(s): 'I', 'me', 'we', 'us'; the *second* person, which represents the person(s) spoken to: 'thou', 'thee', 'you'; and the *third* person, which represents the person(s) or thing(s) spoken of: 'he', 'him', 'she', 'her', 'it', 'they', 'them'. Each of these personal pronouns has a corresponding possessive adjective and possessive pronoun— 'my' and 'our' are the possessive adjectives corresponding to the first-person personal pronouns 'I', 'me' and 'we', 'us' respectively, and 'mine' and 'ours' are the corresponding possessive pronouns. Nouns are similarly classified—*e.g.* '*I, Frederick Smith,* do hereby declare . . .' (first person); 'Do *you, Frederick Smith,* plead guilty or not guilty?' (second person); '*Frederick Smith* pleaded not guilty' (third person). Almost all nouns are in the third person (cf. APPOSITION). Both in English and in German a relative pronoun takes the person of its antecedent—*e.g.* **das Blatt,** *das* **fällt,** 'the leaf *which* falls', **die Blätter,** *die* **fallen,** 'the leaves *which* fall'. See §8, 2.

PERSONAL PRONOUN. See §50; see also PERSON.

PHRASE. A group of words which does not contain a finite verb (thus distinguishing it from a clause, which does). Thus in the sentence 'They kissed under the mistletoe', 'under the mistletoe' is a phrase, as is 'in a bowler hat' in the sentence 'The man in a bowler hat hailed a taxi'. A sentence may contain any number of phrases.

PLUPERFECT TENSE. The pluperfect tense denotes an action or state as completed at or before a past time referred to —*e.g.* 'When he *had finished* his meal he returned home'. Both in English and in German the pluperfect is formed by adding the past participle to the imperfect of the auxiliary verb; in English the auxiliary is always 'had', in German it is usually **haben** (always if the verb is transitive, sometimes if intransitive), but occasionally **sein** (for certain intransitive verbs only)—*e.g.* **ich hatte gewartet,** 'I had waited', but **ich *war* gegangen,** 'I had gone'. The subjunctive of the pluperfect is formed by replacing the indicative of the auxiliary by the subjunctive, the past participle remaining unchanged—*e.g.* **ich *hätte* gewartet; ich *wäre* gegangen.**

PLURAL. A form of a verb, noun, or pronoun (also, in German, though not in English, an adjective) which denotes more than one (cf. SINGULAR). See NUMBER, also §8, 2.

POSITIVE. The positive form of an adjective or adverb expresses the simple, basic form without any notion of comparison—*e.g.* 'sweet', 'noble'; 'sweetly', 'nobly'. See COMPARATIVE, COMPARISON, DEGREE, SUPERLATIVE.

POSSESSIVE ADJECTIVE. An adjective which expresses possession, such as 'my', 'your', 'his', 'their'. See §§114, 115, III, and 116, 3, also PERSON.

POSSESSIVE PRONOUN. See §50; see also PERSON.

PREDICATE. The word or words in a sentence which complete the sense of what is said of the subject. Thus in the sentence 'The dog barked', 'the dog' is the subject and 'barked' is the predicate; in the sentence 'The dog barked loudly', 'barked loudly' is the predicate. The predicate may also express the complement of the verb—*e.g.* in the sentence 'She is a model', 'is a model' is the predicate. Predicates may be compound—*e.g.* 'The prisoner *shouted and struggled.*' See also COMPLEMENT, FINITE, and SUBJECT.

PREDICATIVE ADJECTIVE. As in English, adjectives commonly come before their noun in German—*e.g.* **ein schönes Mädchen,** 'a beautiful girl', **leere Straßen,** 'empty streets': they are then technically called 'attributive'. Sometimes, however, the adjective comes after with a verb (often **sein,** 'to be', or **werden,** 'to become') in between—*e.g.* **das Mädchen ist schön,**

'the girl is beautiful', **die Straßen werden leer**, 'the streets become empty': such adjectives are called predicative, and in German they are invariable (i.e., they are not declined). Certain German adjectives are used only predicatively—*e.g.* **allein**, 'alone', **bereit**, 'ready'. See also §113 and ATTRIBUTIVE ADJECTIVE.

PREFIX. A prefix is a syllable put before a word to affect its meaning; for example, in the word 'befriend' (in German **befreunden**) 'be-' is a prefix. In German, prefixes may be either separable or inseparable (see under these words). See also COMPOUND VERB and cf. SUFFIX.

PREPOSITION. See §292.

PRESENT PARTICIPLE. See PARTICIPLE.

PRESENT TENSE. The present tense of a verb is the tense which expresses an action or state at the present time—*e.g.* 'he *is running*', 'it *does function*', 'he *writes*', 'they *sing*'. Besides being used for what happens or is at the present time, this tense also denotes what is habitually true (*e.g.* 'Some animals *hibernate*', 'Swallows *migrate*', 'He is a man who *says* what he *thinks*') or necessarily true (*e.g.* 'One plus one *equals* two', 'A straight line *is* the shortest distance between two points'). In addition, it sometimes replaces the imperfect tense to produce vividness and is then called the 'historic present'—for an example see §168, 2; and it may also replace the future tense, as in the sentence 'I am going on holiday as from tomorrow'.

PRINCIPAL CLAUSE. See under CLAUSE.

PRINCIPAL PARTS. See §193.

PRONOMINAL. The adjective formed from the word 'pronoun', and meaning like or acting as a pronoun.

PRONOUN. See §50.

PROPER NOUN. See §33.

QUALIFY (TO). A word applied to adjectives; in the expression 'a loud bang' the adjective 'loud' qualifies the noun 'bang'—i.e., it limits or modifies the sense of the noun. See §113, and compare the word MODIFY, used in connection with adverbs.

RECIPROCAL PRONOUN. See §§50, 223.

REFLEXIVE PRONOUN. See §50; see also §§109, 110.

REFLEXIVE VERBS. See §§220–222.

REGULAR. Verbs are said to be regular if they conform to the normal pattern of inflexion; for example, the verb 'to love' is a regular verb, in that its principal parts ('to love, loved, loved') conform to the normal pattern of inflexion—namely, the addition to the infinitive of '-(e)d' to form the past tense and past participle. Similarly in German the verb **lieben** is regular—i.e., weak—in that it follows the normal pattern of inflexion by forming its imperfect through the addition of **-te** to the stem, and its past participle through the prefixing of **ge-** to the stem and the addition of **-t** to it: **lieben** (infinitive; stem: **lieb**), **liebte** (imperfect), **geliebt** (past participle). Cf. IRREGULAR; see also WEAK, and §160.

English *nouns* may also be said to be regular if they form their plural by the addition of '-s' or '-es'—*e.g.* 'shield—shields; class—classes'.

RELATIVE CLAUSE. A clause introduced by a relative pronoun—*e.g.* 'Fay, *who loves horses*, hopes to have one of her own one day' (descriptive force); 'Girls *who love horses* usually long to have one of their own' (restrictive force, = 'Such girls as love horses . . .'). In German, however, such a distinction is not possible because all clauses must be divided off by commas. Since all relative clauses are dependent clauses, the verb comes last in the clause in German. See RELATIVE PRONOUN.

RELATIVE PRONOUN. See §50; see also ANTECEDENT, RELATIVE CLAUSE.

REPORTED SPEECH. See INDIRECT STATEMENT and INDIRECT QUESTION.

SEPARABLE PREFIX. Certain prepositions and adverbs are much used in German as prefixes to verbs, and when separable they are always stressed; for examples see §204. They precede and are written as one word with the infinitive, with or without zu (*e.g.* ˈausgehen, ˈauszugehen), and the past participle (*e.g.* ˈausgegangen), wherever these occur. See also INSEPARABLE PREFIX and COMPOUND VERB.

SIBILANT. A consonant uttered with a hissing sound; in German, **s, sch, ß, x, tz,** and **z** are sibilants.

SIMPLE TENSE. A tense which is composed of only one verb element—*e.g.* 'he laughed'—as distinct from a compound tense, which is composed of more than one verb element (*e.g.* 'he has laughed'). See under COMPOUND TENSE.

SINGULAR. A form of a verb, noun, pronoun, etc., which denotes only one (cf. PLURAL). See NUMBER, also §8, 2.

STEM. The stem is that basic part of an inflected word (see INFLEXION) which remains unchanged throughout a given inflexion, and to which inflexional endings (known as 'case-endings' in nouns, pronouns, and adjectives) are added to show the case of a noun, the person of a tense, etc. For example, the stem of the verb **machen,** 'to make', is **mach** (the ending **-en** here denoting the infinitive form), and of the adjective or pronoun **jeder,** 'every', **jed.** Endings are added to the stem to denote number, case, and gender of German words: thus, in the phrase **dieses kleine Kind,** endings have been added to the stems **dies** and **klein** to denote the nominative (or accusative) singular of a neuter form. See CASE-ENDING.

STRESS. A term used in phonetics (that branch of linguistics which deals with the sounds of speech) to denote the force of utterance given to a sound or syllable; also sometimes called 'accent' or 'emphasis'. In the present work the stress mark [ˈ] is placed *before* the syllable to be stressed—*e.g.* erˈhalten, 'to reˈceive'.

STRONG. A term applied in grammar to (*a*) verbs, (*b*) nouns, and (*c*) adjectives.

(*a*) For strong verbs, see §160.

(*b*) A *strong noun* is a noun which, if masculine or neuter in gender, adds -(e)s in the genitive singular. In the plural, strong nouns either (i) add -e, sometimes modifying the stem vowel—this is known as the *primary* form of the strong declension (see §34, models I, II, and III)—or (ii) add -er, always modifying the stem vowel—this is known as the *enlarged* form of the strong declension (see §34, model IV)—or (iii) omit e in the various endings, sometimes modifying the stem vowel—this is known as the *contracted* form of the strong declension (see §34, models V, VI). See also the Summary of Noun Declension §37, *A*, and the Reference Lists of Nouns, §38, 1–5, and cf. WEAK (*b*) and MIXED (*b*).

(*c*) An *adjective* is declined strong when it is not preceded by a determinative. The strong endings in the nominative singular are -er, -e, -es; for the full declension see §§115, I, and 116, 3. Cf. also WEAK (*c*) and MIXED (*c*).

SUBJECT. The subject of a sentence is that which is spoken of as opposed to the *predicate*, which is that which is said of the subject. Thus in the sentence 'Who killed Cock Robin?', 'who' is the subject; in the sentence 'I, said the sparrow', 'I' is the subject. The subject of a finite verb is always expressed in the nominative case. Besides being a noun or pronoun, the subject of a sentence may be any part of speech used as a noun (*e.g.* '*The poor and downtrodden* continued to be exploited', '*Upon* is a preposition'), an infinitive (*e.g.* '*To err* is human'), a gerund (*e.g.* '*Fishing* is relaxing'), or a whole clause (*e.g.* '*That he should die so young* is tragic'). In German there are sometimes two subjects to a sentence—the grammatical subject, represented by the word **es**, and the real or logical subject, which follows—*e.g.* **Es war einmal ein König**, '(Once upon a time) there was a king'. See PREDICATE, NOMINATIVE CASE.

SUBJUNCTIVE (MOOD). The subjunctive is the mood of indirect statement and of supposed or unreal condition; compare INDICATIVE MOOD. It may be used in main clauses to express a wish or a hope, possibility, doubt, an imaginary situation (non-reality), conditional and qualified statements— see §234; in dependent clauses it is used, for example, to express purpose, and also usually indirect statements and questions—see §§235, 236.

SUBORDINATE CLAUSE. See under CLAUSE.

SUBORDINATING CONJUNCTIONS. See §331.

SUBSTANTIVE. Another word for NOUN. The corresponding adjective is 'substantival'.

SUFFIX. A suffix is a letter or syllable added to the end of a word; for example, in the word 'friendly' (in German **freundlich**) '-ly' and **-lich** are suffixes. Compare PREFIX. The past participle of all strong verbs in German ends in the suffix **-en**—*e.g.* **gesungen** (from **singen**, 'to sing'). Suffixes are added to nouns both in German and in English to form diminutives—*e.g.* **Bächlein**, 'stream*let*'.

SUPERLATIVE. The superlative (or superlative degree) is the degree of comparison of an adjective (§150) or adverb (§274) expressing the highest degree or amount of the attribute denoted by the positive form—*e.g.* **kleinst, schönst** ('smallest', 'most beautiful') are the superlative forms of the simple adjectival forms **klein, schön** ('small', 'beautiful'). The superlative may be either relative, when it denotes the highest degree of any considered (*e.g.* 'He made the *best* offer'), or absolute, when it denotes a very high degree without definite comparison (*e.g.*

'He has the *keenest* of minds'). See also COMPARATIVE, COMPARISON, DEGREE, POSITIVE.

SYLLABLE/SYLLABIFICATION. A syllable is one or more letters, including a vowel or diphthong, forming a complete unit of utterance—sometimes a whole word (*e.g.* 'car'), sometimes part of a word (for instance, the word 'independent' contains four syllables: in-de-pen-dent). When a word is made up of one syllable only it is called a 'monosyllable' or a 'monosyllabic word'; a 'polysyllable' means literally a word containing many syllables, but is used of any word made up of three or more syllables, like the word 'polysyllable' itself, which has five syllables. *Syllabification* is the division of words into syllables. German has strict rules regarding syllabification—see §3.

SYNONYM. A word which is different in form from another, but has the same, or much the same, meaning as it—*e.g.* 'prison' is a synonym for (is synonymous with) 'gaol'.

TENSE. Tense is the distinctive form of a verb to express the *time* the action takes place or the state described is. To indicate time past, one of the past tenses is used, to indicate present time the present tense is used, and to indicate future time the future tense is used. See COMPOUND TENSE, SIMPLE TENSE, CONDITIONAL (TENSES), FUTURE TENSE, FUTURE PERFECT TENSE, IMMEDIATE FUTURE, IMPERFECT TENSE, PERFECT TENSE, PLUPERFECT TENSE, PRESENT TENSE.

TRANSITIVE VERBS. See §160; see also DIRECT OBJECT, REFLEXIVE VERBS.

UMLAUT. In German, the sign ¨, which may be placed over the vowels **a, o,** and **u,** and over the diphthong **au** to form **äu,** resulting in a different pronunciation. When such alteration occurs, the vowel or diphthong is said to be *modified*.

UNINFLECTED. Not subject to variation in form—i.e., invariable. See under INFLEXION, INVARIABLE.

VERB. For general remarks, see §160. For other references, see Index and relevant entries in this Glossary.

VERBAL PREFIX. A prefix pertaining to verbs. See PREFIX, SEPARABLE PREFIX, INSEPARABLE PREFIX, COMPOUND VERB.

VOCATIVE CASE. The case which denotes the person or thing addressed by the speaker—*e.g.* "Lord, now lettest thou thy servant depart in peace" or "O Liberty! what crimes are committed in thy name!" In both English and German the vocative is almost invariably expressed in the nominative case, but cf. English 'Jesu', vocative of 'Jesus', and German **Jesu Christe,** vocative of **Jesus Christus** (§47, 3, note 1).

VOICE. A verb form which indicates the relation of the subject of the verb to the action expressed by the verb. If the subject of the verb performs the action the verb employs the *active* voice; if, on the other hand, the subject suffers the action the verb employs the *passive* voice. Thus, for example, in the sentence 'The police dispersed the crowd' it is the subject ('the police') which performs the action ('dispersed the crowd') and the verb is therefore used in the active voice; but in the sentence 'The crowd was dispersed by the police' the subject ('the crowd') suffers the action (it was dispersed) and the verb is therefore used in the passive voice, 'the police' being the agent. From these examples it will be seen that the passive voice is in fact the active voice inverted, and that only transitive verbs can have true passive forms. See ACTIVE VOICE, PASSIVE VOICE, AGENT.

WEAK. A term applied in grammar to (*a*) verbs, (*b*) nouns, and (*c*) adjectives.
(*a*) For weak verbs, see §160.
(*b*) A *weak noun* is a noun which in German forms its plural by adding **-n** or **-en** to the nominative singular in all cases. Weak masculine nouns also have the ending **-n** or **-en** in all cases of the singular except the nominative. Weak feminine nouns remain unchanged in all cases of the singular. In German, all feminine nouns except those which add an umlaut in the

plural are weak. There are no weak neuter nouns. No weak nouns add an umlaut in the plural.

The *weak declension*, in German, is that class of nouns characterized by the features described above. For models of the weak declension, see §35. See also the Summary of Noun Declension, §37, *B*, and the Reference List of Nouns, §38, 6. Cf. STRONG (*b*) and MIXED (*b*).

(*c*) The *adjective* is weak when it is preceded by the definite article **(der, die, das)** or by the demonstrative adjectives **dieser, jener, jeder,** etc., which indicate the case of the noun **(-r, -e,** and **-s** respectively in the nominative singular masculine, feminine, and neuter)—*e.g.* **der gute Wein,** 'the good wine', **diese schöne Frau,** 'this beautiful woman', **jedes alte Haus,** 'every old house'. The genitive and dative forms, both in the singular and in the plural, have the ending **-en** in all genders, as does the masculine accusative singular; the nominative singular ends in **-e** in all genders, as do the feminine and neuter accusative singular. For the full declension see §§115, II, and 116, 3. Cf. also STRONG (*c*) and MIXED (*c*).

INDEX

The references are to the paragraphs and numbered sections within them, except where page references are specifically given.

declined, 34,IV,XII
ng, pronunciation, 7 (*page* 19)
nicht:
  expletive use of, 338,7(*b*)(*note*)
  position of, 167, 252
nicht nur . . . sondern auch, 340,1(*c*)
nichts, indefinite pronoun, 88, 103
nieder-, verbal prefix, 204,2(*f*)
niemand, indefinite pronoun, 88, 99,2, 104
-nis, nouns ending in, 34,2
nk, pronunciation, 7 (*page* 19)
noch, adverb:
  concessive, 269,4
  = 'still', 'yet', 269,1
  = 'still more', 269,3
  to specify something additional, 269,2
Nominative, 8,4, 9–13, 21
  of definite article, 10
  of **ein** and **kein,** 19
  of personal pronouns, 53
  of **welcher?,** 20
  predicate nominative, 21,2
  use, 9,3, 21
Nouns, 33–49
  abstract, 18,1(*a*), 33
  as imperative, 241,6
  as prefixes, 206, 2
  collective, 33, 43,4
  common, 33
  compound, 33, 40
  concrete, 33
  definition, 33
  derived from adjectives of dimension, 42,6
  ending in -**fache,** 283(*c*)
  ending in -**tel** representing fractions, 43,6, 291,1
  essential parts, 39
  expressing quantity, 285
  foreign, 41,9, 42,9, 43,11
  gender of, 41–43
  general remarks, 33
  in apposition, 49
  infinitive used as, 43,2
  letters of the alphabet used as, 43,5
  mixed, 36, 37,C
  of nationality, 46
  proper, 16,3, 33, 41,7,8, 42,7,8, 43,9, 44–48

reference lists of, 38
strong, 34, 37,A
summary of declensions, 37
weak, 35, 37,B
with verbal force beginning with Ge-, 43,4
Numerals:
  cardinal, 42,5, 279
  multiplication, 281
  ordinal, 286, 287, 289
  remarks on, 280
nun, adverb, 265(*note*), 335,3
nur, adverb:
  idioms, 270,4
  = 'only', 'just', 270,1
  to generalize a statement, 270,3
  to persuade, reassure, 270,2

o, pronunciation, 7 (*page* 16)
ö, pronunciation, 7 (*page* 16)
ob, conjunction in indirect questions, 236, 336, 338,6
ob auch, 336,1
oberhalb, preposition, 321
obgleich, obschon, obwohl, obzwar, conjunctions, 336,1, 338,6(*note* 1)
oder, conjunction, 332,1, 333(*d*)
'of':
  after verbs, etc., 327,1,5
  German equivalents, 326
  how rendered, 300(*notes* 1,2), 321
oft, irregular comparison, 278
ohne, preposition, 303, 308, 330,1
ohne daß, 336,1
Ohr model, 36,XII, 37,C, 38,9
'on', German equivalents, 326
'one', after adjectives, 147
Ordinals, 286, 287, 289
  with personal names, 287

p, pronunciation, 7 (*page* 19)
Participles:
  adjectival, 214,1, 216
  appositive, 159
  as adverbs, 214,3, 250
  as imperative, 241,4
  as nouns, 148, 214,2
  attributive, 216,2
  future passive, 212
  general remarks, 209
  idioms, 215